Nine-Dollar Bill

Jay Jones

Table of Contents

Lacy, my love, I feel you

Preface

My name is Jay Scott Jones. Daddy named me: Jay, after Gatsby, and Scott, after F. Scott Fitzgerald.

Couldn't he have aimed a little higher, say, Homer Shakespeare Jones or Ulysses Tolstoy Jones? How about Quixote Jones? Now, there's a name. Quixote Jones...doesn't it radiate "cool"? With a name like Quixote Jones, I wouldn't even have to *do* anything; the mantle of superstardom would settle on my shoulders like a feather boa on a drag queen. Quixote Jones...girls would swoon upon hearing it pronounced. Quixote Jones would be simultaneously the sexiest leading man in Hollywood and the most fearsome fastballer in the major leagues.

If only I'd been Quixote.

As you will have gathered after reading one paragraph, what follows is not Gatsby, Fitzgerald, or anything close. My name says more about my father than me.

I didn't know I was writing a book. My 9th-grade English teacher read what I'd written over the years and suggested I put together a memoir. Conscientious student that I am, I gave it a shot. Memoirs never appealed to me; I suspected they were written by people lacking the gift and guts to write fiction.

What follows is an accidental, unconventional...something; it doesn't fit the definition of a memoir nor an autobiography...it's an autobiographimoir, a memoighraphy...stories from a life, arranged in roughly chronological order. The first five are written in a child's voice. The tone shifts jarringly toward the end. I wish it weren't so, but when your life takes an abrupt and tragic turn, you can't gracefully feather it in to the fabric of your story; at least I can't.

Have you ever felt like you've lived several distinctly different lives within the whole of your own? I think those who've experienced a sudden loss might say so. Looking back after almost six and half decades, my lives seem clearly demarcated: The first lasted about 50 years, the second one 10, the third three, and now I'm a year and a half into my fourth. These new lives are blowing in too goddamned fast. I can't wrap my head around one life before I plunge into another.

A book made sense for another reason: My son, Jesse, might need it. I am 65, he's five; my mortality looms. I wrote Jesse a 40-page letter before he was born...stories of the fabulous Joneses who live within him and what we live by. This memoighraphy is the word of his Daddy, whoever he is, flaws and all, for another couple hundred pages; inevitably, my corporeal voice will go silent before I've said all I want to say to my son.

I've been asked, "Who is your audience?" and I don't have the answer. My hope is that you dive in, get hooked, and read on. But perhaps I have only an audience of one. And one is enough.

Cover Photo: The book cover was designed by Raquel Key. It is based on a photograph of geezer Daddy and baby Jesse in their angles of repose, taken by Mommy (Lacy Van Zandt). The original photo is in the body of the book.

Author's note: As noted in the Preface, a child narrates the first five stories. His punctuation and grammar are imperfect. He does not use quotation marks. A couple of readers suggested that I "clean up" the prose. I prefer the unsophisticated voice and chose not to alter it.

I Am A Bartender

And A Craps Dealer

My name is Jay and I am 7 years old and I am a bartender and a craps dealer. Craps is not like dookies craps is a dice game. Daddy bought Whiskey that we keep on top of the refrigerator and I have my own stool that I climb to get the Whiskey down. When Daddy's friends come over I get the Whiskey down and mix them drinks Daddy taught me how. I measure the Whiskey with my fingers. All of my drinks have 4 fingers of Whiskey because my fingers are small when I have bigger fingers the drinks will only have 2 or 3 fingers. We have Chivas Regal Scotch that I mix with water and Tanqueray Gin that I mix with Schweppes Tonic Water and Crown Royal that comes in a fancy purple bag that I get to keep when the Whiskey is gone that I mix with Schweppes Club Soda. I have my own swizzle stick and I really like saying those words swizzle stick. We also have Budweiser Beer that we keep inside the refrigerator. Beers are easy I just pop the top.

Daddy taught me to charge $2.50 for Whiskey drinks and 50 cents for Beer and I already have enough money to buy a Spalding baseball glove that costs $19.99 the one with the hole where your Number 1 finger sticks out. Some kids say that if I use that glove my finger will get knocked off but they are crummy baseball players. I am not a crummy baseball player and my finger will not get knocked off.

Sometimes when Daddy's friends come over we shoot craps and it is my job to shout out the numbers when the dice are finished rolling. Daddy says craps is not a quiet game everybody has to holler and have fun and you can't just say 3 or 4 you have to yell these words

1. HaHa I tricked you you can't roll a 1 with 2 dice

2. I yell Snake Eyes

3. I yell Craps

4. I yell Little Joe. Little Joe is on Bonanza and I don't know why he is number 4 but he is

5. I yell Fever

6. I yell Sister Hix Come Out Of The Sticks. Sometimes I tell my little sister Sister Hix come out of the sticks and she gets mad

7. I yell Seven Come Eleven

8. I yell Eighter From Decatur County Seat Uh Wise. This is

my favorite one. Decatur is a town in Texas   and Wise is the county it is in and you don't say of Wise you say uh Wise because   you   have   to   say   it   fast eighterfromdecaturcountyseatuhwise like that

9. I yell Nina Ross You Old Hoss. This is my second favorite one one time we were in a store and there was a big fat lady in a fur coat with red fingernails yelling at the man behind the counter and I told Daddy she is Nina Ross and he laughed

10. I yell Puppy Paws. I don't really like this one I love puppies but it's like a man made up all the rest of the sayings and some little girl who doesn't know anything made up Puppy Paws. Yelling Puppy Paws makes we want to urp

11. I yell Yoleven

12. I yell Boxcars

Mother doesn't think a little boy should be a bartender **or** a craps dealer. Last night Mother and Daddy had an argument and Mother cried and I don't think I'm going to be a bartender or a craps dealer any more.

My Summer Vacation

At the start of the summer my grandparents, Nanny and Daddy Sam, drove from Sweetwater to Post and Mother and Daddy drove from Lubbock to Post and we were in the car with Mother and Daddy. Daddy said the Post football team was named the Post Toasties and we said Nuh uh. Really? Then I saw a water tower with Antelopes written on it and I said Post is the Antelopes not the Toasties. Daddy said I was just spiffing you.

We saw Nanny and Daddy Sam at a park beside a lake and we all hugged and moved our stuff to their car. Mother cried and we hugged her again. Nanny told my little brother Carey that she liked his shoes and Carey said I like your shoes too. Nanny said Lets trade and they traded. Nanny wore Carey's high top Converse tennis shoes with her dress and Carey wore Nanny's golden slippers not just for a minute all day long. Carey was 5 and Nanny was old like 50 but they wore the same shoe size that's how little Nanny was. Daddy Sam was great big and Nanny was little bitty but Daddy Sam acted like Nanny was even bigger than he was.

We hugged my aunt Carolyn when we got to Sweetwater. She couldn't hug us back with her arms because she got polio when she was a little girl and her whole body was paralyzed and she lived in a wheelchair except when she slept and she had a hospital bed in the house. I would be sad if I was paralyzed but Carolyn wasn't sad she was always smiling and laughing. Carolyn was a schoolteacher when it wasn't summer and even when it was summer she taught kids how to speak English on Saturdays. Carolyn went to Hawaii and came home with purple and yellow flowers around her neck she said they were leis not lays. Carolyn and Nanny were best friends even if Nanny was the mother and Carolyn was the daughter. They were bridge partners and they kicked butt that's what Carolyn said and one time they got invited to New York to play in a big bridge contest.

Daddy Sam got us Shetland ponies. Mine was white and was named Snowball. My sister Junie's was silver and was named Silver and one day Silver bucked Junie off and Daddy Sam caught her before she hit the ground like a football player making a diving catch. Carey's was named Pancho and Pancho was too mean to ride. Snowball liked to run me up against barbwire fences and scratch my legs but I still rode him all over. I was gonna ride Snowball in the Sweetwater 4th of July parade and I was sitting on him ready to go but a big horse went crazy and kicked me in the head and in the shin and I got knocked out and there was a little dent in my shin where the bone got chipped off. I didn't get to ride in the parade. Nanny and Carolyn bought me toys.

Daddy Sam told us a secret he was going to play a trick on Nanny. He told us to sit on the couch in the parlor where Nanny and Carolyn and a bunch of ladies were having a bridge party. Me and Junie and Carey started laughing when we heard clomp clomp clomp on the other side of the house. Clomp clomp clomp got louder and we laughed harder. Clomp clomp clomp was coming oh so close and me and Junie and Carey fell all over each other in a pile laughing so hard when Daddy Sam walked in **with Silver.** All the ladies were laughing too there was a horse in the parlor. Nanny just looked over her glasses and said My land Sam and went right on playing bridge.

One time I was taking a bath and Nanny came in the bathroom and tinkled in the toilet right beside me. I was surprised I had never seen a lady tinkle before especially when I was naked but it seemed completely normal to Nanny and we talked about why ladies tinkled sitting down and men tinkled standing up. I understood about men but I didn't really understand about ladies.

Nanny chopped onions with dark sunglasses on so she wouldn't cry. Nanny wasn't really that great a cook not as good as Mother or Grandmommie and I thought maybe it was because she couldn't see what she was cooking with those dark sunglasses on.

Daddy Sam woke up at 3 in the morning for work and woke us up too. He would sing funny songs and cook fried eggs and we didn't understand how someone could be so happy at 3 in the morning. One time Daddy Sam looked out the back door and said Laura Mary your aunt Ada is here. Nanny looked out the back door and all she saw was a great big donkey. Nanny didn't like being up at 3 she said that Daddy Sam's coffee was scared water. Every time I saw water the rest of the summer I wondered if it was scared or not. I didn't think thunderstorm water was scared.

I earned money working for Nanny and Daddy Sam. Nanny paid me 10 cents for every turnip I planted and I planted 20 so that made 2 dollars except when I got to the last one I realized I had planted them all upside down and I had to go back and plant them right side up. I don't think they ever grew up to be real turnips. I helped Daddy Sam dig holes for a fence with a post hole digger and he paid me 2 dollars but I couldn't make the post hole digger go very far into the ground and Daddy Sam had to do it. I liked being alone with Daddy Sam he called me Bud.

We played with Butch and Clete the neighbor boys. Butch was old like 14 and he said **THE F WORD** a lot. He said **THE F WORD** was when a man stuck his weenie in a lady's butt and that's how babies were made. Gross. Butch got stung all over the face by wasps and his face swelled up like a pumpkin's except he wasn't grinning and I thought he got stung because he said **THE F WORD** so much. Butch was a good pitcher he threw the ball hard. He threw rocks hard too and he hit me in the forehead with one and it looked like I had a chicken's egg sticking out of my head. Nanny and Carolyn bought me toys.

At the end of the summer Nanny and Daddy Sam drove from Sweetwater to Post and Mother and Daddy drove from Lubbock to Post and we were in the car with Nanny and Daddy Sam. Nanny and Carey wore their own shoes. We saw Mother and Daddy at the park by the lake and they hugged us. I told Daddy that the name of the Post football team was the Post Hole Diggers and he laughed. I said I was just spiffing him.

On To It

Granddaddy was my other grandfather. Granddaddy's real name was Morris like Morris The Cat and he sorta reminded me of a cat because I didn't know what he was thinking. I know what dogs are thinking...Lets go play, Please feed me, Your face tastes good. I know when dogs like me but I don't really know when cats like me unless their motor is running and it didn't seem like Morris The Granddaddy's motor was ever running. One time we went to see Morris The Granddaddy after a long time and he was eating a sandwich and watching a football game and he barely said hello it was like he had an invisible force field around him like on Star Trek.

Granddaddy got divorced from Grandmommie so he could marry a lady that was younger than Grandmommie. I didn't understand how anybody could divorce Grandmommie she was so nice she was never mean to anybody. Daddy told Mother that Granddaddy was a prick and I didn't really know what a prick was except when you prick your finger and a little blob of blood comes out but I don't think Daddy meant that kind of prick.

I got worried when I thought about Granddaddy being a prick because his blood runs through me right? Did that mean I was going to be a prick? Granddaddy was Mother's Daddy and Mother was definitely not a prick not even close she was about the best Mother in the world. We learned fractions in school and I have 4 Grandparents and 3 of them were the best ever, but 1 was a prick so did that mean I would be 1/4 prick? Could my sister Junie or my brother Carey maybe get all of Granddaddy's prickness and let the other 2 of us be the best ever? Would I want Junie or Carey to be a prick? What if **I** was a prick **already** and didn't even know it? Life is very complicated.

When Christmas came Granddaddy and his new wife sent us Christmas gifts but Mother and Daddy sent them back. I didn't know you could send Christmas gifts back.

Granddaddy's new wife was named Dolores and Daddy said it was very funny Dolores said On To It all the time I mean all the time. Daddy didn't call her Dolores he called her On To It. I didn't meet Dolores and I didn't understand how a person could say On To It all the time.

One day a lady called and I was the only one home.

The lady said Is your mother there?

I said No ma'am may I take a message.

She said This is Dolores Tell your mother that her father had a heart attack on to it.

I said Yes ma'am On to what?

She said Tell your mother that Morris had a heart attack on to it and she needs to come to Fort Worth right away on to it.

Oooohhhh. I finally realized that I was talking to On To It and I understood what Daddy thought was so funny and I wanted to tell him right away. I really really really wanted to laugh but I knew you weren't supposed to laugh when somebody was telling you about a heart attack especially when it was your Granddaddy's. I held my mouth real serious and closed like an O so I wouldn't laugh but my voice got all shivery like it was 13 degrees.

I said Yy-yy-ee-es-ss ma-aa-aa-am.

I laughed really hard after I hung up the phone I'm sorry I couldn't help it. I walked around the house putting On To It into sentences and my dog Soul Sister cocked her head to the side.

I knew it was mean but when Mother got home I told her that Granddaddy's wife called and said that Granddaddy had a heart attack on to it. Then I thought Oh no! Am I already being a prick? I don't think Mother even noticed On To It and I was glad. She just sat down like she was confused and I sat beside her. She cried a little not a lot.

At school I wrote a book report on Old Yeller which was very good but very sad and I added On To It into a couple of sentences and my teacher didn't even notice and I got an A+.

Sister No Hands

Me and Carey got dart guns the kind with the rubber thingy on the end that looks like a little toilet unplugger. If you lick the rubber thingy on the dart it sticks to stuff you shoot like clocks and china cabinets. The darts don't stick on dogs and people we tried that.

Junie got a doll named Sister Small Talk that says I like to play with you when you pull the string on her back. We tried to get her to say other stuff but I like to play with you is all she says. Junie said she loved Sister Small Talk more than all her other dolls. She let us line up her dolls and shoot them with our dart guns. Carey won he licked his dart and got it to stick right in the middle of Sister Small Talks forehead. Carey is good at stuff like that he's only 5 but he still beats me sometimes and I'm older than him.

We wanted to play with our toys but we wanted to go to sleep real fast too because Santa was gonna come and give us more toys. We left milk and chocolate chip cookies out for Santa and Daddy said we should leave beers too and I said Santa drinks beer? Daddy said, By the gallon old pal, By the gallon. I didn't know Santa drank beers.

Me and Carey slept upstairs and looked out the window for Santa and the reindeer and sometimes we thought we heard jingling. Junie slept with Carolyn in the hospital bed.

We woke up and ran downstairs and the milk glass was empty and the cookies were gone and the Budweiser beer cans were empty. Santa had come. We saw our new toys under the Christmas tree but we saw the Baxter dog too and he wasn't supposed to be there. Santa wouldn't have given us the Baxter dog because the Baxters already had him. Somebody had left the back door open and he got in. The Baxter dog always ran low down and scared like he was in trouble even when he wasn't in trouble. He was in trouble this time he chewed the hands off of Sister Small Talk.

Junie cried really hard and I almost cried too. We tried to play with the toys Santa gave us but we were too sad. Mother said We'll get you another Sister Small Talk but Junie said I want *my* Sister Small Talk. Daddy pulled the doll's string and it said I like to play with you. Daddy said Look Sister No Hands can still talk. Junie cried harder when Daddy called her doll Sister No Hands. I thought it was pretty funny but sorta cruel but mostly funny. Daddy was like that he called me Fat Midget.

We started making up things that Sister No Hands would say now that she didn't have any hands.

Carey said How am I gonna tie my shoes.

I said How am I gonna pick my nose.

Daddy said My hands taste like chicken.

Nanny said Don't pet the Baxter dog.

Carolyn said Sister No Hands would still say I like to play with you because she was still the same girl she always was.

My uncle Dave said Hermana De Nada Manos and we said Huh. We said Huh a lot to Dave. Dave said Hermana De Nada Manos was like Sister No Hands in Spanish. We said OK but what would the doll _say._

Dave said Suckaramic.

Mother and Daddy Sam wouldn't make up things for Sister No Hands to say. They didn't think it was funny, but we did and all of us were laughing even Junie who was crying and laughing.

Junie said Take me to the hospital.

Tiger and MeMa

You are my toy Tiger said with his eyes and I thought Oh no I am his toy. He was the cat and I was the mouse. Tiger was my great grandmother MeMa's 18 pound cat. He had green eyes with a creepy black slit in the middle and his grey and black fur was all puffy and dragged the floor like a woolly mammoth. Tiger was a woolly mammoth cat.

When we got to MeMa's I'd look out for Tiger and he would peek at me from around the corner pawing the carpet his body bunching up like a fist. I don't know why Tiger picked on me my brother and sister were even littler than me. Here kitty kitty meet my little brother.

Tiger didn't have claws. MeMa had them taken out because Tiger tore up the furniture. It made me a little less scared of Tiger but not much he still had teeth. MeMa warned us not to let Tiger outside because he would be defenseless without claws against other animals. The idea of Tiger being defenseless seemed very funny but I didn't laugh at MeMa. I wanted to ask MeMa Have you **seen** Tiger but I didn't.

Visiting MeMa made me a little scared even besides Tiger. MeMa walked hunched over her walker and wasn't as nice to us as Daddy Sam and Nanny were. She didn't give us toys. Mom Fisher, my other great grandmother, had sugar diabetes and wasn't as nice to us as Grandmommie was. She didn't make us pies. Are all grandparents nicer than all great grandparents? Is it because great grandparents feel bad?

MeMa's name was Jessie and her husband's name was Jesse.

Daddy told us that MeMa was a fullblood Cherokee Indian and her blood ran through me. I **played** cowboys and Indians, and my great grandmother was a **real** Indian. Mom Fisher had Indian blood but she wouldn't talk about it. Daddy taught us to be proud of our Cherokee Indian blood. He said the Cherokees were the smartest tribe and made up their own alphabet. I would be the Indian next time we played.

MeMa went to church in the woods. She was a Baptist and had pictures of Jesus on her wall. She said it was sinful that Nanny played bridge. I didn't go to church but I didn't tell MeMa that. Mother took us to Presbyterian church a few times but Daddy stayed home and watched football then I stayed home with him. Daddy quit church when he was a kid when the preacher told him dogs didn't go to heaven. I would go where Daddy and the dogs went. Daddy said Decide for yourself about God. I didn't tell MeMa that.

We watched the man walk on the moon at MeMa's house. The man looked like the Pillsbury doughboy in his astronaut uniform and I wanted to poke him in the belly. I watched the man on the moon with one eye and Tiger with the other eye. Not really. I tried to but I was afraid I would go crosseyed. Our bed was a pallet on the floor. I tried to stay awake all night so Tiger wouldn't attack me but I finally fell asleep and Tiger attacked me.

Author's note: The following story, told by my uncle Dave, happened before I was born. Clyde is my father.

MUSTANGS

Dave's burr haircut exposed his most prominent feature: ears that looked like catcher's mitts sticking out diagonally from the sides of his head. Clyde would grab the pendulous lobes with needle-nosed pliers and pull Dave out of bed in the mornings. Dave almost missed the bite of the pliers on his earlobe now. Everything changed when Carolyn got polio.

In 1951, the polio epidemic swept through Sweetwater, Texas, and Carolyn, Dave's older sister by ten years, got infected. She would spend the next two years at a rehab facility in Gonzales and return home wheelchair-bound and quadriplegic. Dave's family seemed to evaporate while Carolyn was away; his mother stayed mostly with Carolyn; his daddy was gone a lot too, and when he was home, he smelled of alcohol more often than before; his brother Clyde, much older than Dave too, by eight years, got hold of a Cadillac, peroxided his hair white, and spent days at a time out in the caves on a ranch near Roby. Mommy Blanche, Dave's grandmother, became his parent by default. Dave would sleep with her, and she'd read him the Bible. She'd rub his legs when he got growing pains.

As much as anything, Dave missed the perpetual flow of family, friends, and dogs coursing through the house. No doors were locked, nobody knocked. There was always a hubbub. There might be a bridge game in one room, a wrestling match in the next, and canine follies spilling into both. There might be five people at dinner or twelve. When Carolyn went away, even the big old house got sad, Dave thought; it groaned and creaked like never before.

Dave was seven years old when Carolyn came home. She seemed to have changed the least of all of his family, except now Dave was the same height as her in her wheelchair. One day, before Carolyn had gotten polio, Dave ran through a pile of smoldering leaves and his coveralls caught on fire. Carolyn swooped in out of nowhere, rolled him on the ground, and put him out without a burn. Dave knew that Carolyn would always look out for him, wheelchair be damned, and it occurred to him that she needed his help right back now.

Clyde gravitated back to the house after Carolyn returned, and the backseat of Clyde's Cadillac became Dave's danger zone. Clyde and his friends would throw lit firecrackers in the backseat with Dave. During his time in the caves, Clyde had captured a snake, a black coachwhip, and would sometimes loose it in the floorboard of the car to terrorize Dave and other unsuspecting passengers.

Clyde's friends were as cruel as Clyde, if less creative. When Dave saw Bryce Hardin, he thought of the toilet bowl because Hardin would dangle him by the ankles over it and flush. Dave would crane his neck to watch the water slurp down the bowl and watch it rise again, then close his eyes when the cool water touched his bare scalp. One time, upside down, Dave hollered at Hardin and called him a "dumbask." Dave was just learning to cuss and didn't have the words quite right yet. "Dumbask" became Dave's name for a while.

As leery as Dave was of his big brother, he ached for his company. Good times with Clyde were the best. The most fun Dave ever had was when Clyde took him to the movie house to see "The Thing." Clyde snuck in his dog, Dirty Ball, under his coat, and Dirty Ball watched the movie from Clyde's lap like a regular person. When The Thing thawed out and turned monstrous, Dirty Ball started barking, and they got kicked out.

Making Dave the Sweetwater High mascot was the brainchild of Bill Washam, Carolyn's boyfriend, who was a drum major in the band. Bill had dearly missed Carolyn and was still worried sick about her. Spending time with Dave was good for both of them. Bill's aunt was a seamstress, and she fashioned a full bandleader outfit for Dave, complete with a red tuxedo jacket and tails. Dave wasn't sure what to make of the whole production, but he wasn't going to argue.

The band director, Mr. Baird, had always wanted to try the stunt of having someone bust out of a drum during a halftime show but never had the opportunity until the big-eared boy came along. He decided to unveil it during the Big Spring game.

Dave fit cozily in the drum. He had to sit with his knees bent, locked together, but it wasn't too bad, just pitch black inside. Before halftime on game night, Bill and the drummer unscrewed the drum skin, and Dave climbed in, dressed in his bandleader outfit, then they closed him back in. Dave could feel every bump as the bass drum on wheels rattled down the ramp from the field house. The drummer couldn't resist banging the drum a couple of times, but it made a "thunking" sound with a little human inside, which wasn't as satisfying as the "boom" it usually produced. Dave hollered, but the drum swallowed his voice.

If not for the press box and stadium lights, you wouldn't know the Mustang Bowl was there, looking from a distance. It was built below ground level and patrons walked *down* to their seats in wooden bleachers set into the grass slope. Personally approved by FDR, it was constructed in 1939 by the Works Progress Administration and was arguably the finest high school stadium in Texas, or the nation, for that matter. In the daylight, viewed from the rim, the Mustang Bowl was a startling sight, like a volcano crater with a football field inside it. At night, under the lights, animated by 17,000 Texas high school football fans, it was breathtaking.

When Dave heard the cue from the band director, he kicked his way through the drum skin and emerged in the middle of the field to the cheers of the crowd. From the stands, it looked like a baby bird hatching from its egg. The colors were electrifying to Dave after the darkness of the drum — the green of the field, the blood red of the Sweetwater band outfits, and the blaze of the lights. Dave realized that Bill hadn't told him what to do once he was out of the drum, and instinct took over. He'd played football on that field since he was old enough to walk, so he ran. Dave ran fast. Dave ran fast and decided he was a running back, and the band was the defense and commenced darting and ducking, shucking and jiving, diving and dashing. He relished the confusion he saw in the eyes of the band members as they peeked down at him over their instruments.

The band members had positioned themselves to form the word "MUSTANGS" in the center of the field when Dave broke free and, at first, tried to maintain their discipline despite the sight of a bald-headed midget in red tails hurtling past their legs. They'd lost their high-stepping confidence, though, and a few sour notes rang out here and there. The letters in "MUSTANGS" began to look like letters in a Halloween ad, all shaky and shivery. Finally, a trumpet player couldn't resist and made a grab at Dave; others followed, and "MUSTANGS" disintegrated. Only a few pieces still played forlornly.

Dave had scampered through the entire band by now and made it to the front of the formation. He realized a few members were chasing him, but they looked cloddish and bumbling in their red boots and tall, fuzzy hats. They'd never catch him. He was beginning to feel a little foolish, however, making all those terrific moves without a football in his arms. A real running back needed a football. It occurred to him that he might be a linebacker instead, and he high-tailed it again, intent on making a tackle. The baton twirlers were first in line, but he would never tackle a girl. He veered away from the tuba that was bigger than he was and the cymbals that looked sharp around the edges. The flute player entered Dave's field of vision, and he launched himself into the boy's chest, pinning him with a perfect form tackle.

Dave had not heard the crowd during his romp, but now, lying on the ground next to the flutist, the roar from the stands engulfed him.

Dave's mother, Mommy Blanche and Carolyn had ringside seats at the game in the handicapped section, just recently erected for disabled World War II veterans. On the car ride home, they were too tickled to be seriously mad at the boy. "Mr. Baird is pretty frosted," Carolyn said, "and he can lump it." Mainly, they just wanted to know what he'd been thinking. Dave kept repeating that they hadn't told him what to do once he broke out of the drum.

Clyde, who would be voted "Mr. Mustang" a couple of years later for his football-playing exploits in the Mustang Bowl, had taken a date to the game, so Dave didn't see him right away. The next morning, he was awakened by the pinch of needle-nosed pliers on his earlobe. Clyde was busting with glee over his brother's escapade. He said, "You blew their doors off, buddy." Dave couldn't remember his big brother ever calling him "buddy" before, and it made his head tingle.

The following year Sweetwater High chose a strawberry roan Shetland pony to be their mascot.

Coachwhip

Clyde Wayne lords a Cadillac
Down a small town Texas street
His bleached hair mocks the color
Of the pearl white leather seat

The hand that drapes the steering wheel
Like it's waiting to be kissed
Teases snakes and prom queens
And breaks noses with its fist

He squires a slith'ry rider
That flicks a forked tongue
Shrouded in the shadows
Seething to be sprung

He spies his baby brother
Who aches for a place to hide
Says, "Hop on in, my little lamb
Let me take you for a ride."

Scummobiles

Daddy Sam, bless his heart, took it upon himself to provide us three grandkids with transportation through our teenage years. He'd been wealthy at one time, but the story goes that he was an easy mark for a hard luck tale and gradually lost his money on loans that were never repaid, bad investments with friends, and the like. He wanted to help everybody till the day he died. I think this dynamic was at work when he set about procuring cars for us. I imagine his negotiation with the seller went something like this: "I'm sure that Pinto will be a fine car, son, once you get it running. $1500 sounds a little low. Will you take $2000?"

Being the eldest of the grandkids, I was the first to experience his generosity in the gift of a car. "I have a car for you, Bud. Come and get it." All I had to do was get from Dallas to Roscoe to pick it up. Flush with *On the Road* enthusiasm and romanticism, my buddy Murphy and I decided to hitchhike. It was late summer, during a smothering Texas heat wave. Mom didn't like the idea, but Daddy was all for it and dropped us off of a morning on a North Dallas freeway. We had provisioned ourselves with a few joints and not much else. Broke college students working summer jobs, we had maybe twenty bucks between us.

Jack Kerouac's *On the Road* was written in 1951; this was in 1980. Times had changed. Hitchhiking was no longer socially acceptable. After about ten hours of 108-degree heat and fifty miles of progress, the only things that burn, burn, burned were our skin and our tempers, and I'm sure we said commonplace things. Cynically (I held a grudge against Dallas for what I perceived to be an aura of gross materialism), I started waving cash to see if that might shake loose a ride, but that didn't work. Waving joints did. We got our best ride of the day from some ranch hands who took us past Abilene. Maybe country folks were more amenable to hitchhikers. We got another ride right away, and, reaching the territory where everybody knew Sam L. Jones, we were delivered to his doorstep.

The Pinto was a faded baby blue station wagon with manual transmission. I'd never driven a manual, so Daddy Sam showed me the basics. I'd learn to drive it on the way home. The Pinto did have an air conditioner, but it blew out before we got to Sweetwater, drenching Murphy's chest with Freon. I figured that its lack of speed was attributable to my clumsy shifting, but that son of a bitch never made it past fifty-six miles per hour on that trip or ever after. Climbing a small hill in the Pinto incited all passengers to lunge spasmodically to help it along. It was an involuntary reaction, like sneezing. You couldn't help yourself.

The battery was dead by the time we got to Dallas. It turned out that it had been set unmoored in its pan, free to slide around like a large hockey puck on a small rink. It cozied up to the radiator and melted. I scrounged up the money to buy a new battery and thought I had it securely mounted, but apparently, the radiator's attraction was irresistible, and it scooted over and melted a couple of days later. I got about a mile into the third battery of the week when the Pinto died again. It was at this point that my first decided to test the resiliency of the driver's side window. My fist kicked the window's

27

ass, and blood fountained into the air, like in a scene from a Monty Python skit. My blood spurted all over a neighbor kid's back seat while he rushed me to a friend's house, where I soaked their sidewalk in blood and vomit until they hied me to the hospital.

The Pinto was a part of me, literally, for two more decades, as glass shards would sprout from my arm periodically when I was well into my thirties.

I never got to experience the infamous explode-on-impact feature of the Pinto, probably because the car would have had to have been operating on a roadway for the opportunity to present itself, and it spent most of its time disabled and disarmed. Curses, punches and kicks did not make it explode.

The Pinto was the prototypical Scummobile, aesthetically appalling and mechanically afflicted. The name originated with a pond scum-colored Buick LeSabre that was a hand-me-down from Daddy Sam's sister. It was an unremarkable vehicle except for its ugliness. My brother Carey, whom Daddy nicknamed "Golden Boy" for his good looks and athletic prowess, didn't want to be seen in it, so he made us drop him off a couple of blocks away from his destination. The Scummobile name stuck and was deservedly applied to every car we had for several years thereafter.

Before I go any further I should acknowledge that our lives with the Scummobiles would have been easier if we'd had a whit of mechanical aptitude or instruction in how to take care of a car. Hell, we didn't know. We were raised by The Anti-Mechanic. Not only did Daddy neglect maintenance on his cars, he willfully abused them. He had a string of company cars that were beta version Scummobiles because he made them so, as some kind of warped punishment of his employer, I think.

Daddy called his company cars "units" (unless I misheard and he was calling them "eunuchs"). I remember him saying one time, "The unit hasn't had an oil change in, like, 25,000 miles. What do you think will happen to it?" It wasn't so much a mechanical question as a philosophical one. The oil light on another company car stayed lit for at least a year, then finally gave up and blacked out. My sister Junie was the unlucky driver during the unlit phase. A thrown rod torpedoed through the engine while she was doing seventy in the middle of unforgiving Dallas traffic. Apparently, the units preferred grungy oil to zero oil.

After we were all off to college, Daddy took a more hands-on approach, beating the hell out of a unit with a 7-iron. As a veteran car batterer, I would have suggested a less lofted club, say, a 2-iron, to inflict the most exquisite damage.

The interior of Daddy's cars were matted in black Labrador retriever hair, deposited by his beloved Soul Sister on her trips to the bars (he claimed she visited 278 bars in her lifetime, Brandy Alexander her drink of choice). The seats were pock-marked from exploded marijuana seeds that popped from his pipe, and Carey later swore that he would get a contact high within five minutes of occupying Daddy's car. Lacking the sense of smell, I was oblivious to the reek. One day, I drove some teammates to a high school baseball game in a company car. One of the guys happened to look in the glove compartment and saw several bags of a green, leafy substance. "Hey man, your dad has a bunch of pot in here!" "No way," I said, "it's pipe tobacco. Daddy smokes a pipe." Because I honestly believed it was pipe tobacco, I was able to convince my friends. It took a couple of more years for me to realize my father really was a soul mate of Cheech and Chong.

A rusty blue Bel Air was by far the most fun of the Scummobiles. She was like a loopy aunt with charming idiosyncrasies. For one thing, you could pull the key out of the ignition while you were driving; the only car I ever had that you could drive and lose its keys at the same time. My favorite feature of the Bel Air was that when you turned the steering wheel "x" degrees to the right, she would honk. One of my usual routes took me through a cloverleaf with a long, circular on-ramp, and she would honk all the way around like she was gleefully shouting, "Look at me, I'm circling, I'm circling!" At first, I tried to take the 360-degree turn in little angles, so the progression was sort of a Morse code of honks, but soon, I embraced the madness and let her express herself in full voice.

Murphy's favorite Bel Air trick was the windshield wiper game. Rain would fall, you'd turn on the wipers and get no response, visibility would finally fade to zero, and you'd decide, "OK, I have to pull over," then she'd flick her wiper arms once, just in the nick of time. This process repeated itself over and over.

Her madness may have been contagious. During my Bel Air summer, I worked as a Schlitz deliveryman in South Dallas. At the end of every day, I climbed, sweat-soaked, into the un-air-conditioned Bel Air, installed a quart of Schlitz malt liquor between my thighs, and fought the Dallas rush hour wars, cussing and shooting the finger at any driver whom I deemed to be an idiot. I quite enjoyed it. Murphy and I still had some faint dreams of baseball careers and felt like we should stay in shape. But what we really wanted to do was drink beer. Our cockamamie compromise was to park the Bel Air about a mile from the liquor store, jog there in the 100-degree heat, and then slug down a six-pack in about ten minutes. We'd walk back to the car with a healthy buzz. I'd just as soon attribute that idea to the automobile.

The Bel Air passed to Junie, in whose hands she became more petulant. The windshield wiper game was not as much fun; making up for missed opportunities in the past, perhaps, the Bel Air wiped the windshield constantly, rain or shine. Toward the end, Junie had to jumpstart the car every time she wanted to drive it. The hood was heavy, so Junie had to stand on it to latch it shut. Every morning and afternoon, before and after school, Junie became an animated hood ornament. She speculated on what the neighbors thought: "There's that loony Junie standing on her car again."

Carey christened his first personal Scummobile Chocolate Thunder, and the name was spot on. It was a dark brown, late model Mercury Grand Marquis Brougham about the size of a humpback whale. Daddy and Dave landed it in Sweetwater; most likely, from the sinister looks of it, after a pimp or mobster rendered it expendable. Carey noticed a couple of oddities right off. While the tires showed tread from the outside, if you spied under the car you could see they were billiard ball bald on the inner half, a disturbing sign in more ways than one. The most intriguing feature lay under the hood, in the form of a large Folger's coffee can lodged in the engine, as if it performed some kind of essential mechanical function. Who knew Folger's made catalytic converters?

Chocolate Thunder's new home was San Marcos, where Carey went to college and belonged to a fraternity. Because it was such an eyesore, Carey's frat brothers would not allow him to park it in front of the house. In an ironic twist harkening back to the days of the first Scummobile, he had to park it a couple of blocks away and walk the rest. A Scummobile owner walked many more miles than the average person.

Carey did demonstrate some mechanical ability, of a fashion, with Chocolate Thunder. One time, a cop pulled him over because a headlight was out. Carey, never shy to diddle with authority (when he was twelve or so, he was nabbed by the police, and asked his name, told them "Knuckles"), disagreed with the cop. "No, the light's not out," he said. He kicked the headlight, it relit, and he was good to go.

The last time I saw the dung-colored heap was when Carey stopped by my apartment in Austin on his way from Dallas. He was transporting a king-sized mattress, tied haphazardly to the roof, and it drooped over the edges like Gilligan's hat. Chocolate Thunder's last road trip was in the role of mini-bus, ferrying half a dozen frat brothers to Nuevo Laredo. Alas, it broke down in Falfurrias. Carey traded a bottle of tequila for a mechanic's labor, but 110 proof did not prove inspiration enough to revive the car, and Carey had to have it hauled back to San Marcos.

Chocolate Thunder received the death sentence for its failure to negotiate the Mexico trip and was executed in a field near Wimberley, broadsided by a Civil War-era cannonball that pierced the driver's side door and came to rest in the passenger seat. Carey lit the cannon's fuse. I was delighted when I heard the news, not so much by the car's demise, but at the method. I wondered if I could get my hands on the bloody Pinto, somehow, and give it the demolition it deserved.

The Scummobile era ended with Chocolate Thunder's cannonball. The quality of our automobiles progressively improved and we siblings evolved into conscientious car owners, erring on the side of more frequent than necessary oil changes.

Mr. Big

Freddie's fingernails unsettled me. They were glossy as if covered with clear fingernail polish. I wondered if he had them manicured to look that way, or if the glaze came from some medical condition, some caustic internal fluid seeping through to his crust, or maybe cards and money flew through his hands so fast that they buffed his nails to a shine.

Freddie Bates was my father's bookie. Daddy named him "Mr. Big."

Mr. Big was in his early 40s, about 5'7", with thin brown hair combed over a receding hairline. A few small scars pocked his chin and forehead. Tinted prescription glasses cast a shadow over his eyes. He had uneven, amateurishly constructed false teeth. Looking back now, I can make a couple of educated guesses about them: One, his original teeth were knocked out by a fist. Two, the dentures were created by a drunkard dentist named Dr. Colter, one of Daddy's drinking buddies who botched the repair of my brother's front teeth when they got broken.

In those days, much of our family commerce went through Daddy's bar pals. One December day, a giant flocked Christmas tree, maybe 12 feet tall, gaudier than any tree we'd ever had before, showed up at our apartment. Daddy hinted that the tree came from a Mafia-related source, and he joked about it, saying, "We should be very nice to those men." He knew the proprietors of a restaurant in

Dallas that was a reputed mob operation; maybe that was the connection.

I met Freddie when I was home for the summer between my junior and senior years at UT Austin, and Daddy got on his Sunday brunch kick. Daddy would invite Freddie over to the condo in Grand Prairie and make his Mexican breakfast or pancakes that looked like tumors or diamonds or footballs, discoursing expansively on his genius creations as they evolved. While Daddy entertained, Mother quietly did the real work, whipping up a spread of scrambled eggs, homemade biscuits, O'Brien potatoes, and usually some kind of specialty bacon Daddy got from a butcher friend.

We'd drink Bloody Marys and watch football. Freddie would fire up a joint immediately after we ate, saying that a heavy meal caused you to lose your buzz. Daddy labeled this the "Batesonian Theory." Carey, who attended a couple of the brunches, proposed the following addendums: "The Water on the Forehead Principle" postulated that taking a shower also caused one's buzz to fade and thus, you had to toke up after bathing. "The Theory of Relativity" held that you needed to be high at any gathering of relatives, say, at Thanksgiving.

Mother didn't like Daddy's or her kid's dope-smoking, but, being married to Clyde since she was 19, she'd learned tolerance at an early age. She enjoyed the brunches and much preferred having her husband partying at home than out in the bars. Mother liked Freddie well enough, but she would never have set him up with a friend of hers if she was a matchmaker. He did have manners, at least when he was sober, but his language became cruder the drunker he got. She preferred him stoned because the marijuana blunted his harsh edge.

My alone time with Freddie came when we'd run errands for booze and groceries in his brand new white Cadillac Eldorado, "the Eldo," he called it. We talked mostly about football and gambling, point spreads, and who we liked in the games. I knew he was from Spearman, up at the tip top of the Texas panhandle, because Daddy would make fun of him for it and said Spearman was a "runty ass little burg" compared to the metropolis of Sweetwater, where Daddy was raised. Daddy accused Freddie of being "damned near an Okie." Freddie didn't volunteer much about his personal history to me.

Freddie treated Mom respectfully and would occasionally bring her flowers, and I liked him for that and for his love of Soul Sister, our black Lab who Daddy escorted to the bars. Daddy told me that one time, a guy stumbled over Soul Sister in The Maple Point. Soul Sister was raven black, and the interior of The Maple Point was cave-dark when you first walked in out of the sunshine...you were damned near blind until your eyes adjusted. The man cussed Soul Sister, and Freddie flew into a rage, spewing spittle and obscenities into the guy's face. The dog was more welcome there than he was, Freddie told him. Daddy said that he was surprised at the vehemence of Freddie's attack. The guy shut his mouth and slunk into the dark. Daddy sent a drink over to his table.

I headed back off to college and saw Freddie just once in the next year or so. I was carless after my latest Scummobile had crapped out, and Mother had found me a used Mazda. Daddy and Freddie met me with it at the Turkey Shoppe (long gone now) near Abbott, Willie Nelson's hometown. They were in high spirits, lit, I'm sure, and I was happy to see them and thrilled to finally have my own ride again. Freddie told me to look in the console of the Mazda and I found a big bag of weed. Yeehaw. That was 30+ years ago now and I still remember vividly that delightful hour.

That was the year Daddy became a drug runner. Mr. Big arranged the gig. Daddy and Mr. Big, accompanied by Soul Sister, drove a van packed with several kilos of marijuana to Florida. Daddy told me about it later and said he did it for the experience to see what that side of life was like; maybe he'd write about it. I'm sure he didn't make a cent on the deal. He said they got pulled over by the cops in Mississippi, and he was worried. Distracted by Soul Sister, the police never searched the van. Soul Sister was rewarded with Brandy Alexanders in dozens of bars along the way. Daddy and Mr. Big caroused with NFL Hall of Fame quarterback Kenny "The Snake" Stabler in Gulf Shores, Alabama. Daddy said Stabler was an interesting cat.

The next thing I heard about Mr. Big was that he was moving to Austin. Daddy said the word in the bars was that the heat was on Mr. Big in Dallas for "passing phony paper," i.e., counterfeiting. Daddy sounded subdued, embarrassed. I got the feeling that they had had a falling out but he didn't say it in so many words.

Mr. Big called me in Austin and told me to see him at The Caucus on Red River. The Caucus (also long since closed) was a hangout for politicians working at the State Capitol, just a few blocks away. Mr. Big's Eldo was parked out front of the two-story white stucco building and I found him in his "office" at a table in the back of the tony club. He bought me a few beers and the bartender treated him with respect, called him Mr. Bates. We caught up on old times, and he said he was setting up a booking operation and would be glad to take my bets. "We'll settle up at a dime," Mr. Big said. He had to explain to me that a "dime" was $1000. I was a poor college student paying my own way with student loans and a part-time job; I would line up with my buddies on the first day of classes every year to get our $150 emergency loans from UT. The $1000 settle-up seemed like an absurd number to me because I would never bet enough to reach it, winning or losing, but I understood that's how bookies worked and wasn't going to argue.

Mr. Big let me bet $50 a game, relaxing his $100 minimum. I started off winning, and, at first, he would offer advice that was usually spot on. I'd analyze the point spreads on Sunday mornings, then call in my bets. After I won a few hundred I boosted my risk to $100 a game and stayed hot, but didn't get any more touts from Mr. Big. Within a couple of months, I'd blown past the dime settle-up. I couldn't believe my luck, and my buddies and I started making grandiose plans for my winnings. Mexico, Vegas and New Orleans beckoned. I was gonna be friggin' rich.

When I talked to Mr. Big about settling up, he said we'd get together soon. I hadn't seen him in a few months, just talked to him on the phone. I figured he probably had high-rollers to handle, and he'd take care of me eventually. Meanwhile, he kept taking my bets, and I kept winning, finally upping my haul to $1800.

Mr. Big kept waffling on my payout and finally said he was going to quit booking for a while, but he would get me paid. His big news was that he and some partners were going to open up a barbecue joint in downtown Austin and told me to come on by; they were just getting it ready. A couple of friends and I visited the bare, defunct lounge that had a small kitchen in the back. Mr. Big treated us to free screwdrivers. The vodka and orange juice looked lonely on the otherwise bottle-less bar. We smoked dope on the patio, ducking the overgrown foliage. It seems funny now, a barbecue joint with a full bar, but that was their plan.

The dirty Eldo was missing a hubcap and sported a couple of dents. Mr. Big's slacks were no longer pressed, and his skin looked sallow.

We drank there for several weeks while Mr. Big and his partners argued about barbecue pits and liquor licenses. I participated in the only work I ever saw done there, cutting pieces of vinyl and gluing them to the tops of a bunch of cheapo, used bistro tables they'd acquired. Mr. Big cussed at the labor, and the tables looked even crummier covered than bare.

One Friday afternoon, I went over there after work, and Mr. Big was all het up, rounding up booze and dope and cocaine for a "pile" that weekend. I asked him what a "pile" was, and he said he and his partners knew some broads who were game to drink and snort coke and fuck all weekend. They shambled in Sunday after the pile, bleary-eyed and snarling at each other, shirts half-tucked into pants, dresses hanging lopsided. My stomach turned.

It was not long after the pile that Mr. Big asked if he could stay with me for a little while till he got back on his feet. The barbecue joint wasn't going to pan out. I was sharing an apartment on the Drag with Murphy, and we said, "Sure." Murphy wasn't around much, and Mr. Big and I spent a few nights drinking beer, smoking dope and playing gin. He had run into some Quaaludes and offered me one. "No sirree bob," I said; beer and dope gave me all the buzz I wanted.

I could shuffle and deal cards pretty spiffily, but I was no match for Mr. Big, whose shiny fingernails flashed as the cards whirred blindingly through his hands. We played gin for a dollar a point, a little scary for me since the most I'd ever played for was a penny a point, but hell, I was up $1800. I'm sure he was the better gin player, but I killed him that week, winning several hundred more dollars that I finally understood I would never see.

Mr. Big got angrier and angrier the more he lost, and I thought he was cussing his luck, but no, he was cursing me crudely, bitterly, calling me a cocksucker and a motherfucker and a cunt, a hundred times over. At first, I joked back at him about it, thinking he couldn't be serious, but he wasn't playing. I don't think I'd ever heard such language spoken in real life, only in movies. I endured his abuse for several nights and never really got mad, it, was so over-the-top. He was (or had been) Daddy's friend, and I respected my elders. I did wonder what would happen if I got fed up and challenged him physically. We were about the same size; I was half his age and much fitter, but I had no battle savvy, and I knew he would fight dirty. He would know how to hurt me.

I returned from class one afternoon to find the Eldo in the parking lot, battered. The front bumper drooped like a pouty bottom lip. The windshield was cracked, and the headlights busted. Inside the apartment, Mr. Big was crashed on the couch, his face bloody and bruised. I asked him what happened, and he said he'd been out with a couple of strippers, Ferrari and Bentley, and one thing led to another.

Hearing Mr. Big say the names Ferrari and Bentley disturbed me because I actually knew them, not from the strip joints, but from the last apartment complex I'd lived in, a place called, ironically, The El Dorado, where all of the apartments opened up to a courtyard with a pool in the middle, and because of the cozy configuration, everybody knew everybody. Their civilian names were Renee and Jennifer, and they were from Copperas Cove. They spoke venomously about "Cove," and said they couldn't get out of there fast enough. My friends and I couldn't figure them out; they were about our age, early 20s, but would usually be lounging around the pool when we were coming and going from class; they didn't seem to be students. They may not have embarked on their careers when we first met them, or maybe they were reticent in talking about it, but their affairs were a mystery to us.

Even among the assemblage of attractive college-age girls at the El Dorado, Renee and Jennifer stood out. Renee was the more classically beautiful of the pair, about my height, 5'6" or so, generously endowed and perfectly proportioned. Seeing Renee in a bikini before class was a better waker-upper than coffee. Jennifer was several inches taller, blonde, and blue-eyed. Her torso slightly outsized her long legs, lending her an aggressive bearing. She was the more outgoing of the two and the more assertive one in their binary clan. Jennifer partied with us more often than Renee did and drank every one of us guys under the table more than once.

One night around the pool, Renee offered to give one of my friends a back rub, and they disappeared into her apartment for the night. Their liaison ended there. Renee and Jennifer were not interested in dating or a "relationship," we gathered. My taste in girls ran to those who presented a more innocent image than Renee and Jennifer's, but I did make a feeble attempt at earning Renee's affection. Still a virgin at age 22, I was acutely self-conscious and wooden with the opposite sex. Renee and I found ourselves alone by the pool one night, and I arched and craned my neck laboriously, wordlessly suggesting that I was in dire need of a back rub. Somehow, my clever ruse did not prove to be the catalyst for my sexual awakening. Renee paid no attention.

It wasn't until everybody scattered at the end of our leases in May that we learned they were dancing at Sugar's, and their working names were Ferrari and Bentley. Strip clubs excited me not one whit; I preferred to have something left to my imagination. I never saw them dance.

When Freddie mentioned their names, I felt a pang of sadness for Renee and Jennifer. I knew they weren't innocent babes, but to be wilding with the likes of Freddie seemed like a dangerous course. Perhaps I was jealous, too, that he'd swooped in on girls I'd met first.

I found myself surprised that my loyalty lay with the girls over Freddie, who was supposed to be my friend.

Mr. Big disappeared that afternoon, and I never saw him again.

I didn't talk to Daddy much during Mr. Big's Austin engagement. I told him I was on a roll betting football and that Mr. Big was opening a barbecue joint, then let it drop. I never did tell him about our temporary living arrangement, nor describe to him the gin games. I'm sure word got to Daddy one way or another that Mr. Big skipped town without settling up with me.

Looking back now, I try to make sense of Daddy's friendship with Freddie and, by extension, mine. One time, Daddy was talking philosophically and said that the driving force in his life was "action." He craved adventure and surrounded himself with eccentric characters; the more outrageous, the better. I think Freddie represented "action" to Daddy. Freddie wasn't particularly smart or endearing or even fun to be around, but he lived on the edge, and that was enough for Daddy.

I think Daddy was also intrigued by the fact that Freddie never worked a day in his life. As his career as a salesman for McGraw-Hill progressed, Daddy had success and made good money but became disenchanted with corporate life. Daddy went into to office less and less, doing almost all of his business out of bars. He would sometimes take off on a lark to Colorado and call into his office saying he was "west of Dallas." Daddy aspired to do as little work as possible and still earn his salary. Freddie was a perfect role model.

The extent of Freddie's criminality, his lack of self-control and spontaneous rage, Daddy didn't see coming. I'm sure Daddy would say he misjudged Freddie on that score.

My father was my hero, despite many transgressions (mostly alcohol-related) that could have, and maybe should have dissuaded my worship but never really did. If Freddie was Daddy's friend then that was good enough for me. After Freddie, I think I became a little more leery of Daddy's friends.

The rest of Freddie's story I got from Mother. Maybe a year after he left Austin, Mother and Daddy got a call in the middle of the night from a bartender friend. Freddie was waving a gun around in a Dallas bar, menacing the customers, and had to be collared before somebody got killed. Daddy drove over to the bar and talked him down.

A few years later, Daddy heard that Freddie had died of some kind of cancer. Daddy didn't go to the funeral.

Following Daddy

I could feel the atmosphere in Daddy's car as if I were sitting there beside him. Daddy would be smoking skunk weed out of a Meerschaum pipe, seeds popping and flaring like shooting stars, sizzling on the purple velour seats, leaving BB-sized black craters. The Sunday New York Times crossword puzzle would be propped on the steering wheel, and Daddy would be lost in contemplation of letters and words. The radio would be silent so as not to interfere with his concentration. Soul Sister, our black Lab, would be in the back seat, basking in her contact high, drooling, dreaming of Dairy Queen Blizzards and deer carcasses.

The Colorado state trooper, coming in the opposite direction, whipped a U-ey, crossing four lanes of traffic to shoehorn himself behind Daddy's car and in front of mine; no signal, no blip of his lights. I had to tap my brakes to give him room. It pissed me off, the arrogance of the maneuver, then I wondered why the trooper would be tailing Daddy. I'd been following him for two hours, and we were both cruising at the speed limit in the right lane like grannies. We were in no hurry on a Sunday morning. Daddy hadn't done anything that I could see to draw attention. Was the trooper targeting Daddy intentionally, or was it just a coincidence?

I wondered if Daddy noticed the cop or if he was in one of his reveries. He'd talked about it earlier in our trip, how sometimes when he was driving, he would get so lost in thought that he forgot his location on the planet. He might snap to after driving for an hour, and for a few seconds, he had no idea whether he was in Tucumcari or Timbuktu, Colorado or Kathmandu. He didn't require weed or a crossword to become entranced sometimes he'd do it stone sober. Those few seconds of mystery delighted him. I've since experienced the lost-in-the-world sensation while driving, writing stories in my head as towns and landmarks passed undetected; the wake-up in who-knows-where is a thrill. And, no, it's not dangerous driving. You're still aware of the texter going 45 in the passing lane, you just might not be able to name the continent you both inhabit.

I was sure Daddy's car reeked of marijuana, and I figured there might be trouble if he had to open his window to talk to the police, but Daddy, the trooper and I drove the 10 miles into Alamosa uneventfully; the trooper never making a move to stop my father.

Daddy and I had met a few days before, between Cuchara and LaVeta, driving in opposite directions. I was on spring break from college in Austin, and Daddy had taken a week off from his job in Dallas. We pulled off on a turnout, and the first thing Daddy said was, "Hey pal, give me $10 for gas." Daddy was going on a week's vacation in Colorado, driving a new Lincoln, with zero dollars in his pocket. He had a Carte Blanche credit card, but none of the gas stations in the tiny mountain towns accepted it. I had less than $100 on me. The year was 1982, before credit cards became ubiquitous, so financing the trip was going to be interesting.

We didn't have any hard and fast plans, only to explore the Sangre de Christo mountain range of southern Colorado, a place Daddy loved since he'd been there as a kid. He would retire to Cuchara

10 years later and rename the Sangres "the Clydes," saying that Jesus had the name for 200 years and now it was his turn. The end goal was Lake Vallecito, in the San Juan range near Durango. We would travel most of the trip in separate cars, happily, each relishing our independence and the option to break off at a moment's notice. Daddy and I enjoyed each other's company but were also perfectly content being alone. Our loner mentality baffled and sometimes infuriated other family members, especially Mother.

We found a cheap motel in LaVeta, twelve miles down the mountain from the more scenic and expensive Cuchara. The first thing Daddy wanted to show me was the site of the Ludlow Massacre, north of Trinidad, where, in 1914, guards from Colorado Fuel & Iron (CF&I), a coal mining company owned by one of the Rockefellers and at the time one of the largest corporations in the country, had attacked and killed two dozen striking miners and their families. Women and children burned to death in a tent fire. Woody Guthrie, one of Daddy's heroes, had written a song about it.

The miners, Daddy said, had been recruited by CF&I from southern Europe to replace miners who had struck before, and we saw business signs with the names of Lenzini, Unfug, and Smircich around Walsenburg, where many of the mines had been located. We explored the old mines and cemeteries and enjoyed pronouncing the exotic names we found, such as Bonicelli, Ciarlo, Dorcas, Hribar, Vucetich, Ozzello, Sporcich, and Koutnik.

The centerpiece of Cuchara's football field-long, dirt road "downtown" was The Dog Bar, where dogs outnumbered bar stools.

We ended our day there, drinking beer. The town dogs were enchanted with Soul Sister's anus.

We both woke up around 4:00 am craving breakfast and ate omelets at an all-night truck stop outside LaVeta.

We got lucky with the weather on that trip. March is the snowiest month in the Sangres, but for the most part, we enjoyed sunny skies and crisp temperatures. That morning on Cucharas Pass, the cloud deck floated below the level of the pass, and we looked down on the clouds shrouding the valley. It felt like we were standing on an island in the middle of a motionless, pillowy sea. We let the silence and beauty wash over us and didn't speak a word.

We drove on south down through the clouds past Monument Lake and on to Stonewall, where we ate green chili cheeseburgers and Daddy told me about the vertical sandstone wall that stretches from Mexico all the way to Canada. Daddy described the huge elk herds he'd seen south of Stonewall, and we drove out for a look, but the elk hadn't descended to the lower elevation yet. We had a nightcap at The Dog Bar.

The next day, I followed Daddy west. I pulled off at Wolf Creek Pass and hiked aimlessly, quickly becoming winded from the altitude, while Daddy drove on to Pagosa Springs, where we'd spend the night.

We arrived at Lake Vallecito the following day, spending most of my remaining cash on a lake cabin. Daddy found a convenience store that took Carte Blanche, and we gassed up our cars and stocked up on beer, bread and lunch meat. Daddy, nodding toward the eye-popping blues and greens and whites of the lake, forest and snow-capped mountains, asked a guy at the gas pump if he ever got used to the view, and the man shook his head and said, "No, I sure don't."

We were the second and third customers at a bar we found on the lake that night. The bartender, who turned out to be the owner of the place, was middle-aged, bald-headed, with a black beard sprouting tufts of grey. He seemed happy for the company. The guy was originally from upstate New York, which was beautiful too, he said, but the mountains didn't make you gasp like the ones in Colorado. He introduced himself as JJ Fischbach. Daddy asked him if he minded if we brought Soul Sister in, and he said he'd be glad to have her. Soul Sister lapped up the Brandy Alexander that Daddy ordered for her.

JJ drank with us, and after a while, we all stepped out back to hit off Daddy's pipe. JJ said that today was a day for celebration because it was the birthday of his twins. He led us into the kitchen and, flushed with pride, showed us a picture of his "twins"— two teenage girls, one black and one white, smiling, with their arms around each other's shoulders. JJ said that they were born on the same day from different mothers.

Daddy drove us to Mesa Verde National Park the next day to see the cliff dwellings of the Anasazi Indians. During the ride, he gleefully recounted the story of the twins. That's why he loved bars, he said, for the stories you pick up. Even after he quit drinking 20 years later, Daddy continued to hang out in bars, content with grapefruit juice and yarns.

We didn't make the hike up to the cliff dwellings because Daddy's knee was aching. He'd torn it up in a football game in his senior year at Sweetwater High and now sported a 6-inch zipper scar along the side of his knee and a metal plate inside it. When we were kids, he'd let us knock on the knee, and we'd hear a leaden thud that sounded unnatural, emanating from a human body. Daddy had a football scholarship to TCU lined up, but the offer was withdrawn when he wrecked his knee (his ambulance crashed in a rainstorm on the way to the hospital). The surgery happened in 1957; today, he'd have been good as new a year after surgery, with only a few arthroscopy scars to show for it.

Another high school football story Daddy told was of looking at himself in the mirror at halftime of a game and seeing his elbow sticking out of the skin. He passed out, came to, had it taped up, and played the second half.

We drove on to Four Corners for the hell of it. Given the choice of four states to pee in, Soul Sister opted to leave her mark on Utah. We circled back through northern New Mexico and up to Vallecito.

JJ was standing on the front porch when we arrived at the bar and said, "Well, if it isn't the Jones boys. Come right in, fellas." Daddy and JJ got to talking about Germany and World War II. JJ's family had lived in Dresden and fled to America in 1937. Daddy said that one of his heroes was Field Marshall Erwin Rommel, the "brilliant" German tank commander nicknamed "the Desert Fox." I wondered where he was going with the story, praising a Nazi to a Jew whose family had barely escaped their persecution, but Daddy ended by saying that

Rommel had treated his prisoners humanely, had not supported the oppression of the Jews, and was among the cabal that had tried to assassinate Hitler, costing him his life. JJ said his father had known Rommel in Dresden, and Daddy said, "Are you shittin' me?" He was as excited as if his 50-1 longshot had just won The Kentucky Derby. JJ said his father had been an automobile engineer and Rommel dabbled with engines, trying to improve his Panzer tanks. JJ said his father liked and respected Rommel.

During all of these bar talks, I was mostly silent and just asked questions. Daddy and I were opposites in a lot of ways. He was a big man, about 6'1" and 230 pounds, gregarious, with a booming voice that reverberated around a room, while I was small in stature and extremely introverted. My voice didn't carry two feet. Daddy once told my aunt that I was "odd as a nine-dollar bill." I told a few stories here and there but was content to listen, laugh and learn.

We had to say our goodbyes to JJ because we were heading back east the next morning. By the end of the evening, Daddy was calling JJ a "kike kraut." Somehow, coming out of Daddy's mouth, it sounded like a term of endearment, and that's how JJ took it. He hugged Daddy, Soul Sister, and me, and made us promise that we'd come back to see him. Daddy said, "You bet your ass we will."

It was on that return trip on the straight, flat strip of road through the San Luis Valley, back toward Cuchara, that the state trooper intervened. The trooper followed Daddy into Alamosa, and when we got into town, I breathed a sigh of relief when he turned right into a strip mall, thinking maybe I'd just been paranoid. Then I'll be damned if another state trooper didn't run the stop sign and jump the curb from the lane the other trooper had just entered, barging in between Daddy and me. I had to slam on my brakes to avoid hitting him.

Now, there was no doubt Daddy was being tag-teamed, and I didn't like it. We resumed our uncomfortable procession out of Alamosa. I wracked my brain, trying to think of a reason they were so interested in Daddy. The windows of the Lincoln were tinted enough that you couldn't see any misdeeds occurring inside his car, and even if you had a view of the interior, you'd have seen a middle-aged man, perhaps smoking a pipe. It just didn't make any sense to me.

I was proud of Daddy for driving straight as a string, exactly at the speed limit. The trooper drove dangerously close to Daddy for highway speed, maybe three car lengths behind. Finally, after about 10 miles, the trooper abruptly executed another U-turn and headed back toward Alamosa.

Daddy and I stopped a few miles down the road in Fort Garland, and I asked him, "What the hell was that all about?" He said, "I don't know, man. Your guess is as good as mine."

We spent one last night at The Dog Bar, then headed back to Texas, stopping in Amarillo to say goodbye. Daddy came from a time and a place where a handshake was a meaningful rite. I felt his big, warm hand envelop mine as he looked me in the eye and said, "I had a blast, old pal. Let's do 'er again." I returned his gaze and tried to match, exactly, the power of his grip. Just before he got in his car he shook his head and grinned and said, "Can you believe JJ's old man knew Rommel?"

What A Cack

In 1991, Daddy retired from McGraw-Hill, and he and Mother moved from Grand Prairie to the condo they'd bought in Cuchara, Colorado. I drove the moving van. After we got them moved in, Daddy set me up with his friend Sid on a fishing trip up to stocked trout ponds on the east of the two Spanish Peaks. On the van ride up, I heard foreign accents, which always pique my interest.

I struck up a conversation with the visitors and learned they were Aussies...Angela, Mick and Rosalie...touring the States in an old Volkswagen bus they'd bought in California. Angela and Mick were engaged; Rosalie was Angela's sister. They were all in their mid-twenties.

I helped Angela haul in the first fish she ever caught, and she was ecstatic. "What a cack!" she exclaimed. (I googled "What a cack," and it does mean "to laugh" in Australian slang; in British English slang, it refers to solid waste matter passed from the body through the bowels. "Cack" will always mean laughter, not shit, to me.)

We had a good time, and I suggested we meet up later at the Dog Bar.

Ange and Rose, as I would come to know them, looked nothing alike. Both were tall, maybe 5'9", but Ange had a cherubic face and curly, short blonde hair. Rose had more angular features, with long, straight dark hair that fell to her waist. Ange was loud and brash; Rose was more soft-spoken. Mick, also blonde-haired, was an inch shorter than Ange, and had a face that looked like a tomahawk, sharp-edged, with a jutting chin and a long, aquiline nose that had been broken more than once. He looked lithe and strong, dead fit. He said he'd been in the Australian navy and was now trying to make a career as a boxer.

Ange commandeered the jukebox, and as we drank beer and talked, I started to get a sense of unease. I didn't hear it, but Mick said that the guys at another table said something nasty to Ange. The men were locals with whom I was acquainted but didn't know. I recognized one of them as the driver of a truck I crashed into as I followed Mother and Daddy from Cuchara to LaVeta a couple of years before. Without signaling, the guy turned in front of me, and I smashed into his trailer as I tried to pass him. Daddy watched it unfold in his rearview mirror and made a swift, worried U-turn. I wasn't hurt, but it was the worst wreck I'd ever been in. The police found the truck driver at fault.

Ange wasn't going to take any shit from anyone; Mick was ready to rumble. I would second Mick. I doubted the locals knew what they were in for...from Mick, not me.

Somehow, thankfully, it blew over.

I had to head back to Austin the next day. As we parted that night, I told them, "Please, please give me a call if you get anywhere near Austin."

A couple of months later, I was home alone in the North Austin house I shared with my friend Key, who owned it. Key was out that week on vacation. The phone rang, and Mick was on the line. They were in Austin. Woohoo, I was thrilled. I gave them directions and they showed up in their VW bus.

I told them I would check with Key, but they would certainly be welcome to stay for a few days. That night, I took them to Dirty Martin's, a classic old burger joint near the UT campus, then the next night we went to Scholz's Beer Garden, where we met up with friends. The Aussies hit it off with everybody, and we had a blast.

I was a little worried about what Key might think. It was his house, and I'd invited these strangers to stay for days while he was away. I told the Aussies, "Key is a great guy, and y'all with love him, but it's his house and his call where we go from here."

Key's first name is Richard, but everyone knows him as "Key," and the name is spot on, somehow. I don't know what he is the key to, what he unlocks, but the name rings true. In our 10 years living together and 40 years of friendship, I have never seen Key do one untoward thing. He's human; he has to have a character flaw of some sort, but I've never seen it. He's as fine a man as I've ever known.

Key is tall, 6'1" or so, slim, has curly brown hair, wears glasses...one of those people who looked the same at age 25 as he does at 65. Calm, soft-spoken, he rarely raises his voice.

I met Key in the early '80s when we worked together at Eczel, an office supply company in Grand Prairie, Texas. I'd just gotten back from a three-month backpacking trip to Europe and was living with

Mother and Daddy until I got settled into post-college life. I started as a temp and soon got hired on full time.

I don't remember a particular hitting-it-off moment with Key; what I remember is our lunches. Once we became friends, we'd go to lunch together, smoke a joint and drink a pitcher or two of beer at the Oyster Cracker, and bullshit about music, the Dallas Cowboys, our families… The workplace had a much looser, freer vibe then than it does now; I know some of our co-workers would be as looped after lunch as we were. One time, the entire office went to lunch after we hit some kind of sales goal, and all of us got rollicking drunk.

I told Key about how I loved Austin, my friends, and the fun we had, the killer live music, and that I would be going back once I got on my feet again. I got offered a position with a start-up office in Golden, Colorado, and lived and worked there for a year. Key and I stayed in touch. Eczel's parent company, Crown Zellerbach, was bought out, and the office supply company went out of business.

I took a modest severance package and moved back to Austin. Key had moved on to a job with Western Paper Company and was transferred to Austin.

We rented a house in Hyde Park and would be roommates for the next 10 years. Our friend Steffen was the third roommate for several of those years.

I'd always raved to Key about Antone's, the legendary blues club, where I'd seen Stevie Ray Vaughan up close a half a dozen times, and any number of other great shows. One time, Bonnie Raitt, whom I loved with all my heart, joined him on stage for an impromptu set. It just didn't get any better than that.

On Key's first night in town, Steffen and I took Key to Antone's to see Marcia Ball, a bluesy piano player who always put on a good show. It was a weeknight. I'd been there on weeknights before and had high times. This night it was stone dead. We were the only customers in the place...a comically lame event. Since we comprised the entire audience, we felt a responsibility to clap particularly loud and do our duty for the band.

Key and I still laugh about that night. He would come to love Antone's, the music scene, and Austin, in its pre-megalopolis days.

Key and Steffen both had the knack for throwing parties; they just knew how to do it somehow, and the energy and fun they sparked made our parties an event. We might have a live band and bocce in the back yard...it might be a "Silly Hat" party... we always had a keg or two. On the face of it, they were probably like a lot of parties, but something magical seemed to happen every time.

There was never a fight at our parties; they were love-ins. One time, after a bedroom or bathroom door had been locked for too long, then a couple emerged, Steffen said, "Why are people always fucking at our parties?"

I think I saw Key as mad as I've ever seen him at one party. A friend of a friend of mine, uninvited, who fashioned himself as a deejay, hauled in a box of records, took our record off the turntable, and put on Kansas or Queen. Several of us looked around, thinking "Huh?"...Kansas or Queen wasn't on our playlist. I happened to be talking with Mother and Daddy, both wearing silly hats, and I watched the scene. Key marched from the kitchen to the turntable, pulled off the offending record mid-song, handed it to the guy, and replaced it with The Band or Los Lobos. I don't know if he said a word. I got tickled by how perfectly Key handled it, and hoped Mother and Daddy appreciated it as much as I did.

One of our parties was attended by a friend from work, in town from our headquarters in Sergeant Bluff, Iowa. I found him in the morning, passed out on the kitchen floor with the bean pot ladle clutched in his hand. He returned to Iowa and told everyone, my bosses included, what a wild-man partier I was; an undeserved reputation that I didn't really mind.

In 1994, Key met sweet Sandra, the love of his life. They would marry the next year at Zilker Park Gardens in Austin. Key wore a tux and Converse tennis shoes. I was the best man, so I had the responsibility of toasting Key and Sandra at the rehearsal dinner, and I completely bombed. I don't remember the details of my speech, other than it was awkward and unfunny, one of the most embarrassing moments of my life. Only through the grace and good humor of Key and Sandra's families was I spared further humiliation.

Key and Sandra raised two beautiful daughters, Raquel and Julia, both gifted artists. For one of Key's birthdays, Raquel crafted a "Silly Walker" clock, inspired by the Monty Python skit. The silly walker's splayed, cockeyed legs constitute the minute and second hands. It is brilliant, and I still believe it would sell thousands if marketed to Python fans. Hanging in my office is a painting I commissioned Raquel to do, of my dog Dakota, chasing buzzards, as was her wont, into the sunset.

I shouldn't have worried about Key's acceptance of the Aussies. He returned from vacation and embraced Mick and Ange, and Rose just like I had.

The Aussies ended up getting jobs and staying for three months.

I think about half a dozen of us guys had a crush on lovely, whip-smart Rose. One friend went out with Rose one night, and they ended up skinny-dipping in Barton Springs pool, a quintessential Austin thing to do. He was going to propose to Rose, but lost the ring down a vent in his truck.

It was Rose who turned me on to "Lucky Jim," by Kingsley Amis, one of the funniest books I've ever read; by extension, I found Martin, his son, whom I've read avidly ever since.

The following spring, Key, Steffen, Steffen's girlfriend, Kelly, and I went to Australia to attend Mick and Ange's wedding in Sydney, and honeymoon on the Gold Coast.

Before the trip, I'd done research on Australia and stumbled upon stories about lethal spiders and snakes you might encounter there. Mick and Ange picked us up at the Sydney airport in Mick's old, beat-up yellow station wagon, named "The Peril," for it and its driver's idiosyncrasies. When Mick opened The Peril's hatch in the airport parking lot, a fist-sized black spider crawled out. Holy shit. They said it was a Huntsman, not particularly dangerous. I would be wary of spiders the rest of the trip.

We spent several days of our trip at the house of Michael and Annette, Rose and Ange's parents. They lived on a lush, green five-acre spread on the outskirts of Sydney. I remember their balcony in the mornings, drinking coffee, recovering from hangovers, struck awake by the ostentatiously colored birds playing bird games among the eucalyptus trees, and then leaning back to watch a horse, languidly lapping water from a pond.

Have you ever met the perfect dog...a dog who, out of the blue, lifts your spirits and fills you with joy? The first perfect dog I met was in Kinsale, on the southeast coast of Ireland. I'd just disembarked from an overnight ferry from England (where I watched 80-year-old Irish ladies drink pints of Guinness Stout at 7:00 am), walked up a hill toward town, groggy, alone, and unsure where to go or what to do. Out of nowhere, an enormous black Labrador retriever came bounding toward me. Non-dog lovers might have been intimidated, but I knew the instant I saw him that he had love in his eyes. He jumped into my arms like a long-lost friend and licked me on the face. It was an almost supernatural moment; I've never been happier. We cavorted for 10 minutes or so, then a car pulled up with a family inside. The father apologized, needlessly, for his wayward pet. I could not adequately express to him the joy his dog had brought me. I was sad to see my buddy jump into the car.

The second perfect dog I met was Gus, Michael and Annette's short-haired fox terrier. Gus was maybe three years old, still had some puppy in him, and had as winning a personality as any dog I've known. Gus would pantingly drop his tennis ball at our feet on the second-floor veranda, and we'd fling it into the far reaches of the property, seemingly impossible to find, and he'd bring it back every time, busting a gut to go again. I'd wrestle with Gus, and he'd bite me just right...a love bite if I ever felt one.

We explored Sydney the way any unfamiliar new place should be explored, if you have the luxury: Led by locals. Sydney reminded me more of America than any other English-speaking big city I'd ever visited. Besides the driving on the other side of the road, and the Aussie accents, it felt like the States, maybe a little cleaner.

Spurred on by Ange, I drove the Peril...my first foray at driving on the left side of the road. I did not like it. The steering column in an Aussie car is reversed, on the right side, not the left. Attempting to turn on the windshield wipers, I would activate the blinkers, and vice versa. I knew that one lapse, one unthinking moment when muscle memory takes over, I could get us killed. I understand you get used to it, but hard-core driver than I am, in left-side-of-the-road-driving countries I will be happy to passenge (spell check keeps putting an "r" on the end of "passenge," but that's one of the joys of writing, making up new words; what sounds better, "to be a passenger" or "passenge?")

The big event of the first week was the marriage of Mick and Ange, of course. I gathered that Michael had some doubts about

Mick marrying his daughter… I didn't know their history together, if perhaps there was some class conflict at work, but I do know that for the entire week we were there Mick wore long-sleeved shirts in warm weather, to hide from Michael the tattoos on his arms (besides those on his arms, Mick had emblazoned on his back, stretching from waist to neck, a prowling tiger…the best tattoo I've ever seen).

Regardless, the wedding came off. Ange rode in on a white horse.

Have you ever been on someone else's honeymoon? I've never had my own, but I had Mick and Ange's, and I'll take it.

We drove The Peril up the coast from Sydney to Surfer's Paradise, stopped off and hiked the Blue Mountains along the way, witnessed the spectacular views of the Tasman Sea, drank our share of VBs (Victoria Bitter, our beer of choice in Australia), and played cricket on the beach.

What a cack.

The Neurotic Onesome

I half expect to hear, someday, the starter at my golf course announce, "Next on the number one tee is the Neurotic onesome, followed by the Smith foursome." I would be the onesome. I almost always tee off before the starter appears, so it probably won't happen.

I love to play golf alone at the crack of dawn, just me and the wildlife. Deer snort and roadrunners cock their heads quizzically at some of my shots. One misty morning, I swear I saw a big horn sheep emerge from the woods. I'm afraid there probably isn't a big horn sheep within 500 miles of the course, but that's what I saw. When you're alone, nobody impugns your hallucinations.

Sometimes, I'll tee off before the morning light has crept in, and I have to guess where my shot landed by the feel of the swing. Sometimes I never see that ball again. I love the quiet of a morning...the "thock" of a well-struck drive against a tree limb rings so clear. Another advantage of the early morning ritual is that I'm through communing with nature and knocking bark off trees by mid-morning, and still have most of the day to fritter away.

Over the years, I have played with other humans in daylight, made friends, and had good times, but I did have one round that scarred me and caused me to scurry back to my crack-of-dawn routine. I was matched up with a foursome of beginners oblivious of golf course etiquette. I consider myself an honorary greens keeper at "my" course, and felt pain as I watched the turf relentlessly hacked and gouged, never a divot repaired. At least the greens were safe from ball marks since their shots never arrived via the air.

At one point, one of the guys shouted for his ball to "come around" after he pull-hooked his shot almost diagonally into the woods. Usually, when you make the "come around" plea, you're asking the ball to curve in a slightly more favorable direction than its current path, not defy the laws of physics. In all my life as a golfer, I've never seen a duck hook change course to a slice or vice versa. How exactly did he think his ball was going to come around? An F5 tornado might have made that shot come around, but the sky was cloudless. Or perhaps drone technology has evolved to the point where drones can snag errant golf shots and fling them toward the fairway.

My clubs have never been cleaner than they were after that round, since I had time to scrub each one 37 times. At one point, I counted 17 shots taken by the Come Around Gang between my first and second one. I did get some experience as a traffic cop, wind-milling other players around our train wreck during the six and a half hour ordeal. I should have worn a fluorescent yellow traffic vest.

I live in fear of being paired with the guy in the tricked-up Harley Davidson golf cart who plays country music, loud, on his built-in stereo. The thought of hearing Tammy Wynette whining "D-I-V-O-R-C-E" while I stand over a tee ball makes me shudder. I'm afraid my hands might d-i-v-o-r-c-e their grip from the club during my follow-through and obliterate DeeJay Hacker's music box. A stereo on a golf course is as apt as a pinball machine in a library.

There are downsides to solitary golf, to be sure. Say, if I've been playing alone for a year, then end up in a tournament, the competition and presence of others is unsettling. I might have the following conversation with myself:

"So these people are just going to stand there and watch while I attempt this crucial 3-foot putt?"

"What if I tell them to go on to the next hole and I'll let them know how it turned out?"

One of my facts of life is that I will never play as well in a group as I do alone. Distractions like waiting or being pressed by a group behind upset my fragile equilibrium. My golf clock is set for a two-and-a-half to three-hour round; when a round drags out to four or more, I get restless.

Playing alone, I get used to jumping in my cart and speeding right away. Then all of a sudden, I'm paired with someone, but lost in my own world, I hop in my cart and drive off without my playing companion. I've found the drive-off move to be very ingratiating with friend and stranger alike.

I've been lucky enough to make five holes-in-one, four of them with playing partners, which is peculiar since the vast majority of my rounds are solo. I have to say, holes-in-one are much more fun with other humans. Pretty girls don't hug you after a hole-in-one when you're playing alone.

There was a stretch of years when a fellow insomniac and I played together at dawn. We became good friends, and one morning, when I was doing a little impromptu grounds keeping, he nicknamed me "Monk," after the OCD-afflicted, poly-phobic television character. My buddy gravitated away from golf after a while, and I was back on my own. I swear I did not drive him away from the game. I swear.

The enablers of my crack-of-dawn golf are the staff at my golf course. I'm sure I'm a pain in the ass for them, arriving sometimes before the lights are on in the pro shop, then playing amongst the mowers. They've won my undying loyalty with their kindness and willingness to let me do my thing. They make me feel good about mankind. They could be hard-asses and declare that the course doesn't open till "x" time, and you have to wait, which is probably the norm. What's the name of this wonderful place? Not gonna tell you.

There is another gentleman who loiters with me now in the pro shop before sunup. We say hello and maybe chat a little, neither of us ever suggesting that we pair up. We understand each other, and I feel reassured, knowing I'm not the only nut job on the premises. We embark separately on our appointed rounds.

"Sit!"

It occurs to me that dogs reveal their character in a couple of definitive acts: How they sit and how they shit. Although I've been involved in the upbringing and care of maybe 20 dogs in my life, I've raised just two dogs on my own from puppyhood. Ignatius ("Igbert") and Mordecai were yellow AKC-registered male Labs out of field trial champions, born 13 years apart. I am not a hunter; they would retrieve Frisbees and squeaky balls, not birds.

A dog's responsiveness to the "Sit!" command says more about the character of the owner than the dog, but Igbert and Mordecai's quirks were still enlightening. I made a half-assed attempt to teach Igbert to sit, but my heart wasn't really in it. I live on a two-acre fenced property where he could roam unleashed; if we lived in a neighborhood, I would have felt more of a need to be a disciplinarian. Igbert's brother Bo would sit. Bo was born at my house, given to another family who alternately abused and ignored him, then returned to me two years later an ill-tempered asshole of a dog, picking vicious fights with Igbert and shunning the attention of humans. But he would sit. After a couple of years of love, Bo would bound into your lap, unbidden.

Igbert would come when I called and was better-behaved than most dogs I knew, so his refusal to "Sit!" didn't bother me. He would look me in the eye, sporting his perpetual shit-eating grin and say, "I love you, man, but there ain't no way in hell I'm going to sit. Dumb butt Bo can sit all day long and think he's got a lick of sense, but we both know better. Challenge my intellect, teach me to play the piano, and then we can talk. I prefer to stand." The only time "Sit!" became an issue was at the vet's office. I am friends with my vet, Trampus, and Igbert's tendency to plop his paws on Trampus's shoulders and lick him in the face when told to sit made me feel sheepish.

I made no effort whatsoever to teach Mordecai to sit. He'd probably never heard the command until one day I was visiting Junie in Plano, and Junie, trying to get a handle on canine follies that were spinning out of control inside the house, instructed five dogs to "Sit!" Four dogs made various attempts to sit. Mordecai, eager to please, jumped into an easy chair and laid his head on the armrest. That's my boy.

While "Sit!" is a learned command, a dog's style of defecation is instinctive, a pure expression of their personality. I appreciated that Igbert and Bo would do their business at the distant corners of my property, as far away from the house as possible. Other visiting dogs haven't been as considerate. Dave's Chihuahua, Beethoven, once did it on my bed. His beady, protruding eyeballs met mine and he said "Kiss my ass, pendejo" as he squatted.

Igbert had things to do and people to see, so he perambulated while he pooped. He felt the need for his smell to attach to my person and would leave his droppings on my walking trail around the fence line. His most nefarious gambit occurred during my tree-trimming obsession. He would surreptitiously leave a pile at the foot of my ladder, and as I climbed, my feet would slip, and I would look down to see brown smudges on each rung below me.

One of my imagined deaths happens like this: I'm standing on the top rung of a 20-foot ladder that is extended to the hilt, bowed from my weight. The ladder is propped precariously against a tree limb that sways in a gusty wind. A swarm of African killer bees engulfs me. I embark on a hasty descent, but my foot slips on a brown patch. My chin bounces off each rung of the ladder as I grab desperately for a hold, but my hands can't find purchase on the slimy crossbars. I imagine the coroner's report: "Decedent died of a broken neck; multiple bee stings on his face; chin and hands smeared with canine excrement."

Mordecai started his business whimsically, spinning around on his front legs until his hiney was situated just right. When he finished, he took a couple of steps, kicked out his back legs, uprooting grass to cover the debris, as mannerly as a society lady. Then a gleeful grin would spread over his face as if he just remembered a hilarious joke he needed to tell me, and he would blast off on a joy run. I never knew watching a dog do number two could be so much fun.

"Are You Shittin' Me?!"

The sport of horse racing first entered my consciousness when I was 13. Daddy and I stood on the pier out behind my grandmother's house in East Texas, late afternoon, casting top-water lures into the pond, fishing for largemouth bass. Daddy looked at his watch and said, "It's time for Secretariat." We parked our poles and went inside. Secretariat was a racehorse attempting to win the Triple Crown (the Kentucky Derby, Preakness and Belmont), a feat which hadn't been achieved in 25 years, but he had to win the Belmont. Daddy and I cheered as Secretariat opened up a lead, then we got silent, not believing what we were seeing, as Secretariat spread-eagled the field, winning by 31 lengths, nearly the length of a football field, an unprecedented margin of victory. Willie Mays had been my sports hero up till then; after the Belmont, my heroes were Secretariat and Willie Mays.

I'd watch the big races on TV after that, and on my 18th birthday, the first day I could legally place a wager, my buddy Kevin and I drove the four hours from Dallas to Louisiana Downs to experience live horse racing for the first time. Horseracing wasn't legal in Texas back then, and the racetrack in Bossier City was the closest venue. Kevin wasn't particularly interested in the races, but my enthusiasm won him over. It would be an adventure, at least.

We bet the first few races and didn't win anything, and after the third race, I met a man on the track apron wearing faded Levis, beat-up rope boots, a ratty, untucked snap-front shirt, and an old, dinged-up cowboy hat. He said, with a Southern twang, that he was from Arkansas and was friends with an owner who'd brought a string of horses to Louisiana. One of them had just won the 3rd race. We met again at the same spot after the 4th and 5th races, and he flashed a wad of cash and said he'd hit those races too. I asked him who he liked in the next race, and he said, "Well, I don't really have another horse until the 10th." He flipped through his program to the 10th race, the last of the day, and put his finger on the number 5 horse. "No fuckin' way", I blurted when I saw the name of the horse: Lucky Jay. Talk about something that was meant to be.

I gushed to Kevin about my meeting with the country boy from Arkansas and convinced him that we should hold on to all the money we had left, pass on the intervening races, and bet our bankroll on Lucky Jay in the 10th. Kevin bought in. I had a little over $100, and Kevin had $20, and we would put it all on Lucky Jay's nose. Over the next couple of hours, we mused about what we'd do with our winnings. On the trip from Dallas to Bossier City, we'd stopped at a Dairy Queen in Waskom, where a snotty lady behind the counter pissed off both of us. We said that after we hit on Lucky Jay we'd go back to Waskom, buy the friggin' Dairy Queen and fire the obnoxious lady.

I'd noticed a horse running in the 8th race named Footstomper and thought it was a funny name. In the post parade, Footstomper bucked and wheeled, acting like a nut, finally throwing his jockey and stomping on him. Kevin and I couldn't help but bust out laughing despite the jockey's misfortune. The race was delayed while an ambulance carried off the jockey, and a new one had to be recruited. I had to place a token bet on Footstomper, despite our vow to hold off till the 10th race. Footstomper didn't hit the board. The track announcer said later that the jockey had suffered a broken leg.

The 10th race approached, and the tote board showed Lucky Jay at 20-1 odds. I giddily placed our bet, $120 to win on the 5 horse. Lucky Jay's odds ticked down to 18-1 and stayed there. I did the math in my head…we'd collect over $2000 if Lucky Jay won, a gargantuan sum of money to us.

Lucky Jay didn't give us much of a thrill. Slow out of the gate, he plodded along at the back of the pack and closed tepidly to finish 5th. We made the long drive home from the track flat broke, a circumstance I would know well later in life.

Looking back, I'm still proud of the bet. We could have bet more conservatively, to place and show, but we took our shot and it didn't work out. Betting a large amount on a stranger's tout, I've learned since, is not so wise, but I forgive myself on that one. I couldn't know it then, but Lucky Jay and Footstomper would be the first of several ironic horse names that would accentuate the comedy and tragedy of my horsey life.

I didn't pay much attention to horses over the next decade, as I busied myself with college and career. I would join Daddy's Kentucky Derby pool, where everyone put in $5 and picked a horse's name out of a hat.

Pari-mutuel wagering was legalized in Texas in 1987, when I was 27, and race tracks began opening in Texas. I started going out occasionally to Manor Downs, a little quarter horse track outside of Austin, where I lived. I dabbled with the quarter horses for a while, but had no affinity for them; the races were too short, just one blast of speed for 400 yards or so. I preferred the looks of the rangier, more elegant thoroughbreds to the blockier, musclebound quarter horses, and the infinite nuance of longer distance races on both dirt and turf.

I gravitated to the simulcast parlor, which televised races from all the big tracks around the country...Saratoga, Keeneland, Churchill, Santa Anita, Del Mar, Belmont. I would print the past performances of the horses from the Daily Racing Form (DRF), study them a little, and head out to Manor. I got hooked and began reading every handicapping book I could get my hands on, books that discussed betting strategies, pedigrees, pace and trip handicapping, how to judge a horse's body language and fitness, and even one about applying Zen to playing the races.

Murphy and our friend Billy Crow would join me at Manor, and we went through a short period of playing just about every race being telecast, on every whim imaginable. There might be four races around the country in progress, and our heads jerked frenetically from screen to screen, trying to watch all of our horses. It took me about two such experiences of losing my bankroll in an hour to recognize the absurdity of playing that way. Murphy and Billy continued to play every race under the sun, and at one time or another, probably placed a bet on every racetrack in the nation. Billy did everything in his life to excess, playing the horses included; he would get drunk and win and lose thousands in a matter of minutes.

The law of averages evened out, and he lost many more thousands than he won, and it became a problem in his life pretty quickly.

I didn't make any huge scores, and didn't lose too much, but had a blast and began to love everything about the game. I found that handicapping suited my personality. I could get lost for hours in the DRF, trying to solve the mystery that each horse race represents.

I took road trips to every track within driving distance, all over Texas, Louisiana, Arkansas and New Mexico. The racing scene in Australia was another matter altogether...Royal Randwick, a vast, beautiful racetrack in Sydney, dwarfed every track I'd ever seen in America. Many racing fans were dressed to the nines, the men sporting tuxedos and top hats, and the women adorned in ostentatious dresses. Racing was broadcast over the radio and featured on the front page of newspapers, as opposed to my home country, where The Sport of Kings had fallen out of favor. The day of the Melbourne Cup, Australia's most prestigious horse race, is a public holiday.

Australian racetracks feature licensed bookmakers where you shop for the best price on the horse you want to bet (in the U.S., all on-track wagering is done with a clerk at a betting window or through a machine; there is one universal price, i.e., odds to win, on every horse). Each bookie had a "spy" standing on a box, binoculars glued to his face, monitoring the odds other bookies were setting. I got a thrill betting a horse at 300-1 odds, a massive longshot whose odds you would never see in America, where the fields aren't as big. My bomber led for about 2 miles of the 2 ½ mile race and finished

4th. I think my friends got a little tired of me begging to go back to Randwick.

In 1996, I read a column by Blackie Sherrod, the legendary Texas sportswriter, who said that "Saratoga is the granddaddy of American racetracks." I had to meet the granddaddy. Murphy was raised in New York and had been to Saratoga a couple of times. I'd played their races from afar but really didn't know much about it. I booked a week-long trip to Saratoga; Murphy would join me for the last few days.

On the second day of my inaugural visit to Saratoga, before Murphy arrived, I heard that Cigar, who had won 16 races in a row and was arguably the greatest American racehorse since Secretariat, was going to work out on the track in preparation for a race in California, where he would be shooting to tie the American record of 17 straight wins. I arrived at the track before dawn on the misty morning, one of maybe 30 people out at that hour, besides the exercise riders and trainers. Everyone was on the lookout for the "big horse" and sure enough, he ambled up "the wrong way," clockwise, around the outside rail, in preparation for his workout, when he'd turn and run counterclockwise around the track.

Accompanied by his trainer, future Hall of Famer Bill Mott, and ridden by the best jockey in the business then, future Hall of Famer Jerry Bailey, Cigar was full of himself, bucking and playing right there in front of me. I couldn't believe it; I could have reached out and touched him.

Normally when horses work in the morning there is a buzz of activity, dozens of other horses either working or going the wrong way, preparing to work. On this morning, everything came to a dead stop when Cigar broke off into a slow gallop around the first clubhouse turn. By the time he'd reached the backstretch, he was running full throttle, and we could see his dark mane flowing in his self-generated breeze. The only sound we heard was Cigar's hoof beats, faint at first, then louder and louder as he rounded the far turn and barreled out of the mist, striding through the finish line right in front of us again. Mott clicked his stopwatch and said, "One twenty-seven and three." Cigar had worked seven furlongs (7/8s of a mile) in one minute, twenty-seven and three-fifths of a second...racehorse time.

Saratoga hosts a breakfast on the patio starting at 7:00 am, where racing fans eat and watch the horses work out. That morning, it was presided over by a lady named Mary Ryan, a racetrack veteran, whose voice was transported via loudspeaker throughout the track. She talked about the history of Saratoga, famous horses, trainers, and general horse minutiae. I found Mary and asked her if she saw Cigar's workout. She said no, she'd just gotten there. I filled her in, and she reported it to the growing crowd. I was proud to have provided the scoop on the hottest horse in America.

I couldn't wait to get back to my room and tell everybody about Cigar. I called one friend back in Austin, and he said, "Oh, cool," but he wasn't as thrilled as I hoped he'd be. Then I called Daddy in Colorado, where it was about 6:00 am. Daddy was an early riser like me, and I found him awake. When I told him what I saw, he said,

77

incredulously, "Are you shittin' me?!" You know how, when you're jazzed to tell somebody something and their reaction makes all the difference in the world, as if they legitimize your excitement? Daddy's spontaneous joy made all the difference to me that morning.

A couple of years later, I took Daddy to Saratoga. He had recently undergone disk fusion surgery, and suffered from pancreatitis, so he dealt with severe pain and wasn't as mobile as he'd have liked. I made runs to the betting windows to place his bets. He couldn't get comfortable at the picnic tables where we sat, out in the park by the paddock, so we borrowed a chair from our hotel.

Despite the pain, Daddy had a blast and "got" Saratoga like I did. We ate breakfast on the patio and watched the workouts a couple of mornings. Daddy got on a kick out of pointing out to me the "fatties" in the crowd, as if obese New Yorkers were fatter than those anywhere else in the world; he didn't mean it as an insult, rather as a nod of kinship. Once a fat man himself, he rued the weight loss he suffered from his ill health. Daddy said he had a fat man's personality.

Daddy died of pancreatic cancer two years later in 2000. I'll always be thankful that we made it to Saratoga together.

A few days after I saw Cigar, I stood with my arms propped on the rail by the track, facing away from the 130-year old wooden grandstand, just after dawn, reveling in the peace, admiring the beauty of the horses, listening to their whinnies and knickers and snorts, to the coos and smooches of the exercise riders. A man walked up beside me and said, almost in a whisper, "It's heaven on earth, isn't it?" I told him he read my mind. We stood side by side for a few minutes, silent. He'd already said it all.

On one of those splendid mornings, a lean, hawk-nosed horse trainer named Barclay Tagg caught my eye. Unlike some of the trainers on the grounds, he sat a horse like he belonged there (I learned later that he was a former steeplechase jockey). I'm sure it was just my imagination, but he seemed to take a little more care with his horses than some of the other trainers I watched. He wasn't a big-name trainer, didn't have a large stable of horses, and was known as a turf specialist. I started watching for his name in the entries and betting on his turf horses, who usually outran their odds. One day, he had a two-year-old horse running in a sprint race on the dirt, not his forte, and I dismissed the 30-1 longshot. The field was brimming with expensive horses from the most famous trainers in America. Barclay's horse won, and I told Murphy to punch me if I ever ignored a Barclay Tagg horse again.

Another Saratoga character I loved was "Little" Andy Serling, a former Wall Street stockbroker who was a guest handicapper at morning seminars held at a restaurant across from the track. A short guy who walked with his chest out, he carried himself like Napoleon, I decided.

Little Andy openly ridiculed jockeys' rides and trainers whose methods he disapproved, but the main thing I appreciated was his passion for horse racing and how hard he worked at handicapping, watching endless race replays of past races to get an edge. Little Andy gave me direction and inspired me to work harder.

The horse racing bug fully infected me after the Saratoga experience, and I began going out to Manor every weekend I could to play the races.

In 2002, I entered my first handicapping contest, held at Retama Park in San Antonio. I didn't know much about it other than that the top two finishers would win a free trip to Las Vegas and participate in The National Handicapping Championship (NHC). I had zero expectations and was intimidated when I visited with people who'd flown in from New York and California to play in the contest. I knew I was out of my league. Early in the day, I hit a 57-1 longshot. I was in second place behind another guy who must have hit the same horse, and we were well ahead of the pack. I didn't hit much else the rest of the day, but my score held up.

All the players were gathered around watching the last race of the tournament and I heard a few people grousing about us leaders "stabbing" (not really handicapping, but betting the longest shot on the board on a prayer) and it pissed me off. I actually liked and bet my own money on the 57-1 horse, who was only about 25-1 when I bet him; a bunch of money must have been bet late on another horse, driving my odds up; and my hit came early in the day, before a player would be stabbing. "Kiss my ass, fellas", I thought.

I left Retama with a check for $3000, second-place money, and a free trip to Vegas. Horseracing had provided me another "Are you shittin' me?!" moment. Daddy would have been over the moon for me.

The winner of the Retama contest was a gentleman named Trey Stiles. Trey and I visited that day, and in later contests, and became friends. Trey parlayed his early success into stardom in the handicapping world. As of this writing, Trey has qualified for the NHC a record 22 times, was inducted into the NHC Hall of Fame, and now appears on TV as the track handicapper at Sam Houston. Besides being a brilliant horseplayer, he's as gracious and generous a man as I've ever met.

The NHC was held at Bally's in Las Vegas on a weekend in late January. About 250 of the best horseplayers in the nation gathered in their Sports Book, surrounded by dozens of big screen TVs showing races from all over the country, cheers and groans ringing out all over as races were run. We played for two days for a $100,000 purse and the title of Handicapper of the Year. On the first day, after about six races had been run, a drunken man, another contestant, plopped down in the seat beside me, said he'd had a few drinks on a plane that was late from Iowa, then immediately passed out. At least I wasn't going to finish last, I thought.

I held my own and, going into my last bet on Sunday, was within shouting distance of the top ten and a share of the purse. I'd picked a longshot "mudder" who was running on a sloppy track, and he had the lead at the top of the stretch before fading. Whew, what a hoot. I came in 37th place.

Some Vegas Sports Books offer a "future" wager on the Kentucky Derby. You are betting on the Kentucky Derby months in advance, when there are still hundreds of horses in play because the field hasn't been narrowed down yet, so the odds are much higher than when the race is run on the first Saturday in May. Another reason the odds are inflated is that thoroughbreds are fragile creatures, and it is extremely difficult to maintain their fitness and soundness for months at a time. Some horseplayers believe a future wager is a sucker play. I bet $30 on a horse that my man Barclay trained named Funny Cide, who had won a couple of minor stakes races restricted to horses bred in New York. Funny Cide didn't fit the profile of a Kentucky Derby winner because he wasn't royally bred nor had high-profile connections, but I trusted in Barclay and had to take a shot at 125-1 odds.

Funny Cide ran well in his prep races and made it into the Derby field, going off at 12-1. I was thrilled for Barclay to have a horse in the Derby, but wasn't sure he could win. Because I would make a big score on the future bet if he won, I hedged my bets by betting him "under" (to come in 2nd or 3rd) in exactas and trifectas. Murphy and I watched the race from my house in Bertram, and I hollered myself hoarse, scaring my dogs, when Funny Cide fought off the two favorites to win the Derby. As delighted as I was for Barclay and for winning $3750 on my future bet, I felt a twinge of regret for not putting him on top in other wagers. Even after a big score, horseplayers often lament that it could have been better if only they'd bet it right.

Funny Cide destroyed the field in the Preakness and had a chance to become the first Triple Crown winner in 25 years, but finished 3rd in the Belmont. Still, it was a joyous ride.

The following year, I entered several handicapping contests in Texas, but didn't do any good until the last one at a dog track in Harlingen, way down in south Texas. The six and a half hour drive through scrubby country bored the hell out of me, but it was worth it as I squeaked into the final NHC qualifying spot, earning another free trip to Vegas. I reveled in my brilliance on the drive home, the 400 miles passing unnoticed.

I had a blast in Vegas again in January, but didn't do as well in the contest, finishing 87th.

Flush off last year's win with Funny Cide, I had to make more Derby future bets. Murphy was sold on a horse named Smarty Jones. I wasn't a believer, even though the name was pretty damned ironic (me being a Jones boy). After two straight years of qualifying for the NHC, I thought I was a big-time handicapper and felt I could have made the case that I was one of the top 100 or so horseplayers in the nation. Big-time handicappers don't bet on names, as compelling as they might be. I told my mother, my sister Junie and my brother Carey about Smarty Jones and they loved the name, so I bet $10 for each of them, as well as $20 for Murphy on Smarty to win the Derby, at the same odds as I got on Funny Cide, 125-1. I eschewed joining in the fun and didn't bet a cent on Smarty Jones for myself.

Murphy scared my dogs that year, rattling the walls exhorting Smarty Jones to the wire to win the Derby, while I turned pale at my own stupidity and arrogance. "You're Smarty Fucking Jones alright", I thought. I was happy for Murphy, and when my phone started ringing with calls from Mother, Junie and Carey, I regained my enthusiasm; to have them get such a kick out of a horse race gratified me. They knew I didn't bet on Smarty and each sent me $100 to salve my feelings.

I went to see Daddy Sam in West Texas the following weekend. He didn't approve of gambling, but was thrilled about the Smarty Jones experience and praised me up one side and down the other for my prescience in betting the Derby winner for the family. I tried to tell him I was the dumb ass who didn't bet a penny on Smarty Jones, but he wouldn't hear it.

I didn't know it then, but my dissing of my namesake must have angered the racing gods.

I attended only a couple of handicapping contests the next year, in my attempt to qualify for the NHC the third year in a row. My last chance came at Sam Houston Park in Houston. When I got there, I found myself seated beside a table of eight, which turned out to be a man who'd recruited seven family members as his proxies; the guy was basically playing eight entries. I wondered how you beat a guy with eight entries. I'd heard of people teaming up before, but that seemed ridiculous. I had always played just one entry, all on my own.

Late in the day, I was in 2nd place, ahead of the eight-headed monster and everybody else but one guy, a public handicapper I respected. Only the contest winner would qualify for Vegas. In the last couple of races, I thought for sure that I hit on an 11-1 winner, but somehow he lost the head bob, then another longshot came in 2nd but got fouled in the stretch, and I was sure he'd be moved up to

1st. Alas, no change. I finished 2nd in the contest, having given it a good run, and if not for a couple of tough beats, I might have made it to Vegas again. I was copacetic; tough beats were part of the game.

The last hurrah for horse racing in Texas came with the Breeders' Cup at Lone Star in 2004. Neighboring states began approving slot machines at their racetracks, and a percentage of the slot revenue was funneled into racing purses, which soon dwarfed those in Texas. Texas horsemen fled to the larger purses, naturally. The Texas state government, backed by the powerful Baptist church, an enemy of horseracing to begin with, was never going to approve slot machines in Texas (although they happily support the ultimate of sucker bets, the lottery). Texas racing began its descent into irrelevance, where it stands today.

Texas racetracks cut budgets to survive, and one of the victims was the handicapping contests, which dwindled to just a couple. If I were going to continue to participate, I would have to do extensive travelling on weekends, which didn't suit my lifestyle, or play contests online, which came into vogue about that time. I tried a couple of online contests, but they lacked the camaraderie and buzz of the on-track events, and I had no success in them. My participation in handicapping contests petered out after the Houston tournament. With no more free Vegas trips, my Kentucky Derby future betting dried up as well.

I settled into a routine of playing the races from home, where I could watch the races on satellite TV and wager through an online account. I played just about every weekend, and Murphy would make the hour drive from his home in Austin about once a month to my place in the country, which he dubbed "Bertram OTB" (OTB: Off-track betting). We played the races in perfect comfort; it was a sweet deal. Our racing year still revolved around our 10-day trip to Saratoga in late July.

One of the best times I ever had in my horsey life had nothing to do with gambling. I'd always wanted to see another classic American racetrack, Keeneland, in Lexington, Kentucky, visit the horse farms, and find out if the grass really was blue (I didn't see it; I supposed the season and the light have to be just right). I thoroughly enjoyed Keeneland, although it could never replace Saratoga as my favorite track; it wasn't as spread out as Saratoga, and I felt a little claustrophobic among the wall-to-wall racing fans. I visited Coolmore Stud, one of the pre-eminent horse racing operations in the world, and watched million-dollar horses copulate. I was glad to have experienced it once, but that was enough.

The highlight of my trip was my visit to the Kentucky Horse Park, where I got up close to dozens of different breeds of horses, from tiny ones that could ride in the backseat of a car, to the monster Percheron, Shire and Clydesdale draft horses. The Hall of Champions, where former racing stars are housed and pampered, is the main attraction. I visited in 2004 and saw my old buddy Cigar again and the grumpy old war horse, John Henry, who won 39 races in his storied career. It's rare to see a racehorse even run 39 times these days, much less win that many. As his keepers paraded Cigar in front of fans in a dirt-floor pavilion, with replays of his races playing in the background, emotion welled up in me and I found myself crying. I don't cry easy.

My racing fortunes turned a little sour after the Funny Cide and NHC years. I keep scrupulous records of my wagering activity, and after several winning years, a losing streak took hold. I felt like I was still learning every day, and handicapping well, it just seemed like I lost every head bob and had an inordinate number of horses disqualified. I figured that they would even out in the long run.

If a horseplayer can achieve a "masterpiece," where he melds handicapping and betting a race exactly right, I authored mine in 2008 on a horse named Jose Adan. I'd seen his first race as a "baby," a 2-year-old horse, and he did things a 2-year-old horse wasn't supposed to do, fighting through trouble and charging through a tight spot up the rail like a seasoned veteran. I put him on my "watch" list.

Jose Adan went off at 14-1 odds in the Arlington-Washington Futurity at Arlington Park in Chicago, facing more experienced stakes horses. If I ever "knew" a horse was going to win a race, it was Jose Adan that day. I made the biggest bet of my life, before or since. I'd learned my lesson with Funny Cide and did not hedge one iota. I bet $100 to win, and another $200 on him on top in "exotics" wagers...trifectas, superfectas, Pick 3s and Pick 4s. A $300 bet might not sound like much to high rollers, but it was a huge bet for me.

Jose Adan came through, closing late, full of run, to win a thrilling finish. The track announcer called him "magnificent." My

Mother watched the race with me as I jumped out of my skin with excitement. I had hit *everything* for the first time in my life. I had no idea how much I would win, and that's one of the joys of horse racing, waiting for the big payoff numbers to light up the tote board. I guessed I'd won $10,000 to $15,000 with all the exotic bets, but I couldn't know; it might be even more.

The "Inquiry" sign flashed, indicating the stewards were looking at a possible foul in the race, but I wasn't really worried. I watched the replay and saw that the 2nd-place finisher had soundly bumped another horse; that horse would be DQ'd. Jose had closed on the far outside, and his trip looked pretty clean, except for one slight bump with another horse. I'd seen much worse infractions summarily dismissed, so I still wasn't worried.

The Inquiry seemed to take forever, never a good sign. Finally, the official results flashed…Jose Adan had been disqualified as well as the 2nd-place horse; a double disqualification. In the tens of thousands of races I've watched in my life, I've seen only a handful of double DQs. Spitting mad, I stomped out to the yard so as not to cuss in front of my mother, who was angry too.

The next year, I was DQ'd out of an $8000 Pick 4 at Belmont; I'd been DQ'd out of the two biggest scores of my life.

The lows of horse racing are as agonizingly painful as the highs are electrifying.

In 2009, I bought an 8-week-old yellow Lab puppy and named him Mordecai, after a maniacal child in "Raising Arizona," one of my favorite movies. The puppy was registered as Mordecai Jones. Two months later, I was perusing the Saratoga entries, and who do I find...a first-time starter named Mordecai Jones...very weird. If that horse had been entered at any of 50 tracks around the nation, I would never have noticed, but it was entered at Saratoga. Mordecai Jones, the horse, was female. I placed a token bet on her and she lost that race and 31 of 33 other times she raced, but she always tried hard and often finished in the money, an admirable horse. The truly brilliant Mordecai Jones was the one who slept in bed beside me every night.

In 2011, my horseracing life took another downturn, through the power of politics. Greg Abbott, then the Republican Attorney General of Texas, and now the governor, achieved the goal of his personal crusade and formally outlawed Advance Deposit Wagering (ADW) in Texas, meaning that horseplayers could no longer bet online; we would have to go to a racetrack to do exactly, precisely what we had been doing from home. Manor Downs had long since closed, so the nearest race track to me was 100 miles away in Fredericksburg. I would have to drive 200 miles to bet on the races.

The law made no sense to me. Why would a lawmaker inflict this hardship on the taxpayers of his state? Horseracing was still legal after all. Wasn't the conservative ethos less government regulation, not more? Abbott's law had a hugely negative impact on my lifestyle. I drove the 200 miles most Saturdays, when the biggest races occur, putting a ton of miles on my car, fighting the vagaries of Texas weather; a Saturday night social life evaporated, since I had to be in the car.

Am I a gambling addict? I don't think so, but that could be another of my delusions. I believe I have an addictive personality, having drunk and smoked dope almost every day for 25 years before quitting both cold turkey 12 years ago. I still smoke cigarettes. In my defense, I do keep detailed records of money won and lost, and the losses have not severely injured me financially (I paid off my house in 11 years and retired early). 95% of my bets, losers that they may be, are placed only after copious study. I don't like losing, but I don't get depressed about it; temporarily insane, but not depressed.

One unexpected benefit I've realized from my devotion to handicapping is that my math skills have improved immensely over time. I've spent so much time buried in numbers that I'm now able to do a significant amount of math in my head. Call me Rain Man. I believe horse playing has made me a better money manager in real life as well. Lately, I've come to believe that I could improve kids' math and money management skills by taking them to the track, and I think about opening a sort of horsey Montessori school. I picture a table full of children in the simulcast parlor with their heads buried in the DRF, pens stuck behind their ears, DRF ink staining their tiny, innocent hands. I would use a riding crop as my pointer.

I think about my friendship with Murphy and wonder if we would be as close without the horses. We played high school baseball together 40 years ago, and racing has been the one constant in our friendship since. Over the years, many of my other friends and I have drifted apart as life responsibilities intervened. A day at the races gives Murphy and me a defined meeting place and time. I am grateful that Murphy's wife, Sharon, does not begrudge his horseplay with me, or our yearly Saratoga trip; sometimes she'll take off on her own trips while he stays home.

When we were in our early 20s, Murphy and I drove from Texas to New York and back, and one morning we got up, got in the car, and drove 500 miles without either of us saying one word. We weren't mad at each other, just lost in our own thoughts. We both appreciate the beauty of silence. At the track, we have an unspoken understanding that there is a time to talk and a time for quiet study. We've shared picnic tables at Saratoga with non-stop chatterers and had to relocate.

Murphy has evolved from the play-every-race maniac of 30 years ago to a much saner player than I. He doesn't bet a lot, but still gives himself a chance at a score. I guess his horse playing evolution mirrors his personal maturation. He has raised two great kids, thrived in his career, and earned a PhD. Deep down, though, I think we both know that his apparent prudence and wisdom are just a façade, masking a contentious lunatic who would argue with a tree stump if he thought he could get a rise out of it. I owe Doctor Murphy a blanket apology for all my bad-beat rants and sulks over the years; he handles tough losses much more gracefully than I do, which I attribute to the patience he learned raising kids, while I remained childless.

I still love to play the races. My girlfriend, Lacy, loves horses and hates horse racing, but she is heroically tolerant of my passion. I think she would love the mornings at Saratoga, and I hope she'll accompany me one of these days.

Author's note: The old man in the following story is my grandfather, Daddy Sam; his son, my uncle Dave.

Watermelon in the Bathtub

She was a beautiful creature. Her head was streamlined and elegant, as opposed to the swollen, brutish head of the male. Later, the old man would put on his reading glasses and admire the artistry of the diamonds on her back with the wonder of a child marveling at a butterfly wing.

She could kill a child, though, and he could not abide her sunning where his great-grandkids played. She was a big sucker, maybe four feet long and thick as a summer sausage. With sadness, he sighted the rat-shot-loaded .357. His 91-year-old arm held steady and his rheumy old eyes aimed true. He'd imagined blasting all over creation like Yosemite Sam, but he killed her with one shot.

A mockingbird, dive-bombing the ground, had alerted him to the snake. The old man had been in one of his reveries, shoulder propped against the door jamb, staring out the glass door. You never knew what you might see out in the country; usually nothing but brown old west Texas, but if you were lucky, a roadrunner, a coyote, a mammatus cloud, a bobcat. Today he saw an angry bird.

He'd been thinking about his dreams, trying to make sense of them. In the first dream, he was standing in a cafeteria line, starving, piling food on his plate. When he got to the end of the line, the cashier took his plate from him. The aggravating procession repeated itself over and over again, like a film stuck in a projector. In the second dream, a mild-mannered friend turned murderous, butchering scores of people. When his friend finally approached him, the old man thought he was a goner, but the killer said he would be spared "if you improve your posture." He attributed the dreams to another new medicine the doctors were trying out on him.

He was afraid the snake might be in Ole Mexico by the time he got out there, as long as it took him to find the pistol, corral his walker, and shuffle across the yard to where it lay. His feet were damned near permanently asleep, so he had to raise them exaggeratedly to know that they were off the ground and moving. It was like having rag dolls where his feet used to be.

As he clomped down the ramp to the sidewalk, he looked over at the rock fence he'd built when he'd moved out there, after Laura Mary died, and cussed himself for the hundredth time. The idea was to separate the yard from the pasture, but he'd dimwittedly constructed a home for snakes near the Rattlesnake Capital of the World. Building a stone wall near the house had been the dumbest thing he'd done since his drinking days forty-some-odd years ago, back when he'd taken the controls of that little Cessna and bounced it twenty feet off the runway, trying to land. He'd had no more business piloting a plane than the man in the moon. Or the time he'd gotten drunk and bought an armada of motor scooters in a bar. The old boy was down on his luck, and it seemed like a fun idea at the time. Laura Mary hollered to high heaven but quieted down when he reminded her that she'd jumped off a diving board in her cocktail dress and eaten Thanksgiving dinner through a catcher's mask. He ended up donating the scooters to the Shriners for parades.

Hoisting the slack and clammy body of the diamondback tested his sketchy balance and recalcitrant limbs, and he almost wound up on the ground beside it. He pictured his son or a neighbor arriving to find him marooned in the dirt beside a dead rattler. The thought of his son gave him an idea of what to do with his kill. He managed to get the snake into the basket of his walker with the pistol and started the trek back to the house.

He almost lost his balance again when he tried to twist his hunched torso up to see the sandhill cranes, but he could barely look a man in the eye anymore, much less see the sky above. Ah, well, he didn't need to see them anyway; the hearing was the joy. He never could understand why the call of the sandhill so stirred his emotions. It always amazed him how impossibly far their voices carried, and something in the timbre of their call suggested a vulnerability that made him want to cry.

The old man took a moment to give thanks for his hearing. He was losing every bodily faculty he ever had, but he could still hear just fine.

He aimed the walker at the AstroTurf-covered plywood ramp he'd built for the dogs a few years back. Precious and Shorty were both crippled from arthritis and struggled climbing the stairs. He'd built the ramp at the same time he pulled the frame and box spring out from under his bed, lowering the height and making it easier for the dogs to ascend to their snuggling spots beside him.

One day, just after his back surgery, he was following the dogs up the ramp. Rain had made the AstroTurf a little slick. Precious lost her grip and slid back down into Shorty, upending him, then both dogs tobogganed like incompetent skiers into the old man, knocking him down. The three prone stooges looked at each other with the same question in their eyes: "Can you get up?" and the same answer: "Nope." Then they all agreed, "It's up to you, old man." The dogs had sheepish grins on their faces, and he got to laughing too.

He rose, wincing, in stages, from his back to his stomach, then to all-fours, then to his knees and finally to his feet. His surgery stitches ripped out as he lifted them up the ramp.

The old man felt like he had a moment of clarity after the dog pile, and the truth was that he could no longer take care of Precious and Shorty. He had the vet come out with his syringes, and the old man looked his buddies in the eyes as they closed for the last time. Once, when he was younger and he'd had to euthanize a couple of his dogs, he'd hugged them from behind, but their eyes were on the vet, a stranger, and they cried out. Their howls broke his heart, and from then on, whenever he had to put an animal down, he made sure his face was the last they saw.

His youngest son came to live with him soon after the dogs died. He thought of his son as a boy, but his son was getting to be an old man himself, in his sixties. He knew he should have been grateful to the boy for moving out there to help him, but he'd lived alone thirty years now and was past the point of wanting or tolerating a roommate. He'd been perfectly happy alone. He loved his son, but that didn't mean he wanted to live in the same house with him.

The old man became convinced that the boy was the loudest human on God's green earth. Everything his son did came with a clamor. The TV was always on and always too loud. Every door slammed. Out of the blue, the boy would cut loose with a thunderous belch, then add on some improvised bellering at the end of it. Sounded like a stricken donkey.

They had running arguments with each other about the most inconsequential things. When Holy Lands Mini Golf opened in Sweetwater, the boy thought it was the funniest thing he ever saw, and would make up stories about where, amongst the mangers and shepherds and camels, a golf ball might travel. The old man knew the proprietor from church and thought the fellow was odd, but the more the boy carried on about the miniature golf course and the crackpot owner, the more vociferously the old man defended him.

Home repairs brought out the worst in the two men. The old man had been a carpenter, meticulous and exacting, but about all he could do any more was direct his impatient and artless son, and it offended him to see his handiwork bastardized by duct tape and haphazardly driven nails. The old man took to referring to his son as "Shortcut" when they were feuding, rather than the customary "Bud," which he called every male in his universe. The boy's retaliatory nickname for his father was "The Toothless Wonder."

Back inside, the old man was anxious for his son to return from the grocery store so he could spring his surprise. When the younger man walked in, the old man said, "Bud, an old boy brought us a watermelon. Can you fetch it from the bathtub?"

The boy muttered about the idiocy of putting a watermelon in a bathtub, but headed back to the bathroom. The old man cackled when he heard a yell and the clatter of the shower curtain rod bouncing off the tub.

Daddy being Daddy, standing; Carolyn in her wheelchair; Nanny to the left

The author, age five, with his mother, Beverly

*My grandfather, Daddy Sam, and his
son, my uncle Dave*

Daddy, in his "uniform", in Rosita, Colorado

Reverend

I loved Reverend. He was the first cat I ever understood. What I understood was this: Reverend wanted to kill me and eat me.

A couple of years after I'd moved out to the country, a tiny tabby kitten showed up in the yard. He couldn't have been more than a few weeks old. I was out playing with the dogs and spotted the kitty before the dogs did. He walked right up to me, and as I stooped to pet him, my dogs, Igbert and Bo, 90-pound Labs, came thundering across the yard to investigate. The kitty, outweighed by 179 pounds, did not flinch or cower; he stuck his nose right up against theirs. I admired the kitty's pluck and decided he could stay. I named him Cat Verbeek (Beeks), after Pat Verbeek, a Dallas Stars hockey player who was the smallest man on the ice and started the most fights.

A few weeks after Beeks settled in, I stepped out on the porch to find him conducting a huddle with two black kittens. Their three noses were almost touching. Beeks told the visitors, "This is a pretty cool place if you don't mind dogs. You should join me." The kitty that accepted Beeks' offer was all black except for a white patch of fur on his throat that looked like a priest's collar. I named him Reverend.

Rev grew to be a big ol' boy, weighing about 15 pounds. Beeks, also a male, was maybe two-thirds of Rev's size. I am a dog person, not a cat person; the dogs lived inside, and the cats lived outside.

A hard lesson I learned about country cats is that they'll wreak carnage on a bird population. Kitty Boy, Rev's and Beeks' predecessor, an older cat I inherited with the place, wasn't much of a hunter, so the depredations of my new cats took me by surprise.

I had grown to love watching the cardinals, red-winged black birds, and finches that frequented the two bird feeders I kept faithfully supplied. One day, I ran out of feed, and my restocking trip to the local stores proved fruitless. I arrived home to find dozens of red-winged blackbirds and cardinals arrayed across the top strand of my goat wire fence like a Comanche war party lined up on a butte. They chirped angrily at me. The birds said, "Hey Asswipe, where is our food? You can't feed us every day for years, then cut us off cold turkey." I felt guilty then, but not near as guilty as I felt when I began seeing piles of feathers strewn about the yard after Rev and Beeks had gone hunting. I took one of the bird feeders down to try to limit the slaughter, but I was never able to create an environment that wasn't lethal to the birds, and I felt remorseful about it ever after.

Beeks' hunting style was straightforward. He would stalk, kill, and consume his prey, birds mostly. I'd hoped the cats would kill snakes, but I never saw them do it. The closest snake encounter I ever witnessed happened one evening about dusk. I was standing on my front porch and saw Beeks under the live oaks, about 15 yards away, crouched over something I couldn't make out in the twilight. He pawed tentatively a couple of times. After a couple of minutes, I realized his target had to be a snake. I felt relief not hearing any rattles. After a few more minutes of intense concentration, Beeks suddenly back-flipped like an Olympic gymnast; I guess the snake had struck. I couldn't help but laugh despite my concern for Beeks; I'd never seen a cat do a backflip and was impressed with his agility.

He couldn't have practiced that maneuver, it just came to him. Beeks retreated, uninjured. I tiptoed over and saw a 2-foot-long bull snake slither away toward the fence.

Killing was more of a game to Rev. He would hide under the birdbath, and when a bird lit, he'd reach a paw up and knock it into the water, then snatch it before it could right itself and take wing. He preferred to torture his victims, which became larger and larger over time. He graduated from birds to frogs to cottontails to squirrels, and liked to bat them around with his paws, letting them think they were on the verge of escaping, then pounce on them again. It pissed him off when I'd rescue one of his playthings and his hazel eyes blazed with anger.

I did get on Rev's good side once. Early one morning, I was washing dishes and glanced out the kitchen window to see Reverend sitting under a mesquite tree at the back of the yard. I looked up again a minute later, and a giant blonde coyote stood in Rev's spot, and Rev sat on a mesquite branch above the predatory canine. I walked out toward the coyote, shouting and waving my arms, thinking he'd flee as soon as he saw me, but he just looked at me, then up at Rev. Finally, when I got within about 20 yards, the coyote slunk away and jumped the fence. Rev descended from his perch and said, "Oh man, just when I had the drop on him!" but he trotted along happily beside me, and we both knew he wasn't going to kill and eat that coyote.

Rev continued to maraud up the food chain until he discovered jackrabbits. Every few months, I'd find a floppy-eared, big-footed jackrabbit, every bit as large as Reverend, disemboweled on the back steps or the dog path around the house. I didn't know that domesticated cats killed jackrabbits.

One time, Rev went missing for several days, and I got worried; he never missed a meal, even though he fed on something a half a dozen times a day. At last, I found Rev splayed out on the ground by the fence, blood matting his thick black fur, and little white, viscous chunks that I thought might be brain matter peppering his skull. He could barely open his eyes. I thought Rev was dying, either hit by a car or mauled by a coyote. I rushed inside and soaked a towel in warm water so I could clean him off and assess his injuries. I gently dabbed the blood and brains off him, but didn't find any gashes or punctures or broken bones. Then Reverend popped me on the chin with his paw. The son of a bitch was fine; he'd gorged himself on some colossal kill. Had Rev managed to take down a wild hog or a buffalo, I wondered.

My littlest dog, Spunky (renamed "Thelonius Spunk" by Dave), a Corgi mix, was terrified of Rev. Whenever Rev saw that the dogs and I were coming into the house, he would station himself at the top of the stairs and take swipes at us as we passed. They weren't playful spars; his claws were extended, meant to draw blood. Any creature who knew Rev walked with a hitch in his step up those stairs. "Take that with you," Rev said, after he popped you. Spunky had been blinded in one eye, either from a Rev slap or a battering from a Labrador retriever's wagging tail. Dave also called her "Gotch-eyed Spunk." She learned to wait at the bottom of the stairs until I opened the door, then bolt up the steps past Rev and into the house.

I think the ultimate goal of Rev's porch-swiping exercise was to trip me so that I'd crash headfirst into the stone wall and knock myself out. Then he could open my throat.

The only creature immune to Rev's bullying was Beeks. I never saw the bigger cat pick on the smaller. Sometimes they'd stalk and pounce on each other playfully, like the cute, harmless kitties they weren't, or I'd find them intertwined, sleeping peacefully.

Dave was a cat person and when he visited he'd wrestle and talk shit with Rev, then come inside, arms dripping blood. Dave is a tough old coot from West Texas, but he took to wearing leather work gloves when he petted Rev. Dave loved Rev, and Rev loved Dave. I think Rev wanted to kill and eat Dave even more than he wanted to kill and eat me.

Rev wasn't a murderous rat bastard all the time; he could be charming and sociable. Mother was not a cat person but gamely introduced herself to Rev, who was uncommonly gentlemanly that day, allowing himself to be cooed to and caressed, drawing just a slender dribble of her blood.

When I played Frisbee with the dogs or drank beer at the picnic table, Rev would join me and observe the proceedings. I didn't realize it then, but I'm sure that he was scrutinizing us for vulnerabilities that he might expose. Was Igbert limping? Did Bo just break his neck running into a tree? Is Jay drunk enough to be caught unawares?

Igbert and Bo were brother Labs; Igbert yellow and Bo black. Igbert got the brains.

You know how when you pull up in front of your house, and if anything is even slightly off kilter, like an open gate or a missing shingle, you notice it immediately? One day, I came home from work and something looked different. The front window blind was raised, and not just a foot or so, but all the way up to the top of the window. My first thought was that maybe my friend Kevin had visited and raised a blind for some reason. I called Kevin, who said no, he hadn't been by. I was baffled. Later that evening, I heard a commotion in the living room and found Igbert standing on the couch, pawing the drawstring on the blinds. Igbert had figured out how to catch the drawstring between his claws and pull it down.

Igbert was also a superior athlete to Bo. Both were avid Frisbee catchers. Igbert was a little taller and lankier than Bo, who was stockier, more musclebound. In football parlance, Igbert was built like a wide receiver and Bo like a linebacker. Igbert was Jerry Rice, the greatest pass catcher of all time, and Bo was Lawrence Taylor, one of the fiercest tacklers ever. Igbert was flat-out spectacular in his athleticism. I could throw two Frisbees, one right after the other, and he would catch the second while still holding the first in his mouth. He got so good that he would show off for fun. He had a couple of signature moves: One was the hooked marlin, where, at the top of his leap, he'd thrash his head back and forth, brandishing the Frisbee.

The other reminded me of a motocross biker turning his steering wheel at the top of a jump; Igbert would kick out his butt so he'd spin in mid-air.

Bo just ran over your ass. Bo did everything with blind gusto. Kevin and I had been playing with the dogs one steamy Texas summer day. Black Bo became overheated and chugalugged the contents of the full 5-gallon water bucket. A couple of minutes later, Kevin and I heard what sounded like an earthquake and looked over to see Bo impersonate a firehose, ejecting five gallons of water in a gush that would have knocked a man down.

Bo might not have been a genius, but he had heart. Near the end of his life he was blind, suffered from crippling arthritis and congestive heart failure, but would still drop the Frisbee at my feet and wag his tail, wanting to play. I started calling Bo "The Black Knight," after the character in "Monty Python and the Holy Grail" who had both of his arms and legs chopped off, but still wanted to fight ("It's merely a flesh wound").

One day, I was at the back of the yard throwing the Frisbee for the dogs, and Reverend was near the house, 50 yards away, sitting in the grass watching us. I flung the Frisbee in his direction for the hell of it. The Frisbee would never come close to such a small target; the distance was too far, and the disc too fickle in its flight. The Frisbee flew straight and true, however, right at Rev. If the dogs weren't charging, it would have landed, spinning, on top of his head. But the dogs were blitzing hell bent. Igbert, ever alert, saw Rev at the last moment and swerved to the side, but Bo, single-minded zealot that he was, didn't see anything but the Frisbee and splattered Reverend, who bounced across the yard like a kicked can. Rev collected his senses and scampered through the fence. After I stopped laughing, I went over and apologized and tried to coax Reverend back, but he just glared at me through the wire and would not come.

When I find myself sulking about how unfair life can be, I try to remember that, at least one time in my life, I witnessed an episode of exquisite justice.

A couple of days later, we were out in the yard after a round of play. One Frisbee lay on top of the other. Reverend sauntered over and squatted on them to take a crap.

Rev and Beeks died about a year apart; I found each of their bodies beside the house. My vet suspected bladder blockage, which sometimes occurs in neutered males. I never saw them in distress or would have taken them in for treatment. I cried as I buried them in their hunting ground. Birds rejoiced. Reverend would never kill me and eat me. I would miss the challenge of living in his domain.

Master Bath

All right, it's been quiet in there too long

Master might need me to save him

I nose the door open

Interesting, indoor fog

Master looks safe enough

A little silly, to be honest with you

Lying naked, water up to his chin

Master giggles, an invitation

I lap lap lap warm, soapy water

Tastes manly, yes, but I like it too

My Cucking Fareer

PLAVSHK is my name for a game I made up, where you strike random keys on your keyboard and try to pronounce the "words" that show up on the screen. I stole the word PLAVSHK from Lionel Essrog, Jonathan Lethem's Tourette Syndrome-afflicted character in *Motherless Brooklyn*. I favored a Jerry Lee Lewis piano style to create the jumbles of letters, raking my hands across the keys with a dramatic flourish, sometimes pounding the keyboard with my heel like Jerry Lee. Careful you don't tip your chair over if you try this maneuver. The oddball guttural sounds that came out of my mouth when farting around with newfound words kept me tickled for hours.

If I weren't playing PLAVSHK I might be stoking my obsession with Spoonerisms, in which the first letters in a word group are transposed to form a more entertaining or enlightening phrase. Here are a few examples:

--Smart farming = Fart smarming

--Walmart = Malwart

--Chicken and dumplings = Dicken and chumplings

--Dog food = Fog dood

--Ground beef = Bound greef

--Shaving cream = Craving sheam

--Food Mart = Mood Fart

--Grilled Cheese = Chilled Greese

No, I wasn't a crackpot linguist. The scene of most of my PLAVSHK and Spoonerism activity was at my desk in Austin, early in my career at PTI/PTT/MCI/WorldCom/Verizon, which I will refer to henceforth as WorldCon for brevity's sake. I had my own office in the late '80s, before the corporate world became entirely cubicle-ized, so I could speak gibberish and cackle as loud as I pleased.

The cult classic movie "Office Space", a spoof on everyday work life at a software company, was filmed in those very offices after we moved. I like to think that the filmmakers tapped into the aura of absurdity still emanating from my chamber.

I took the job with WorldCon when I was in my mid-20s, after graduating from UT with an undergraduate degree in English, a 3-month backpacking trip to Europe, and then stints in Dallas and Colorado working for an office supply company. I wanted to settle in Austin, a city I loved, and needed a paycheck.

I took the job with WorldCon and stayed for 27 years.

The slack time mentioned above was not representative of my entire career. I'd say I worked my ass off 60% of the time, humped the 8 to 5 gig 35% of the time, and was PLAVSHK-ly bored the other 5%. When I look back on a quarter century of corporate life, my best memories have almost nothing to do with work. I was never inspired by the goal of making money for a corporation, and I am somewhat disappointed in myself and embarrassed that I spent almost half my life in the corporate world. My weaknesses and/or character flaws that made for an extended corporate career were a desire for financial security, not being enough of an asshole to get fired, the ability to get along with people, communicate well in writing, and the capacity to bullshit my way through stuff I didn't understand.

Early in my career, I was excited about business travel, to see the country and have fun on the company's dime. The proudest moment, hands down, in my father's career as a salesman for McGraw-Hill was when he took a bunch of friends to the horse races at Louisiana Downs for a "sales meeting." They partied and gambled all day, and Daddy got away with expensing all of their losing tickets as customer perks. Imagine having your company pay your gambling losses. I was never as brazen as Daddy, but I wanted to see what I could get away with. On my first business trip, to Washington D.C., I went to a swanky jazz club in Georgetown, spent about $40 on the cover charge, $80 on dinner and drinks for one, and another $20 on a club t-shirt. I submitted all of those charges on my expense report, and they were denied. Chastened, having had to cover the Georgetown spree out of my own pocket, I played my next trip by the book, but ended up getting the worst chewing out of my career for expensing an $8 shoe shine.

It turned out that frugality was foisted only on the working grunts; executives were another matter. A few years later, I accompanied another boss, an up-and-comer in the company, to a meeting at the Broadmoor, a luxurious resort in Colorado Springs.

We played golf and got massages during the day, then one night I watched my boss go on a drunken, naughty rock star rampage, throwing everything in our suite that wasn't nailed down, including the mini bar refrigerator, out the 3rd story window. My boss's boss, who would later become Executive Vice President of the company, sat by and snickered. I wondered how many thousands of dollars the room-trashing cost. During this same period, we were laying off 10,000 people at a time and giving employees 1% raises.

The weird thing was that my boss's outrageous behavior enhanced his reputation in the company, like a politician getting name recognition, and his ascension into the upper echelon of management escalated after that. A Masters of the Universe egotism that I haven't witnessed to such an extent in any other walk of life oozed from many of our executives, and I think that was a component of my boss's tirade and subsequent approbation, but I still never comprehended the code.

My career came to a crossroads about that time. Over the span of a couple of years, I got job offers in Colorado, Missouri and Virginia. I turned down the first two, but thought seriously about taking the job in Virginia. It would have meant more money and responsibility, and it felt like it might be an adventure. I was young and free, so what the hell. The position was Operations Manager, running a 500-person call center and supporting the sales team.

The guy who offered me the job assumed I was going to take it and started prepping me on my initial responsibilities. We were opening up a brand new building, and the Sales Managers had come up with a whiz-bang opening ceremony to get the salespeople jazzed. My role in the kickoff would be to amp up the shenanigans by dressing up in a clown suit. Clown suit? Me? The decision that had been causing me so much angst became a no-brainer...no way.

My management career ended with the clown suit episode, and that was fine with me. I didn't belong there in the first place. The idea of "managing" people was alien to me, and I couldn't discipline another person if my life depended on it. I'm happy to say I never fired anyone.

I transitioned into the role of Project Manager (PM), whose duties I performed for my last 15 or so years at WorldCon, still feeling like an impostor. My projects revolved around installing voice and data networks and blah, blah, blah in corporate and customer sites. I was then, and remain, a technical idiot, with not a whit of schooling in IT shit and no affinity for it; moreover, I have strong Luddite tendencies, disdainful of cellphones and texting, which I believe breed rudeness, distraction, disrespect for words and language, and horrendous driving. I believe that in a few hundred years, human fingers will evolve into styluses, at which point soccer will be the *only* sport played on the planet because you can't catch a football or baseball with styluses.

I had to have been the only employee of 200,000 in one of the largest telecommunications companies in the world who did not carry a cell phone.

I think I inherited my how-things-work instinct from my father, who, about 30 seconds into one his rare attempts to work on one our cars, got pissed off and threw his wrench at our other car, denting its door. I have similar technical aptitude and patience. Lacy, whom I met a couple of years before my WorldCon career ended, assumes that, because I led technical projects, I am adept at troubleshooting computer problems. I've told her several times that she'd be better off consulting a 4-year old, but she persists. My advice, invariably, is to turn her machine off and back on.

Despite having no tech savvy, I was good at my job. I learned that you didn't have to be a technical wizard to lead technical projects. One of my few strengths was that I had no problem saying, "I don't know, but I can find out." I didn't have many answers, but I knew who did. One of my co-workers described me as having a "bulldog mentality," which I wouldn't have ascribed to myself, but I liked the idea and decided maybe I do.

My business travel curtailed once I was out of the management path, and that was fine with me, too. I had come to despise the sheep-herding aspect of air travel. If I believed in torture, my method would be to place the evil-doer in the middle seat of a packed airplane on the DFW airport runway on a 110-degree August afternoon, the terminal in view but unreachable. To this day, if I need to travel anywhere within 1000 miles, I'm driving.

Shortly after I settled into the PM job, I enjoyed one of the most satisfying experiences of my corporate career. My IT department was co-located in Austin with the telemarketing center, and I had a cubicle right next to the salespeople. It was another one of those sales kickoff events, similar to the clown suit episode, and the Sales Manager had a crackerjack idea: A parade up the main aisle of the office led by Bevo, the University of Texas athletic mascot, a burnt-orange longhorn steer, followed by the UT marching band. The Sales Manager was from New Jersey. Are cattle house-trained in New Jersey?

You know how it is in life, you breathlessly anticipate an event, but it never really pans out as thrillingly as you hoped. I *knew* what was going to happen, and yet Bevo extravagantly exceeded my expectations. Bevo pissed and shat his way up the carpeted aisle of our balloon-festooned hallway, then goosed by the band playing the Texas fight song right behind him, got excited and began throwing his head around like he was being attacked by bees, flailing his 3-foot long horns, and slinging gobs of slobber on grossed out bystanders and their cubicles. The handlers of the agitated steer almost lost control of Bevo, who threatened to perform a one-animal stampede before they reined him in. I pictured cubicle walls falling like dominoes. Bevo emptied his bladder and bowels on the way out of the building.

The company brought in carpet cleaners to erase Bevo's brown and yellow stain, but his 50-yard trail stubbornly remained until the carpet was eventually replaced. I had never felt such joy going into work every day, skipping delightedly up Bevo Lane.

One weird thing that never felt quite right about office life at WorldCon was the vaguely incestuous feel it had. I knew at least 15 couples who met and married there, as if the office were the only place on earth where one could meet one's mate. I also found it unsettling, being in a meeting with both halves of several married couples.

If I had to name an actual work event that proved gratifying to me, it would be about a two-year stretch in the MCI days, when we peasants in the field were given the freedom to make decisions and drive our projects without much input from management. We had a core team of maybe 20 people from several different disciplines (voice and data technicians, programmers), who worked our asses off, not because we were told to, but out of pride of ownership. We'd work countless all-nighters and build a 500-seat office from scratch in as little as a month's time. I've participated in all manner of teams in my life, especially in sports, but that was as dedicated an outfit as I ever had the honor to join. After management got involved and layered their bureaucracy into the equation, the same job would take six months to a year.

I'd been buying company stock at a 15% employee discount for at least a decade and had accrued several thousand shares, as well as stock options from my management days, and the stock had risen substantially over those years. Feeling flush financially, I wanted to buy a racehorse, pursuant to my dream of getting my picture taken in the winner's circle at Saratoga. Racehorses are about the most precarious investment known to man, but I had a dream. I found a bloodstock agent who ran an ownership syndicate, and I was pretty far down the path toward becoming a horse racing mogul. Then along came Bernie.

Bernie Ebbers was the owner of WorldCom, a telecommunications company that was actually smaller than MCI, but somehow managed to acquire us; I never understood how that worked.

We didn't know much about Bernie other than that he was some kind of corporate maverick, a billionaire Canadian who wore boots and jeans to work. After a year or so, we started hearing reports from our co-workers in Mississippi, where Bernie officed, that he would go into the break room and count coffee filters to see if they matched the number of coffee packets, suspecting theft. Shortly thereafter, the company stopped supplying office coffee, and we had to bring it in ourselves. I knew then that I should have sold every bit of company stock I had, but I didn't.

Bernie would start off our corporate meetings with a prayer; it turned out that as he was invoking God, he was also cooking the books, which led to the largest corporate fraud and bankruptcy in American history at the time. Everybody I knew had company stock, and we all got burned. The saddest story was of a friend of mine who was in his 60s, just on the verge of retirement, but his entire 401K was in company stock and he was completely wiped out. It wasn't a wise financial decision to have all his savings tied up in one stock, obviously, but it had worked for 30 years, and he saw no reason to change.

My horsey dreams evaporated (a couple of years later, the bloodstock company with which I'd been negotiating sold one of the racehorses I might have invested in for $6 million). I figured I lost about $200,000 on paper, and that was my first lesson on how little "on paper" means when it comes to finances. My 401K was diversified, so I wasn't completely wiped out, but I did feel like I was starting all over. That was another excuse I had for staying so long at WorldCon...I still had a paycheck coming in and needed to keep it.

My experience in the corporate world made me wonder, where did the myth arise that big business ran like some well-oiled machine? I witnessed fraud, gross inefficiency, waste, and especially, stultifying bureaucracy. I never worked in government, but I can't believe the red tape there could be any worse than it was in my later years at WorldCon.

Reductions in force (RIFs) were a fact of life we all had to deal with, usually several times a year. I experienced at least 100 RIFs in my career, and found out after the fact that it came down to me or another person a couple of times. I saw countless friends led out of the office by Security with a box in their hands, sometimes right before Christmas; the insensitive timing didn't matter to the company. It always pissed me off that the stock price would invariably rise after the company laid off 15,000 employees. Another RIF repercussion was that we survivors had to pick up the slack for those who'd been axed, so the workload ratcheted up every time.

I transitioned to telecommuting for about the last eight years of my career, and those were the hardest working years of my life because I treasured the privilege of working from home. I'd moved out to the country, 40 miles from Austin, and hated the traffic-congested hour-long commute to and from the office.

Telecommuting had its own comedies. One time, I was leading a conference call of about 30-40 people, including my boss and several higher-ups. It was cool spring day and I had the windows open, and my call was joined by an unexpected attendee, a young donkey that I named Zorro, for the white "Z" emblazoned on its butt. Zorro stood in the neighboring pasture right beside my fence, maybe 30 yards away, and cut loose with a spectacular, drawn-out, bawling heehaw. I guess the wind was just right to carry his voice in my direction because his aria resounded loud and clear, and the conference call went dead silent. I continued leading the call as if nothing had happened.

Of the millions of words I wrote in my corporate career, the majority came in the form of project plans, the PM's self-created bible that summarizes the ownership and timeline of a project. I wrote maybe a thousand of them in my career, taking great care to word them just right. As I was writing my 900th project plan I realized that noboby actually read the damned things; they didn't have the time or inclination, and I didn't really blame them. The true purpose of the project plan, I learned, was to keep the PM on track.

The best piece of corporate communication I ever read was created by my best friend at work. He inserted in his weekly report of accomplishments a paragraph of nonsensical technical mumbo jumbo, couched in corporate buzz words like "synergy" and "cloud" and "modularity", that meant absolutely nothing. We gleefully watched his passage of utter bullshit propagate up the management chain and finally land on a VP's weekly report. I'm surprised that

WorldCon didn't mount a marketing blitz around his "product" and charge $149.99 a month for it.

I generally had about 50 projects in my queue, which I thought was excessive. I talked to PMs with other companies who gasped when I told them how many projects I was working on; they usually had fewer than a dozen. One day, I counted 18 conference calls on my calendar, about 15 of which I was scheduled to lead. I can't bitch too much, though, because the five or six other PMs on my team had a similar workload. About half of the projects could be knocked out in a month or so, but the other half might last many months, or even years. I got in the habit of waking up at three or four in the morning to catch up on the prior day's work or prepare for the next, and my sleep pattern has been wrecked ever since. Even three years "retired" now, I still rise in the middle of the night.

My boss was a champ, another reason I stayed at WorldCon as long as I did. She was an Iowan, legendary within the company for her work ethic; nobody worked harder. She trusted me to run my business and never interfered, only jumping in if I asked for help. Sometimes we'd go for a couple of months without speaking, other than on staff calls. I'd had maybe 20 bosses in my career up to her, but we stayed together for 12 years as she took me through at least a half a dozen organizational changes. A dozen years in the corporate world with only one boss borders on the bizarre.

In August of 2013, I finally decided I'd had enough of the WorldCon bureaucracy and felt like I should do something more personally fulfilling. I told my boss that I would like to be RIF'd when the next round came up. It was a tough call because I had a pretty good gig outside of the workload and uninspiring subject matter: I worked from home, made good money, and got five weeks of vacation a year, which was as important to me as anything. I used every one of my vacation days and will never understand people who leave them on the table. After 26 years at the company, I would be eligible for a severance package worth half a year's pay.

Months passed without a RIF in our organization. Friends in other groups were still being laid off in droves, but I could not get canned. It crossed my mind that, if I could get myself fired, I'd get the severance package that way. I'd have to do something outrageous, like cuss out an executive, but I didn't have it in me to do something like that.

Finally, I was assigned a project to audit thousands of data center circuits nationwide, a mammoth, tedious, brain-deadening undertaking. The audit was supposed to be done annually, so theoretically I'd finish it in December, then start the same process all over again in January, a Sisyphean task as appealing to me as dressing up in a clown suit. I protested to my boss, who said she'd explore other options, but that was the end for me. I submitted my resignation in March of 2014, leaving without the much-coveted severance pay that would have covered my expenses for a year.

At age 53, I retired.

The Wave

I walk a country road almost every day and wave at people passing in cars.

Daddy Sam lived in the country and waved at people from his pickup truck. He would lift his hand slowly off the wheel, like an Indian chief in a bad, old cowboy movie saying "How." Daddy was the most aggressive waver I've ever known. He would reach his whole hand over the steering wheel toward the passer-by, almost confrontationally, and wave. He would shoot the finger at friends.

Thinking back, I guess I did wave from the road as a kid. When I was about eight years old, in Lubbock, Texas, my friend Greg and I came up with a game. I think we must have just learned how to shoot the finger...Greg probably taught me because I was a naïve kid, always the last to know, from Santa to sex. Of course we had no idea what it meant. We would ride our bikes around the neighborhood and simulate the most horrific collision of Schwinns the world has ever seen, our bikes crashed and twisted by the side of the road, our mangled bodies splayed out among the wreckage, our middle fingers extended. Not one car ever stopped to assist or scold.

When I wave now, conventionally, most people wave back. Ladies are my favorites because they wave with their whole hand and sometimes enthusiastically, like they're really glad to see me. I get tickled. Why, thank you, I'm really happy to see you, too.

Every once in a while, somebody will point at me with their finger, as if they are choosing me for their football team, and I really enjoy that one, too. I want to say, "I'm in, buddy, let's go."

Men generally wave with a studied nonchalance, too cool, or too busy with more important business to wave with their whole hand. One or two fingers are all they can manage. I don't know the physics of hand muscles, but I think it actually takes more thought and effort to raise one finger than it does to raise all five. It would be just like us males to exert ourselves more to appear to care less.

Waving to anybody under 20 is a different experience entirely. When I wave at the young, I usually see a confused look on their faces, as if they're thinking, "What the hell is this guy doing? I'm just minding my own business, and this doofus waves at me." Some tentatively wave back while others speed up to escape. Why is waving such a foreign concept to the young?

(In my first draft, I wrote, "My instinct says it's technology's fault. If I carried some giant emoji around and flashed it at them they'd probably be hunky dory." I was taken to task by Murphy, the father of two "Generation Z" kids, who "have expressed, fairly convincingly, why such generalizations are lazy and rarely stand up to scrutiny...you get your old person card as soon as you say it." I think Murphy's kids are right. Blaming technology for youthful behavior is unfair. But the question remains, why don't they wave?)

If somebody is driving way too fast on my road, I don't wave. It's their punishment for speeding. What happens is, they feel a sense of loss at not being waved at by me, and, chastened, don't speed in the future. No telling how many lives I've saved.

Decamping

"Is this your dog?" the lady asked.

"Yes, ma'am."

"Well, he just peed on my potato chips."

I started to launch into a profuse apology, but she stopped me.

"That's alright, we're best buddies now. He brought me his Frisbee. What's his name?"

"Ignatius...or Igbert. A Jones dog never has just one name."

"After Ignatius Reilly?"

"Yes, ma'am, you got it." I was delighted that she named the protagonist of *A Confederacy of Dunces*, a book I love. 99% of the time, when I told people my dog's name, they stared vacantly as if they were thinking, "What a silly name for a dog." This lady had made the best first impression on me of anybody I'd ever met, bonding with my dog and connecting his name to literature.

"Please quit calling me ma'am. I am Sara, and this is August." She motioned over to the tent where an enormous man had just emerged. I had noticed him the night before, but had not spoken to him. August nodded. I introduced myself.

I wondered if I'd offended Sara by calling her "ma'am." I'd been raised to address my elders as "sir" and "ma'am," and Sara was probably a few years older than me. I'd never considered that by addressing a lady as "ma'am," I was obliquely referring to her age. I'd have to think about that.

"Did you try to kiss a wolverine?" Sara asked, gesturing at my face.

I chuckled at the image, but had no idea what she was talking about at first. I touched my bloody upper lip. "Oh. Yes Ma'a...Yeah, I slept too close to a dreaming dog," I said.

Sara was mid-fortyish, with long, curly blonde hair, disheveled after a night in a tent. Her hands were a little beat up and calloused, but still feminine; her occupation involved outdoor manual labor, I decided. She threw Igbert his Frisbee while we talked, and after he dropped it at her feet, he would leap to Sara's eye level so that she could get a close-up gander at the grin plastering his face.

"Fortuna doesn't torment this Ignatius, does she?" Sara said, referring to the Roman goddess of luck whom Ignatius Reilly blames for the downward spiral of his fortunes throughout *Confederacy*.

I laughed. "No, she sure doesn't."

The occasion of our meeting was an annual campout called Springfest, near Round Top, Texas, about 90 miles east of Austin, hosted by Anders Saustrup, the father of my friend Steffen, who invited me out. I had met Anders once before, but saw him only in passing at the campout. I knew maybe six people there, out of the 80 or so attendees. The campers reflected Anders' diverse interests: There were botanists, historians, university professors, musicians, and Texas Democratic Party movers and shakers. Many of them, including Steffen, had camped extensively all over the world.

I had arrived the afternoon before, completely unprepared to lodge outdoors. I hadn't camped out in 20 years; it wasn't a part of my lifestyle. I had no tent or any other camping accoutrements. I figured Igbert, Bo, my other dog, and I would sleep in the back of my Volvo station wagon. The only food I brought was a few snacks I'd picked up at a convenience store.

My primary preoccupation was with the safety of my dogs. I didn't let my dogs run loose in public very often. We lived on a couple of acres of land out in the country, about 40 miles northwest of Austin, where they could run to their heart's content, so I didn't feel guilty about letting them be homebodies.

Igbert and Bo had come into my life just after I'd moved out to my place. Kevin, my best friend from high school, his wife Anna, and their one-year-old were living with me while they waited for their house to be built. Calpurnia, their female black Lab, was pregnant; their male, Boo, a yellow Lab, was the father (yes, a Boo and a Bo in the same family). Kevin didn't know exactly how far along Calpurnia was in her pregnancy, and one day I came home from work and opened the door, flabbergasted to see white feathers floating in the air and blanketing the floor. It looked like a bomb had gone off in a henhouse. The living room couch had been disemboweled, its springs exposed. A couch in another room had been similarly eviscerated.

I heard whining and found Calpurnia in a bedroom with one live yellow puppy and one dead one beside her. A third animate puppy lay on the floor. Calpurnia arose, weak and agitated, and I followed her into the living room, where she sniffed the floor frantically. I could not figure out what she sought until I moved an ottoman and found a black puppy whimpering beneath it.

My heart hurt for Calpurnia and the desperation she must have felt as she tried to dig out a birthing nest. Anna arrived, and we created a makeshift home for Calpurnia and her puppies in a cardboard box. I buried the dead puppy out in the yard.

I kept the biggest yellow puppy and named him Ignatius. Kevin found owners for the other two, but Bo, the lone black one, came back to me a couple of years later after Bo's family didn't pan out. I came from a dog-loving family, but these were the first dogs I would raise on my own.

A few weeks later my front gate was accidentally left open and Boo bolted during a thunderstorm and was struck and killed by a car on Highway 29, a couple of miles away. Kevin and I lifted Boo's battered body off the side of the road and into the bed of his pickup, where his blood trickled over the bare, ribbed steel. We bawled as we dug Boo's grave behind Kevin's house.

The way some people tossed out the phrase "my dog got run over" had always irritated me, as if it was just one of those things, like a light bulb burning out. I believed that if you tried hard enough, cared for your dog just a little bit more, took that one extra little precaution, then your dog would be safe. I said to myself, "I'll be goddamned if one of my dogs *ever* gets run over."

Anders' campground was at least a mile from any paved road or traffic, so I had no real reason to worry about my dogs, yet I couldn't help but watch them attentively. Igbert and Bo had a blast among the dozen or so other dogs, exploring freely, sniffing earth and butts and food, leaving their mark where they deemed appropriate, behaving like perfect gentlemen. I'm certain they were more popular than me. One of my friends surveyed the canine troupe and said, "Igbert is the best-looking dog out here. He seems like the smartest and happiest one of the bunch." The compliment pleased me more than my friend could know. No matter what else I'd done in my life, at least I had raised one happy creature. Bo was happy too, just not as radically exuberant as Igbert.

I'd been living alone out in the boonies for about six years by then and had begun to manifest hermit tendencies. I had hermit dreams, in which I would have a dream and tell it, not to other humans, but to characters I created in subsequent dreams. My social life happened mostly in my head. I wasn't used to being in a crowd of people, and all of the voices at the campout confused me. I felt an irrational need to try to assimilate all of them at once, and the effort left me frazzled.

At supper time, steaks and sausage sizzled on grills, beans bubbled in campfire cookpots. My inner Nazi decreed that since I hadn't contributed food or helped with the preparation then I shouldn't partake of other campers' cooking, although I had a couple of offers to "dig in." I stole out to my car and ate stale sandwiches from triangular plastic boxes. I was one fun dude. If only I'd brought a date to impress with my Clark Gable-like savoir faire.

That night, I drank a few beers to try to loosen up and loitered on the fringes of the campfire, behind the musicians and storytellers, never sitting. I thought about how Daddy would have been right in the middle of them, telling stories, singing his ass off. I pictured him happily bumming food off strangers, charming them so thoroughly that they would have felt lucky to have served him.

I heard stories about "Ann" and "Molly:" Ann being Ann Richards, the former Texas governor, and Molly was Molly Ivins, a political columnist I read faithfully, who had nicknamed George W. Bush "Shrub". Being a liberal Democrat, I should have been in hog heaven listening to their insider stories, but by then, my self-inflicted alienation had consumed me. I felt like I did not belong and retired early to my "tent."

My bed in the back of the Volvo didn't prove as cozy as I'd imagined. I tried to sleep, contorted between two dead-to-the-world 90-pound Labs. Igbert churned his legs in his sleep, dreaming, just about every night. On this night, while he frolicked in Dog Paradise, he managed to drag a claw from my nostril to my upper lip, drawing blood that I wiped on my sleeping bag; another flailing paw scraped me down the forehead and cheek. I had forgotten about it by the next morning and glanced in a mirror to see what looked like an Indian who had used an arrowhead to apply his war paint rather than a finger.

Before daylight, I gave up trying to sleep. I took a leak and fed the dogs before driving 20 miles into La Grange, in search of real food. No restaurants were open yet, though, and I ended up with a tankard of bitter coffee and a cellophane-wrapped blueberry muffin. I meandered through the countryside as the sun rose on a cool, cloudless morning. I thought about heading back home right then, but decided I should say my goodbyes at the camp before fleeing. I would tell my friends that I had a commitment in town, which was a lie.

When I arrived back at Anders' place, the campers were stirring, brewing coffee with chicory, frying bacon and eggs in skillets on camp stoves. That was one time in my life when I was grateful for not having a sense of smell; if I'd inhaled succulent aromas, I might have cried.

Ignatius disappeared, and that's when I met Sara and August.

"Ya'll found yourselves a secluded spot," I said to Sara.

"Yeah, last year we camped with everybody else the first night," Sara said, "but August woke the entire campground with his snoring, and we learned our lesson. August snores...like an angry bull."

The loudest snorer I ever knew was my buddy Billy Crow, who was 40-50 pounds overweight, had a severe case of sleep apnea and would sometimes drink a case and a half of beer in a day. When we'd go on road trips and share a room with Billy, we learned to try to go to sleep or pass out before Billy did, lest we be kept awake by his stentorian snoring. One time in a New Orleans hotel room, a friend didn't pass out in time and the next morning we found him balled up under the bathroom sink, cowering from the cacophony. I think Billy's wake-up radius might have been 20 yards or so; he could have woken up the occupants of surrounding tents, but not a whole acre's worth of people.

While Sara and I were talking, August performed his morning ablutions. He appeared to be younger than Sara by six or eight years. He was shirtless, so I got a good look at his physique, which resembled that of a sumo wrestler. He stood 5'10" or so and weighed about 380 pounds, I guessed. Unlike some obese people whose rotundity is centered in the gut, August was huge from head to toe; every part of his body seemed to be busting out of its skin. His Michelin Man arms swung around his massive torso when he walked, and, at rest, hung slightly out and in front of his girth as if he were preparing to bear hug a barrel.

I told Sara about Billy's snoring, and she said, "August, tell Jay about the bull."

"Right. Well, Sara and I love to camp." August's voice surprised me. It was higher-pitched than I expected from such a large man. He massaged Sara's neck absent-mindedly when he wasn't gesturing to highlight the story.

"We had a campsite reserved at Garner State Park, but the Frio River had flooded the campground, and it was closed. It was late at night and we were beat. A friend of a friend had some land nearby and allowed us to spend the night in his field. We found a spot on high ground, but it was too muddy to set up the tent, so we slept in the truck. Sara took the cab, and I slept in the bed with the gate down."

"In the middle of the night, I woke up from a dream of earthquakes and grizzly bears. I glanced out the back of the truck and saw the earthquake grizzly bear...a big ol' black Angus bull, 10 yards away, bellowing and stomping, throwing his head around, flinging gobs of slobber in the air, snorting steam like in a cartoon. He was one mad mamma jamma. He thought I was another bull, infringing upon his territory, and he was gonna show me who's boss."

"That dang bull lowered his head to charge, and I had to move quick. I scrambled out of the bed and into the cab. I could feel that SOB right on my ass. The second I got the door closed, he whooshed by. Took the side mirror clean off the truck."

I laughed and shook my head.

"I never knew what my snoring sounded like. Sara had tried to describe it...like a locomotive, like an injured lion. Sometimes I wake myself up snoring, but I hear only the last snatch of sound as I come to, like my body is teasing me. Now I know."

"It's weird, being so disruptive while I'm unconscious. It's as if everyone else knows me better than I know myself, in one particular way."

"Is there a cure...for the snoring?" I asked.

"We're working on it," Sara said, winking at August.

"How do you handle the racket?" I asked Sara, feeling a twinge of uneasiness as I spoke. Was I getting too personal? Might I offend August? I am an intensely private person, loath to volunteer much about myself until I know someone for say, six or eight years; I'm usually ultra-respectful of others' privacy in return, but Sara and August had melted my defenses, loosened my tongue.

"Oh, I've tried everything under the sun, ear muffs, plugs.... They help a little."

Then she said, matter-of-factly, "You know, it's amazing what love will allow one to abide."

I would like to say that I realized I did belong at the campout after all, that my place was out back of the farmhouse, set off from the crowd, next to my friends Sara and August; that I encamped beside them and we talked about books and dogs and dreams all day long; that I learned what Sara did with her hands, and when night fell, I got to hear August snore. But I didn't. I told them my lie, ran away home and never saw them again.

Author's note: How could you not love a place called "Casa de Risa"? The name fit. A dozen vivid stories come to mind when I think of the cottage on Baffin Bay, south of Corpus Christi, so I had to write about it. Steffen's aunt Willie, prescient in more ways than one, bought the place for $500 in 1940 and christened it Casa de Risa. In charming disrepair when I wrote this, it has since been razed and rebuilt from the ground up by family and friends...nothing slapdash about it now, but the vibe remains.

Casa de Risa

I know a place on Baffin Bay
Ain't fancy, ain't got cachet
There is a Riviera near
But French ain't spoken there

Slapdash shack sits atop a dune
Sports a bar from an old saloon
Bedrooms are festooned with bunks
Feels like a camp for drunks

AC hasn't graced her yet
You wear a sheen of sweat
From the loo, you hear a shout
Bloody hell!
Black snake on the shower spout

135

Clothes fall off like autumn leaves
Cares blow away in the breeze
Life's bullshit don't light your fuse
Feet forget the feel of shoes
You can have your Martha's Vineyard
You can have your Waikiki
Gimme Casa de Risa
Down home, funky, free

If a pool game suits your vibe
Head on over to the local dive
The 8-ball rolls a wobbly route
Through dead flies lyin' about

Fixin' dinner is a form of play
You coax your groceries from the bay
Specks bite shrimp and plastic bling
Crabs grab chicken necks on string

There's kids and dogs, and dancing bears
Dancing tables, dancing chairs
Dancing on the patio, dancing on the dock
Dancing, dancing, dancing, dancing, dancing 'round the clock

Clothes fall off like autumn leaves
Cares blow away in the breeze
Life's bullshit don't light your fuse

Feet forget the feel of shoes
You can have your Martha's Vineyard
You can have your Waikiki
Gimme Casa de Risa
Down home, funky, free

Clocksucker

I fear my attic.

The last time I set foot up there, a decade ago, wasps swarmed around my head. As I ducked them, I stepped off a beam and onto the drywall ceiling, which will support the weight of one of those 3-inch tall green army men that I played with as a child, but nothing heavier. I crashed through the ceiling, but rather than dropping into the hall closet like an indoor parachutist, my arms lodged on cross beams, almost pulling them out of their sockets. An exposed nail impaled the fleshy underside of my forearm. I dangled from the ceiling for a moment before lifting my punctured limb off the nail and completing my descent.

I ended up paying a local handyman several hundred dollars to patch the hole in the ceiling. He did a crappy job and I paid another guy a few hundred dollars more to have it done properly.

A bland, round Timex clock hung above my kitchen sink. The original owner of the house had installed it when he built the house in 1983. I bought the house in 1995 and let the Timex stay because it told time and because its cord ran up through a half-dollar-sized hole in the ceiling up into the attic. After 34 years, the Timex groaned and died. I had inherited a hand-painted floral clock from my mother, who passed away three years ago; it held sentimental value to me, and I wanted to put it up. I tugged at the cord of the Timex, but it would not shake loose. I wasn't sure if it ran to a socket or was wired in, so I didn't pull too hard.

I consulted with Murphy, told him about my attic aversion, and he suggested I might cut the cord of the Timex below the ceiling and cap it off. We agreed it would be a good idea to turn off the kitchen breaker first. I pondered this potential solution but decided against it; I have a healthy respect for electricity and didn't want to create a fire hazard.

I would have to brave the attic to find the terminus of the Timex cord. My attic is a pain in the ass to access. The particle board-covered, shoulder-width black hole is sequestered in the upper corner of a bedroom closet. Everything in the closet has to be removed to make room for a ladder. I cleaned out the closet, committing myself to the attic expedition.

As I wrestled an eight-foot-long shelf through the cluttered bedroom, it clattered off the whirling blades of the ceiling fan.

I own three ladders, two outdoor ones that are too tall to maneuver into the room, and a stepladder, which is not tall enough to reach the black hole. I scoured the house for a way to boost the step ladder.

The last time I had attempted creative laddering was 30 years ago when I was locked out of Key's house. I thought I might get in via a 2nd story window. I was drunk. I found some heavy-duty beer coolers in the garage and decided that I could build a platform out of them. I climbed my cooler ladder to the edge of the roof. As I heave-hoed to lift myself onto the roof, the coolers slipped from under my feet and down we tumbled. I drove myself to the hospital with two broken metacarpals in my left hand.

I looked over at a cooler that I had extricated from the closet. The cooler said, "Hey Jayroe, long time, no see. I'll be glad to boost you up to the attic. Let me grab a couple of buddies."

Wiser and more sober than I was in my youth, I declined the cooler's offer and instead placed the step ladder on the seats of two opposing metal folding chairs, which held firm but did not raise me quite as high as I needed.

That afternoon, I half-heartedly checked out a few pawn shops in search of a cheapo 6-foot ladder, but the idea of owning four ladders seemed absurd. I borrowed one from the maintenance shop of the apartment complex Lacy manages.

The assault on the attic would occur, I decided, when my mind was at its most steel-trapish, when I was hyper-alert after four cups of coffee…about 4:00 am. The temperature in the attic would only be about 95 then, rather than the 145 degrees it would register on the August afternoon. I live alone; my dogs would be the only witnesses.

To get the ladder into the closet, I had to remove one last item, a 10-foot-long wooden clothes-hanger pole. As I guided the pole out of the room, it clanged off the whirling blades of the ceiling fan.

I donned sweat pants, a long-sleeved shirt, a baseball cap, gloves, and a white dust mask before heading up into the attic. I tested my flashlight. I had the clever idea of placing an alarming clock underneath the hole in the ceiling to help lead me to my target site, which was halfway across the house from the attic portal. The staccato beeping of my alarm clock sounded exactly like the timer on a bomb in a terrorist movie that the hero disarms with one second to spare. It accentuated the sense of danger I felt, and I was relieved when it went silent as I climbed the ladder.

When I got a foothold in the attic, I turned on the light and surveyed the metal roof innards, the beams and rafters and joists. I didn't know exactly what a joist was, but I found that I liked saying the word out loud. I didn't see any wasps. I was reminded that I had the attic re-insulated a few years ago. The surface was covered in two feet of wooly grey snow, hiding the flat plywood boards that I had planned to tread across to reach the clock cord hole. I would have to step on the slender beams of the frame instead, which I couldn't see either. I remembered that the prior owner of the house had told me that he thought he had hidden a loaded pistol up there and never retrieved it.

I rummaged through the insulation around the edge of the attic hole, but didn't lay my hand on a gun. I shined the flashlight in the direction of where I thought the cord ran, and thought maybe I saw an electrical box, but couldn't be sure. I would have to get closer. The path I decided to take was where the rafters, slanted at a 45-degree angle, joined at the bottom of the roof; there had to be a solid beam there, slightly wider than a tight rope. The clearance was about three feet high, so I hunkered down and did an imitation of those '70s "Keep on Truckin'" cartoon dudes whose torsos lean way back while they walk and their legs lead the way. My hips would be sore for a week after.

As I trucked awkwardly and gingerly, hands grasping for rafters, I began sweating, and my glasses fogged up from my breath trapped by the mask. I lay the flashlight down, unmasked myself, and wiped my glasses. The flashlight had sunk deep into the insulation, and it took me a minute to find it.

Torch back in hand, the beam illuminated something shiny, a three-foot-long snake skin. I lifted the skin with the flashlight, hoping it would disintegrate from old age, but it was wholly intact, glistening, fresh. I wondered if the snake was bedded down beside me, flicking its forked tongue, thinking that today might be its lucky day, that a giant, oafish rodent had blundered into its den.

Oh well. I shined the flashlight toward the cord hole and saw clearly the electrical box and clock cord, tucked just under the eave. The plug was partway out of the socket. Eureka! I was still about 12 feet away and couldn't get to it, but at least I knew what to do...get the hell out of the attic and pull the cord from the kitchen until it released.

I made it out of the attic safely, sweating profusely, legs shaky. I smoked a cigarette on the front porch, happy that I'd survived the attic and wouldn't have to go back up again.

I pulled hard, then harder on the Timex cord but the son of a bitch would not come free. The hole in the ceiling widened and bits of sheetrock rained down into my eyes. Could the cord be tied around a rafter, I wondered. It must have been angled in such a way that I wasn't able to apply enough leverage to extract the plug. I thought about ending the whole charade right then and there by punching a hole in the ceiling, but I stifled my urge for violence.

I would have to go back up into the attic after all.

So, how would I reach the plug? I wasn't going to try to belly my way blindly down to the outlet under the eave; the path was too obscure and the space too tight. I needed a very long arm. What about my fishing pole? It had a metal tip on the end, and if I happened to touch the tip to the exposed part of the plug in the outlet, I might fry. The fishing pole was too flimsy to wield reliably anyway.

It occurred to me that if I found the pistol, and my karma exerted itself in its own peculiar way, I might simultaneously shoot myself, get snake bit, electrocuted, then crash through the ceiling and break my neck. I imagined a TV show where my death was amateurishly re-enacted, then viewers would text in their vote on the actual cause of my death.

After my apocalyptic vision, I remembered the ten-foot clothes hanger pole. If I could attach a hook to the end of it, I might be in business. I found a metal plant-hanger hook in my toolbox, wrapped it in electrical tape to stifle its conductivity, then taped the hook to the end of the pole.

Harpoon in hand, I advanced on the whale. On the march to my roost, my staff ricocheted off the whirling blades of the ceiling fan. I scrabbled my way down the perilous path, said hello to the invisible snake, and snatched the cord out of the socket on the first try.

Back down in the kitchen, I pulled on the clock cord, and it slid right out, as if it had been yearning to surrender all along. I thought about taking the Timex out to the yard and beating it to pieces with a 4-iron, but repressed my violent impulse. I laid the old clock to rest in the garbage can.

Mother's clock now hangs where the Timex once did. It is battery-operated. Cordless.

So, that's how I pulled a plug. Now let me tell you about a light bulb that needed unscrewing…

Beverly Jones

Beverly Kay Jones passed away on Saturday, October 18, 2014, at the age of 75.

Beverly was born to Morris and June Pruitt in Lamesa, Texas, on February 9, 1939. When she was ten years old, the Pruitts, now a family of four after the birth of Sandra in 1941, moved to Sweetwater, Texas. There, Beverly met and instantly disliked a smart-alecky fellow fifth-grader named Clyde Jones. She went on to attend Sweetwater Newman High School, where she was a baton twirler and Homecoming Queen in her senior year. Beverly and Clyde became sweethearts in high school and were married on June 7, 1959.

Beverly gave birth to son Jay in Arlington, Texas, in 1960, then daughter Junie in Amarillo in 1961, and son Carey, also in Amarillo, in 1963. The Jones family moved to Lubbock in 1965, then to Richardson in 1969, as Clyde prospered in his job with McGraw-Hill. Beverly, who had been a stay-at-home mom, went to work as a secretary in the early '70s to help make ends meet. Beverly and Clyde later lived in Grand Prairie after their kids went off to college.

Clyde christened Beverly "Alpine Bev" with their move to Colorado in 1991, upon his retirement. Clyde set about building his Colorado "empire", eventually buying property in Cuchara, Rosita and Walsenburg, and they lived in all three places during their Colorado years. Alpine Bev grew to love the mountains, people and wildlife of southern Colorado, and was the gracious hostess (and bouncer when necessary) of many a wildlife gathering.

Beverly's beloved Clyde died at home in Walsenburg in July of 2000. Beverly nursed her husband with saintly patience and compassion to the end. In her time as a widow, she settled in Rosita, where she communed with deer and the occasional bear, worked home improvement projects, read voraciously, visited friends, and took trips with her kids. She spent winters with Junie in Plano.

Beverly was the consummate lady, exuding class and grace at every turn. She loved to shop and dressed exquisitely. Another nickname Clyde bestowed on Beverly was "Queen", and it could not have been more appropriate. She was a superb cook and shared her table liberally. Beverly had an unerring sense of right and wrong and was not afraid to express her opinion. She was physically brave, selflessly putting herself in harm's way more than once when others were at risk. She fought cancer twice in her life, beating it both times with grit and good humor.

Beverly was the best mother one could ask for and was immensely proud of her kids (who hit the jackpot on parents, it must be said). She was best friends with her mother, June, who died in 1996. Beverly shared everything with her dear sister, Sandra Walker, and found the brother she never had in Clyde's brother, Jesse David Jones. She had friends all over creation, and especially close to her heart were her niece Shelli Dill, her nephew William Haskell, Sam Jones, Jeffrey Jones, Dorian Jones, Melinda Hervey, Nora Henson,

Sharon Scott, Paula Padilla, Lacy Van Zandt, Glen Bakken, Mark Winnubst, Anna Stubbs, and Joe and Sue Ozzello.

Beverly was laid to rest on a crisp, clear October morning in Rosita, Colorado, now forever beside her Clyde.

Mother's Air

What would Mother say? That was the question we had to answer. For the first time in our lives, we couldn't ask her. Carey, Junie, Lacy, my aunt Sandy and I had been at Mother's bedside that afternoon and shared our grief at her passing.

Mother loved us children unconditionally, in our own separate ways, but at the end, she most yearned for Carey's presence, and he'd driven in from Colorado, although her condition seemed stable. I was the eldest, responsible, reliable, infallible, in Mother's mind. Junie was her best friend, her happy hour and museum running buddy, who also managed the day-to-day complexities of endless doctor's appointments and overflowing pill dispensers, and who shouldered the emotional burden of nursing a cancer patient who is also your mother. Toward the end, Junie's and Mom's roles reversed, and Junie mothered Mother. Carey, who had been Mother's primary companion in Colorado after Daddy died, was the youngest and most trouble-prone. Mother, Daddy and Carey once took a trip together when Carey was seven or so, and Daddy reported that Carey had gotten 18 spankings during the trip. Daddy exaggerated every number in his life tenfold, but we got the point. Carey still has a recording of Mom's voice on his phone, from one of her last nights. She'd been in and out of consciousness and convinced herself that Carey was out on the town late at night. "Carey, it's 1:30 in the morning," she says, agitated. "Where are you? You need to come to Junie's or the hospital, now!" Carey had been faithfully rotating hospital shifts with Junie and me, and was asleep at Junie's. We laughed about it the next morning, Mother most of all.

Mother had beaten cancer twice already; underlying the femininity and grace of Beverly Jones was an indomitable will. I think we all inherited a kind of root optimism from Mother and Daddy, and, dedicated to helping her overcome her latest health challenge, we thought only of the battle. "What ifs" didn't enter into the equation, so we began facing them for the first time that October afternoon.

Mother had lived with Junie in Plano, Texas, for the last two years, but she would rest permanently beside her husband, our father, Clyde, in a cemetery where elk grazed next to tombstones in Rosita, Colorado. How would we get Mom to Colorado? At the hospital, I threw out the idea that we should drive her there ourselves, and Carey was ambivalent. That night, as we sat around the table on Junie's back porch and discussed it more seriously, the idea started to grow on all of us. We invoked the memory of Call's final trip back to Texas with Gus in *Lonesome Dove*. Junie's friend Nora said the scheme was "crazy ass and poetic."

But what would Mother think of us driving her to Colorado? In the end, the decision came pretty easy. Mom would want to be with us every step of the way, and if that meant us driving her to Colorado, so be it. Mother was game.

We got fired up, Carey especially, and when Carey is excited, look out. He is the most extroverted and emotional of us kids, capable of tornadic energy. We started making calls to check the legality of transporting a body across state lines. Carey's buddy Mark, a lawyer who had helped Mom with her will, had his doubts. We didn't need to be reminded that if there were a state in the union that would have punitive, draconian laws on the books, it would be Texas. Junie called a friend who had once worked in a funeral home, and he was dubious as well. On the positive side, Lacy's cousin had transported both of his parents home in a pickup truck, one across state lines. Maybe we'd have to do it outside the law, but we were doing it, by god. Mother would have agreed; Daddy would have preferred we break a few laws along the way.

The next morning, we called the funeral home, they said our proposed transport was legal; we just needed to carry a death certificate in case we were stopped by the police.

So, what car would we drive? We measured Mom's and Carey's SUVs, and neither was long enough for a casket. My Volvo station wagon, the oldest and least roadworthy of all of our cars, came closest to a fit. I elected Carey, who is more socially adept and persuasive than I, to convince the funeral home to let us test a casket to see if it would fit in the Volvo. He pictured us re-enacting the funeral parlor scene from "The Big Lebowski", where the John Goodman character raises hell, slamming his fist on the table and bellowing obscenities, but the negotiation was very civil, and Carey swung the deal. Our contact at the funeral home went beyond the call of duty in letting us jimmy a display casket into the Volvo, but the box was about six inches too long. When we got back home, I found some levers on the passenger seat that allowed me to tilt it forward another half a foot or so. We thought the casket would probably fit, but we wouldn't know for sure until the morning of the drive.

I had just about decided to get rid of the Volvo a few months before because repair bills were mounting, and it had developed a mystery rattle that three mechanics couldn't solve. They concluded that, whatever the defect, the car was still safe to drive. In the couple of days before the trip, I got it as road-ready as I could, changing the oil, inflating the tires, and topping fluids. One thing I would never be able to do would be to rid it of dog hair. Labrador retrievers shed copiously, and four Labs had occupied the Volvo in its 14 years. Lab hair had infiltrated every pore of the vehicle.

Dog hair would adorn Mother's casket. It reminded me of the funeral of Grandmommie, Mother's mother. Daddy, Mom and I rode in the procession in my Mazda, its velour seats a dog hair magnet. I think Daddy pictured us on the front row, heads bowed somberly, onlookers behind us aghast at our fur-festooned funeral suits. He named us "The Dog Hair Family".

Our funeral home hero came through again, meeting us at 5:30 on a Tuesday morning. He wheeled out Mom's casket, and it fit in the Volvo with a couple of inches to spare. Carey and I high-fived each other.

The drive to Colorado was fairly uneventful, thankfully. No breakdowns or wrecks, which I had tried hard not to let myself envision. Junie didn't feel right about driving the Volvo, so Carey and I took turns. There was no room for passengers in the Volvo besides Mom. I played Mom her favorite song, "Harvest Moon", a slow, gentle, romantic Neil Young tune that Carey had turned her on to. Part of the chorus goes like this:

> "Because I'm still in love with you,
> I wanna see you dance again
> Because I'm still in love with you.
> On this harvest moon"

I apologized to Mom for a transgression that had always bothered me. Daddy and Mother took me and my friend, Murphy, on our first Vegas trip while we were in college. We men were a little looped and eager to get to the tables. We walked fast and charged through a door, leaving Mother a couple of steps behind so that she had to open the door for herself. She was angry and hurt, and she cried; that was no way to treat a lady. Hurting Mother's feelings was unconscionable, and I told her again that I was sorry.

I recalled our devastating day with Soul Sister, our beloved black Lab, who tackled us when we performed Monty Python "silly walks" (I know, this is the second mention of "silly walks", in a book riddled with Monty Python references. "Monty Python's Flying Circus", televised on PBS Sunday nights, was the one guaranteed meeting spot for the Jones family, when I was a teenager; every one of us a devotee.). Soul Sister developed oral cancer when she was 13, bled from the mouth and couldn't eat. Mom nursed her devotedly, but finally decided Soul Sister was suffering too much; it was time to put her down. Daddy couldn't bear it and left town. Mother and I tearfully drove her to the vet, and when Soul Sister resisted, like she knew what was coming, and we had to drag her out of the back seat, we were shattered. Sweating and bawling, I dug Soul Sister's grave in her favorite park, near water, which she loved. At one point, a cop drove up and asked what we were doing. Mother was not going to tolerate any intrusion and said, "We're burying our dog. Can you please leave us alone?" The cop said, "Yes, ma'am," and left.

I asked Carey what he talked about on his shifts with Mom, and he said he reminded her of "taco nights" from his childhood. He loved her greasy corn tortilla tacos, but would try to omit the lettuce, tomatoes, and onions. Mom always caught him and made him include the garnishments. He talked about all the shit she put up with from Daddy, like on Christmas trips when we'd be all packed and ready to go, and Daddy made us wait for hours while he was at the bars, finally showing up way late and drunk. It happened more than once, and we, kids, started demanding that we go on our own, but Mother would never leave without him.

The casket-bearing Volvo drew gawks and double-takes from riders in passing cars during the 13-hour drive. I waved and smiled back, and Carey said he did the same.

Separately and as a family, we'd made the Dallas or Austin to Colorado drive hundreds of times and knew it by heart. Valley Pecan in Chillicothe was one of Mom's favorite stops for their pecans and gifts. Mom loved to shop. We drove by our childhood house on Janet Street in Amarillo. When we were kids Daddy had told us about Stanley Marsh, the eccentric Amarillo millionaire who'd created Cadillac Ranch and the even sillier "Floating Mesa," a huge mesa with a white band across the top that was supposed to create an optical illusion, but which looks like a mesa with a white band across. The "Floating Mesa" and the barren terrain impart a whimsical otherworldliness to the 30-mile Boys Ranch Road stretch, by far my favorite leg of the drive. Sometimes I'd go 110, stereo cranked to the max, singing my guts out. I didn't do 110 with Mom. The rest area on Boys Ranch Road beside the Canadian River was another Jones haunt, where we'd let the dogs out to stretch their legs. They always got stickers, but we stopped there anyway.

The only canine folly occurred when we were eating lunch in Amarillo. Carey's dog, Oscar, ate a sack full of snacks that a friend of Junie's had packed for us. A Jones trip without a canine folly would be like a Marx Brothers movie without a joke.

Dave was an hour and a half late meeting us in Amarillo, which pissed us all off; he had the shortest distance to travel and the fewest logistical hurdles. If Dave says, "I'll see you Saturday," there is a chance he'll see you Saturday. There is an equal chance that he'll see you Friday, Sunday or the next Saturday. Dave has as much affinity for time as a camel has for an iPad. You can't stay mad at him, though, because he means no harm, he's just absent-minded, and his defense of loved ones is legendary within the family. At Daddy's bachelor party, an acquaintance of Daddy's, much bigger and older than Dave, disparaged Daddy, and Dave laid him out; he'd stood up for all of us similarly, if less violently, at one time or another in our lives.

I rode with Dave, and within 15 minutes, the rest of the caravan was out of sight. I learned that Dave drives 60 miles an hour pretty much all the time, no matter whether the speed limit is 75 or 30.

Carey's girlfriend, Paula, her best friend Bertha, and several other friends met us at the entry to the Navajo development, where she and Carey lived, outside of Walsenburg, Colorado. We'd made it. A merrier ending to a funeral procession has rarely been witnessed.

I had rationalized a way not to tell the next part of the story. Carey is the only person I've told till now. It's not pretty, but it's one of my strongest memories of the trip and I have to tell it true.

We embarked the following morning on the last leg of Mom's journey, from Walsenburg to Rosita, a drive of about 80 miles. Colorado backroads miles aren't like freeway miles; they're slower and often more perilous. Carey led the five-car caravan, and I took up the rear with Mother. Carey turned right out of Navajo, which meant we were taking Yellowstone Road, rather than the paved "city" route through Walsenburg. Yellowstone Road is a washboardy, pothole-cratered, teeth-rattling, 20-mile dirt road with beautiful mountain vistas, teeming with wildlife. I apologized to Mom for the rough ride, but she would have chosen Yellowstone, too.

I wasn't accustomed to hopping in the car for two hours after my morning three-cups-of-coffee. I started feeling its diuretic effects, and the bucks and shudders of Yellowstone Road made me wince. The relief when we hit pavement again was short-lived.

There is not one single gas station between Yellowstone Road and Rosita, nor even a decent pull-off, and besides, I was driving the car of honor in a funeral procession. What the hell is the protocol when the chauffeur needs to pee? This driver held it for about an hour and a half. By that time, I was sure I was doing internal damage, it hurt so badly. I found an empty, wide-mouthed tea bottle in the floorboard and used it to unburden myself while going sixty on a windy mountain road, with my defenseless mother beside me. Visions of the infallible son plunging to a spectacularly humiliating death flashed through my mind.

It turned out Carey was hurting like me, and hit the ground running when we made Rosita.

The next part of the story is as ticklish to tell as the last, for entirely different reasons. The last thing I want to do is write some maudlin Hallmark card moment, but we saw what we saw. Fall was late coming to the Wetmore Valley that year, and all of the trees were still green in mid-October; all of the trees except for the cottonwoods flanking our cabin, which were blazing amber. When we topped the last hill entering Rosita, we saw Mother's place lit up in gold, like a fairytale house. There was not another "turning" tree in the entire valley except for Mom's.

We buried Mother that afternoon at the Rosita cemetery, on one of those Colorado days so clear and crisp that jet contrails cast a shadow on the ground. Mother's friends streamed in, mostly on foot from their homes nearby. Carey bravely conducted, welcoming everyone and telling Mother stories until he got choked up. Dave stepped in and started telling more Clyde-centric stories, as did another friend, and it felt a little awkward. I think it bothered Carey the most; it was Mother's day. But it was understandable, Daddy lay right there beneath our feet too. Junie got us back on track, speaking eloquently and affectionately about Mother, setting things right. Still afraid of public speaking at age 54, I managed one monotone, tongue-tied story. Mom would have said I did fine.

Sitting in a tractor off in the background were two burly, bearded men, father and son, who would finish the burial. After the service, Junie, Carey and I walked over to visit and thank them for their patience, and the elder mountain man said he would take care of our mother like she was his own.

Daddy had nicknamed Mom "Alpine Bev" when they moved from Texas to the mountains, and the nickname came to fit, not in a muscular, lady lumberjack kind of way (Mom was a petite, proper lady), but as a lover of the mountain country, characters, and wildlife. She especially loved the elk that grazed in her yard, and would now repose in their midst. "Alpine Bev" was home.

Queen, Ascending

There, there, my babies, everything is all right
Your mother is safe, aglow in the light
We fought like the dickens, now we go rest
The parting is hard, but it's all for the best

Your father awaits, and I'm on my way
I'll join him where heaven's hell-raisers play
Fresh in his uniform, ensconced on his throne
Planning a party to welcome me home

My angels with paws, berserk in their glee
Will break all the laws of propriety
Unwitting bystanders better take heed
Lest they endure a tail-wagging stampede

Mother, exemplar of effortless grace
Will cradle me in her gentle embrace
Whispering softly, caressing my skin
Oh glory be, to be mothered again

There, there, my babies, everything is all right
Three heroes you are, divine in my sight
Do what you do, keep the light in your eyes
When I see you again, I'll make chocolate pies

Ocotillo Autobahn

If you're ever 'round Amarillo
Bound for New Mexico
And need to break the monotony
I'll tell you right where to go

Head west out of town on Forty
Paint a Caddy at Cadillac Ranch
Get the hell off the interstate
Bear off at the Bushland branch

Get a load of Floating Mesa
S'posed to play a trick on the eye
A flat-top beaut of a butte
Suspended in the sky

You might see all kinds of shit
Unmarshalled by the law
Rattlesnaketornadotarantula
The ghost of a Comanche squaw

Chorus:

Jack up the volume on your radio
Till it won't jack no more
Jam the pedal to the metal

Yodel till your voice gets sore
Look out, loafers and laggards
Katy didn't bar the door

The road snakes hills and mesas
Ocotillotumbleweed
Nary a tree to block your view
Buddy, it is built for speed

Top a hill you can see to China
And, by god, you'll be there soon
It's like riding a rollercoaster
A rollercoaster on the moon

Hey, dig your doggie in the window
Jowls flappin' like a flag in a gale
Ears splayed out like airplane wings
Bedazzled by a thousand smells

Chorus

Like all good things, the road plays out
Time to button up your shirt
Pat your electric hair back down
Smooth the wrinkles in your skirt

But if you ain't ready for reality
Ain't ready for the fun to end

There is one thing that you might do
Turn around and drive it again

Chorus

Author's note: Junie is the ostensible narrator.

Fucking Meringue

I am not one prone to swear
Perturbed, I might say dang
Ladylike, genteel until
I face the prospect of meringue

Fucking meringue

My mother and her mother
Meringue'd like breaking sticks
I sense their disapproval
As I flounder with the mix

Fucking meringue

Their chocolate pies resplendent
With luscious, silky peaks
My frost sometimes resembles
A desert of buttocks cheeks

Fucking meringue

My brother does the easy part

A chimp could stir the fill
Should he attempt meringue
…Now you're talking swill

Fucking meringue

Then there's that little tin of sin
Rat bastard cream of tartar
A pinch awry fucks your pie
So where's the nearest bar?

Fucking meringue

The holidays I once prized
A shitstorm of goddamned pies
I think that next Thanksgiving
I'll jam the egg beater in my eyes

Fucking meringue

Jesse David Jones

Jesse David Jones, of Roscoe, Texas, died on February 26, 2023, in Round Rock, Texas, in the bosom of his family. He was 77.

He was known variously as "JD", "Dave", "Jesse", "Sweetwater", and "Baby Brother." It was appropriate that he was known by multiple names because he bestowed them by the score upon every creature he loved. Those gifted with Dave's love knew it beyond doubt because he declared it vociferously. If you weren't a part of his blood family and he loved you, he might try to adopt you. If you crossed one of Dave's loved ones, you were looking for trouble. His niece, Junie, said it right: "You don't mess with anybody Dave loves."

Dave never met a stranger; he would invite everyone within earshot to a family wedding or birthday party.

Dave loved animals. He took particular joy in naming his own pets and renaming yours. Among Dave's beloved pets were Rose, Beethoven, Rattler, Jimmy, Douglas, Bob, Wheezer, Winnie Mandela, Scotty, Southpark, Onique, El Chapo, Kitty O, The Flying Menendez Brothers, Tugnutt, and Rollo.

He loved music and had an eclectic taste, enjoying anything from George Jones to Taj Mahal; Frogman Henry to Santana; he passed along his love for music to several generations of Joneses. Dave loved attending the New Orleans Jazz and Heritage Festival and treasured the shows that his friend Mila Beth staged in Sweetwater.

Dave would break into song at the drop of a hat and loved to sing to his granddaughter Audrey and great-nephew Jesse.

Dave faced daunting physical problems over the last couple of years of his life, but never lost his unique exuberance. As the surgeries mounted, he worked up a set list of songs to sing as he was wheeled into the Operating Rooms.

Special mention must be made of Lacy Van Zandt, who nursed Dave heroically through the surgeries. He thrived under her care, and they became blood.

Dave was born January 13, 1946, in Sweetwater, Texas and graduated from Loraine High School in 1963. He was a proud veteran, having served in the US Army, stationed in Germany from 1964 to 1967. He attended Arizona State University for one year, then worked for the Texas Highway Department and Texas State Water Board in Austin, Texas, from 1969 to 1996. After he retired from the state, he lived for a year in Bertram with his nephew, Jay, then moved to Roscoe to take care of his father, Sam, and lived there for the last 27 years of his life.

Dave was preceded in death by his sister Carolyn, mother Laura Mary, brother Clyde, and father Sam. Zelma Blanche Blansett, "Mommy Blanche," his grandmother, owned a special place in his heart. Mommy Blanche mothered Dave when his parents were away for a year at a rehab facility in Gonzales with Carolyn, who had been stricken with polio.

He is survived by sons Sam, Dorian, and Jeffrey, daughters-in-law Irma, Michelle and Nicole, grandchildren Ashley, Sammy, Bradley, Rowan, Audrey, Tory Bell, Dorian, Darius, Marcellus, David, great-grandchild Rhea, nephews Jay, Carey and William, nieces Lacy, Paula, and Junie, former wife Lourdes, and great-nephew, and namesake Jesse.

Dave had a legion of friends, chief among them his lifelong mate Lance Hall, who stood by his mercurial friend through high times and low. "Big Frank" Biggers, Wrangler Little and Mila Beth Gibson were also close to Dave's heart, and he loved them all dearly. Cousin Jimmy Sansom and his wife Faye meant a lot to Dave as well.

Jesse David Jones was an American original, eccentric, maddening at times, true blue, hilarious, and busting with life. We mourn our earthly loss, knowing that heaven just got a helluva lot more fun.

A Memorial service will be held for Dave at the McCoy Funeral Home in Sweetwater on Saturday, March 25, at 2:00 pm.

Dakota

Dakota was a gangly, big-boned, muddy-coated yellow Lab. I preferred the more classic Lab look...broad-headed and chested with a shiny, definitive coat. But that was OK. I needed a running buddy for my prize puppy, Mordecai; Dakota didn't have to be a star.

Lab puppies are about the funnest creatures on earth, but they will wear your ass out with their energetic shenanigans and I felt like I needed to get him a partner to take some of the play-load off me.

I'd been scouting around and my barber mentioned that she had a customer who was getting divorced and had a one-year-old female yellow Lab that needed a home. It sounded good to me, and I drove to a large brick house next to a country club in Georgetown to meet the dog. Upon entering, I noticed several framed posters of Republican National conventions. A middle-aged man and lady seated me in their finely appointed living room, and while the woman went to retrieve the dog from its kennel, the man started to pitch me on the Texas Tea Party. Not interested, I steered the conversation away.

I asked the dog's name, and he said, "Dakota. We bought her from a puppy mill in South Dakota, so that's where we got the name. We were going to go through PetSmart, but we cut out the middleman and got a better deal." Puppy mills are large-scale dog-breeding "factories" that prioritize profit over the health of the animal; known for overcrowded, squalid conditions, and unsound breeding practices, they are a blight on the industry. Bragging about buying a dog from a puppy mill was one of the most tone-deaf statements I'd ever heard uttered.

I'm not saying his political affiliation had anything to do with him being a gaping asshole...that was just the scene I encountered. I would have been equally appalled had he been a Democrat, a Civil Libertarian, or a Communist.

Dakota slunk in, seemingly cowed by her owners. I called her, and she came to me and immediately rolled over on her back. She loved to have her tummy rubbed, they said. I rubbed her tummy.

Despite my distaste for the man and Dakota's unimpressive looks and questionable breeding, I couldn't turn her down; she seemed like a sweetheart. I agreed to take her. They would drop her off at my house the next day.

When they arrived in their Beamer, I opened my front gate to let them drive in, but they didn't enter. They stopped on the shoulder, shooed Dakota out of the back seat of their car and drove away.

The last thing I'd asked them about Dakota before I adopted her was, "Does she have any medical conditions I need to know about?" "No, no," the man said, "she's clean as a whistle." The next day, I was working from home, and as Dakota slept peacefully by my chair, she peed a river.

I took her to the vet, who diagnosed urinary incontinence; we put her on Proin, which she would take for the rest of her life.

I wasn't enamored with the name, Dakota, especially knowing the story behind it, but I don't believe in changing a dog's name once they know it. It would only confuse the dog. We Joneses have always taken great pride and care in naming our dogs, but sometimes you have to take what you get. Dakota did get amended to Kody over time.

Dakota and Mordecai became fast friends; she turned out to be the perfect mate. Dakota weighed about 90 pounds; Mordecai ten pounds less. Mordecai was smarter...I think they both understood that...so Dakota usually followed his lead, and deferred to his dominance. Mordecai got the place beside me in the king-sized bed, and Dakota slept on the far end.

The only time Dakota asserted herself was when Mordecai harried her endlessly, playfully, till she'd had enough, then Mordecai learned who the real boss was, and would run for his life. That was another thing they both understood...Dakota could whip Mordecai any time she chose.

The timidity she displayed at her original owner's house disappeared. She slunk no more.

When she got mad, Dakota was a fierce fighter. One day, Junie was visiting with her female Labradoodle, Wally, and she and Dakota were tugging at a Frisbee, but it wasn't play; it was a death match, both their mouths bleeding finally from the endless, no-holds-barred tug of war. Over the years, Wally and Dakota had half a dozen vicious fights, and Junie, Carey and I all got bloodied trying to separate them.

Dakota was sweet-natured with every other creature she encountered....kids could crawl all over her and she wouldn't turn a hair.

Dakota didn't have retriever instincts; whenever she happened to grab the tennis ball that I'd been throwing to Mordecai, she'd take it and run off, daring me to chase her. Game over. She was a bird dog of a sort, though...if a buzzard alit near the house or flew close by, she would bark at it, and chase it off.

Dakota developed arthritis when she was about seven years old. I gave her a shot of Adequan every month to treat it, and it seemed to free her up, ease her creakiness. My first attempt at giving her a shot inspired the "Run Away!" poetic experiment. Coupled with Proin and Mordecai's seizure meds, I was spending about $400 a month on vet bills; no sweat, the dogs were worth it.

When Dakota was 11, her health began to deteriorate. She lost her appetite and her incontinence reappeared, despite the meds. I took her to see my vet, Trampus, on a Friday. He suspected bladder cancer and ran blood work...we'd get the results back in a couple of days. He prescribed pain meds to get her by until we knew the proper course of treatment.

I feared she might have only a few months to live. She was worse again on Saturday; I told myself it might be weeks. On Sunday, I knew it might be days.

I woke up Monday morning, Labor Day, and she was so weak, I knew. Today is her last day. I frantically called every vet's office I could find within 100 miles, trying to find some last-ditch relief for her, or to put her out of her misery. Every last one of them was closed, even the emergency clinics. We were on our own.

Could I put her down myself? The only firearm I owned was a .410 shotgun that Dave had given me for killing snakes. I couldn't conceive of putting a shotgun to her head.

We went outside and Dakota struggled down the front porch steps, then squatted painfully and peed something brown. Oh lord. Then she nosed her way into the shrubs beside the house, hiding. She was going off to die. I'd never seen an animal do that before, but her intent was clear. She was going off to die.

What do you do when a pet you love goes off to die? Do you respect their wish and leave them alone? Do you lie with them and comfort them? I did both. I'd walk around the yard for a few minutes, then lie in the shrubs with her and try to soothe my sweet girl. I made this circuit a half a dozen times, holding my tears in check as well as I could.

Finally, I walked out to the front fence, 40 yards from the house, and when I turned around, I saw Dakota, crawling up the driveway to meet me, in agony every inch. The dam burst inside of me and I bawled, and groaned involuntarily, from the heart, and bawled. I am bawling and groaning now as I write this 10 years later. It was the bravest, most heartbreaking thing I've ever seen in my life. I felt like I did not deserve the honor of her love.

Lacy arrived. We got Dakota around to the water bucket out back and comforted her as she expired. Lacy hugged me tight and whispered in my ear, "It's OK to cry. Let it go."

Why do some of us have the instinct to fight back tears? Yes, Daddy scolded us boys for crying over minor injuries and insults, but I don't think that's the cause. I think crying takes practice. I didn't have much to cry about my first 40 years. Crying comes easier now. I've had practice.

Run Away!

A bottle of airplane booze

Dwarfs

The vial of medicine

I'm supposed

To inject

Into

My dog

I plunge the needle

Into the tiny bottle

But it doesn't reach the mark

A fingernail

Tantalizingly

Short

Of

The

Itch

I'm stuck...

Not by the needle

Yet

But I fear

I will

Impale myself

In the armpiteardrumeyeball

How does the needle
Reach the healing balm?
I fumbleclumsilybefuddled
Give up

Oh wait
What if…
I turn the vial
Upside down?

Voila!

Loving brown eyes
Gaze up at me
Trusting
Unconditionally

Are you making me a treat?
Not really

She does not comprehend
That her master
Is
An
Idiot

She does not comprehend

That I

Will attempt

To insert

This wickedpointything

Into

Her body

If I

Were her

I would

Run away! Run away! Run away!

Mordecai's Brain

It had to have been the single weirdest minute of my life: Sleep, death, pain, blood, then sleep again, all within one minute.

Sound asleep, I was awakened by a commotion on the bed, then a wall-shaking crash. I sprang up to find my bedmate, Mordecai, thrashing violently, teeth bared, his head jackhammering the floor. My first sleep-fogged thought was, "Am I watching Mordecai die?" Out of the blue, my big, happy, healthy dog was in agony. I began stroking him gently on his side, telling him "It's OK, buddy," when he reached around and bit me hard on the hand. Bewildered, I stumbled into the bathroom to stop the blood and collect my senses. I was surprised how much it hurt. I saw my pale face in the mirror, then I went back to sleep.

Back to sleep, meaning I passed out. I guess I was in shock, presumably from the pain and blood, but mostly stupefied that my sweetheart of a dog, whom I raised from a puppy and who sleeps beside me every night, had bitten me. I swear, in our seven years together, it had never entered my mind that he would bite me. Mordecai doesn't have a mean bone in his body and spends most of his life with a shit-eating grin on his face, permanently happy. His worst character flaw is excessive licking. He has never bitten anything in anger.

I knew I hadn't been out long because when I came to, Mordecai was still distressed, reeling drunkenly about the room. I realized he wasn't dying. He'd had a seizure, the first in his life.

I trust Trampus implicitly. Back when I barely knew him, shortly after he opened his practice, he came through for me on a moment's notice. My beloved Igbert and Bo, Mordecai's predecessors, were suffering and too crippled to be transported. Their time had come. Trampus came out and did the deed gently and compassionately, while I cried harder than I've ever cried in my life. I'm sure vets are schooled in bedside manner, but his kindhearted spirit transcended training.

Although we've become friends, Trampus still calls me "Mr. Jones" because that's how his mamma raised him, I guess. Every once in a while, he'll slip and call me "Jay," and I get a kick out of that.

The dumbest question I asked Trampus that morning was whether Mordecai would remember biting me. Did I want him to remember and feel guilty about it? I hated to admit it, but I was a little afraid of Mordecai at that point. I'd wince involuntarily just before my hand touched his fur. No, Trampus said, a human or dog is basically unconscious during a grand mal seizure and would have no recollection of what happened. I'm sure my fear was a self-preservation instinct, and it subsided in a few days.

Trampus said that Mordecai might have another seizure right then, or never again in his life, but most likely he'd have a few more over the following day or two (he did). He suspected that at

177

Mordecai's age, the cause was more likely a brain tumor than epilepsy, which would have presented itself earlier in life.

The brain tumor diagnosis scared the hell out of me, but Trampus's prevailing message has been, "We got this." Whenever I've called him, desperate or sad, he has reassured me that we can manage this deal.

Trampus has educated me over the seven months since the first attack. He drew me a picture of waves rising and falling to depict the seizure pattern; the wave crests, a cluster of seizures occurs, releasing the pressure, then it builds again, to the next event. The rumor that seizures could be caused by flea medicine is nonsense, he said. He advised against brain surgery. The cost is $15,000 to $20,000, the stress on the dog was severe, and the success rate was poor. The scariest thing he said was that in the direst cases, a dog could seize and never stop. Even after sedation, they return immediately to the seizure and die from the prolonged trauma. Please God, not that.

We've jiggered with the dosage of his main med, Zonisamide, to control the episodes as best we can, and can add another type of med, as necessary. I write down the details of each event to gauge whether the seizures are becoming more severe, and monitor the spacing between them. The interval between attacks shrank from 24 days to 14 days on the last two cycles.

Mordecai has had about 25 seizures now (he would have over 100 in life), all triggered when he's asleep. A look of abject fear and confusion darkens his face, his neck arches painfully; he seems to be trying to back away from it, and sometimes he even tries to run from it. One time in bed, I felt a rustling and he vaulted over me, wiping out everything on the bedside table (lamp, clock, phone, books), before crashing to the floor. Once the convulsion begins, he bares his teeth and thrashes like a hooked shark for maybe a minute. Mordecai doesn't pussyfoot. Every seizure is "A Clockwork Orange" violent. After the convulsion, he lies rigid, all of his limbs splayed stiff. His bladder empties. His mouth is closed like he's holding his breath. I know he's coming out of it when he opens his mouth to breathe and his limbs relax. He's communicative but still in a danger zone because he has no sense of balance and careens all over, anxious to escape. I try to hold him to me, but he's a strong, eighty-pound Lab wanting freedom and bangs into furniture and walls.

Since I got over my fear of Mordecai, I can't help but pet him during his seizures, and my body is a bloody pulp of punctures and gashes. Not really. I learned my lesson on the first attack to just stand and observe, clearing any hard or dangerous objects from his tornadic path. If you take just one thing from this story, let it be this: Do not touch an animal having a seizure.

After the convulsion and recovery, he clings to me desperately, circling and stepping on my feet when I walk. One time, he stood with his paw on my bare foot for minutes.

I've tried to seizure-proof the house, but there's only so much I can do. I removed the bedframe and put the mattresses on the floor so he'd have a shorter fall, unhinged the glass door from the entertainment center, moved a heavy plant from a table to the floor... but he still batters furniture and draws blood on most of his seizures. He's cut the same eye twice in different places. Of course, if he were an outside dog, he'd probably be much safer, but every Jones dog in history has had full household privileges like any other family member, and that's not going to change.

My latest strategy when he's in the midst of a cluster of seizures is to move into the living room, push the furniture to the walls, leaving a clear thrashing ground, and cover all hard edges with pillows and blankets. The most dangerous time is the *first* seizure of a cluster, which comes out of the blue, absolutely unpredictably. Once he has one, I know he'll have a few more over the next day or two, and I can try to soften them.

One irony is that two of the people dearest to me, Junie and Lacy, have been afflicted with seizures. Junie began having them in her teens. The only one I saw came while I was driving her and some friends home from a sleepover, and she had a convulsion in the back seat. I freaked, driving ninety through neighborhoods till we got to a friend's house. Junie eventually got her seizures under control through medication.

Lacy is a different story. She had epileptic seizures in childhood so severe that, after all remediation failed, she was given the rarest and most radical possible treatment, a hemispherectomy; almost half of her brain was removed. It would take a book to tell Lacy's miraculous story, but she came out on the other side a lovely, thriving woman.

Junie and Lacy have helped me understand what Mordecai feels before, during, and after a seizure. It is comforting to know that he's oblivious to the agony I witness. He fears and hates the attacks, undoubtedly, but at least he's not aware when his body whacks out.

My proximity to seizures makes me wonder, am I the catalyst? Is there something about my aura or personality that causes creatures to collapse into uncontrollable convulsions? It would certainly explain the performance of some of the racehorses I bet on. Wait, I didn't know Lacy and lived at least fifty miles away when her seizures began, so I can't take the blame for that. Whew.

The good news is that Mordecai is pretty much his old self between bouts. He still flies after the "Squeak" ball and makes it talk on the way back. He still uncorks spontaneous "joy runs" around the yard. He still farts, then looks over his shoulder at the invisible culprit. He still gazes into my eyes with the earnestness of a love-struck teenager. He still opens the front door like a human and bounds in, beaming, his expression saying, "Aren't you glad to see me!"

Over the moon, buddy, over the moon.

Please Pet Me

It comes without a warning
The monster I can't see
I know it's there, I know it's there
I know it's after me

I run away
Run away
Run away
RUN

Then
I don't know

What happened

I'm so happy to see you
Did the monster get me?
I'm so happy to see you
Is the monster gone?
I'm so happy to see you

Please don't leave me
Did I do something bad?
Please don't leave me
If I did, I didn't mean to

Please don't leave me

Please pet me, no, don't
I don't know if I like being touched right now
Please pet me, no, don't
Why am I covered in piss and shit and slobber and blood?
Please pet me, no, don't

Please pet me, no, don't
Please pet me, no, don't

Please pet me

Igbert catching a frisbee

Igbert on ice

Reverend and Beeks

Dakota chasing buzzards; painting by Raquel Key

Mordecai and frisbee

Murphy and Sharon, 40 years ago, in Mexico

My brother, Carey, and his wife, Paula

25 Years

Sometimes you just know. I was a first-time homebuyer looking for a quiet place in the country. I'd looked at 20 or 30 houses, mostly east of Austin, around McDade and Bastrop. Nothing clicked, so I expanded my search to the northwest of town. As soon as I saw it, I knew I'd found the place: A blue frame house sitting on a rise beside a creek on a tree-lined county road, 40 miles from Austin, out in the boonies. Water tinkled in the creek. The only other house I could see was a quarter mile away, a grand two-story manse built in 1906. I wanted a place where I could raise dogs, and the two fenced acres would be dog heaven.

When I stepped into the house for the first time, a Boxer was giving birth to puppies in a wooden box in the kitchen. Home.

The interior suited me fine, nothing fancy, three bedrooms, two baths. The owners had children, and one bedroom was painted Pepto-Bismol pink and another glared blood red and white. Rooms could be painted.

I inspected the inside perfunctorily; I wanted to be outside among the live oaks, the biggest a century-old granddaddy that shaded the wooden deck out the back door. A cottonless cottonwood stood out front, along with six newly planted silver maples that ran along the caliche gravel driveway. Out back, four cedar elms ran in a row atop a small land terrace and a large mesquite twisted up out of the earth at the back of the yard. What made the backyard unique was the circle of about ten yuccas, a couple over ten feet tall. I would fall in love with the white blossoms that sprouted in early spring.

I bought the house, southeast of Bertram, in 1995, and it has been home for 25 years. I have a recurring dream that I've sold the house and am moving into some weird new place, and I think, "You idiot, what have you done?"

One reason I wanted to be out in the country was to be closer to wildlife. I've had encounters with everything you might imagine in the Texas hill country...deer, foxes, coyotes, turkeys, snakes, wild hogs, raccoons, possums, roadrunners, armadillos, buzzards.

I've also run into one creature I did not expect to see. Not long after I moved here, I was out before dawn one Sunday morning, heading toward Georgetown for migas at Dos Salsas. A quarter of a mile up the road, I flipped on my brights to see a ghostly apparition crossing the road directly in front of me. It looked white in the glare of the brights. My first thought was, "That is a cat". My second thought was, "That cat is bigger than Igbert." A mountain lion, I couldn't believe it. The big cat bounded effortlessly in about three strides from one fence line to the other, never quickening despite being spotlighted. Cool as the other side of the pillow. His tail seemed as long as his body. He cleared the fence with the ease of a man stepping up a curb and was gone.

I called Texas Parks and Wildlife to report the sighting, and they sounded skeptical. "Are you sure it wasn't a deer?" Uh, yeah.

A few years ago, I arrived home just after dark one night, got out of the car and heard a baby crying out back of the house. Huh, a baby? Do I even know anybody with a baby? But the sound was unmistakable, a baby was crying in the backyard. I hustled around the house expecting to find this mysterious baby, but nobody was there. Then I heard a deer snorting beside the fence. I went inside, got my flashlight and searched all along the fence until I finally spotted, on the far side, a dead fawn in a thicket of seedlings. I didn't know fawns vocalized like human babies. I felt sorry for the doe. I couldn't know for sure that the predator was a cougar. It could have been a bobcat or coyote.

There was nothing else I could do that night. I checked back the next morning, and the fawn's body was gone. I wondered how close the killer had been when I was searching the night before.

A couple of nights later, I opened the sliding glass back door to feed my cat, Edith. Just then, a deep, menacing feline growl emanated from somewhere out in the darkness in the direction of where the fawn was killed, near the creek. Edith never moved faster in her life, skittering straight to the top of the granddaddy oak in nothing flat. The growl lasted maybe five seconds and seemed to quiver and shift in the air as if it was on the move. I researched mountain lion behavior and found a passage that said they would hide out in creek beds and growl into dead tree trunks to diffuse the sound and confuse their prey.

A couple of months Lacy left my house before dawn and called me two minutes later, saying she'd seen a big cat and two cubs cross the road in front of her.

I have mixed feelings about the mountain lion encounters…a healthy fear for my loved ones, human and animal, but also a sense of privilege to taste the real wild.

Domesticated animals have entertained too. One day, I came home from work to find a lanky longhorn steer in my backyard. The first thing I did was scan the fence line for a hole or damage where the longhorn must have entered, but I didn't see a break. As I wandered out toward the animal, it took off running and hurdled the four-foot-tall goat wire fence like Edwin Moses. I called Daddy Sam out in West Texas that night to tell him the story, and he said, "Oh, so you had a jumper." I grew up a city boy, I admit, and didn't know about jumpers.

It reminded me of a sign I saw in Arizona: "Watch for darting cattle." "Darting" cattle? Cattle can dart? I guess if they can dash and hurdle, they can probably dart too. What other cattle signs have I not seen? "Watch for pole-vaulting cattle," "This stretch of highway adopted by The Cattle of Mensa." It would be fun to draw the pictures for those signs.

I do know about cattle thieves. I'd ordered some running shorts, and the vendor emailed me confirming that the shorts had been delivered. No shorts. I called the Bertram post office and talked to the lady who delivered my mail (a small-town perk, talking to the lady

191

who delivers your mail). She said she'd hung the package on my mailbox. It aggravated me that someone would steal a package from my mailbox. It would be the first crime I'd experienced out here.

My post lady called back the next day to tell me that she had found the package, empty, by the side of the road, soggy, like it had been chewed. She said, "Mr. Jones," she said, "there's been a cow on the loose and I think it ate your shorts."

Little did I know that my house stood at Demolition Junction. Cars and trucks go careening off the road willy-nilly right in front of my house. County Road 322 (CR322) takes a modest jaunt to the northwest, just where the creek crosses the road, and the drivers here can't seem to handle it. It's like my stretch of road has been transported into a video game where the drivers think, "I'll try not to wreck, but what the hell, it's a game." Boom.

Standing at my front gate today, I see three fresh separate sets of freshly gashed, smashed cedars. The crashers almost always wreck on the opposite side of the road from me, but one guy over-corrected and took down part of my fence. I heard the impact and ran out to see what happened, but he was driving off when I got there, and I couldn't catch him.

One foggy dawn, Lacy and I were saying our goodbyes out front before she left, and we heard a sports car floor it a half a mile up the road. "Idiot," I said. The road was damp from mist, and the guy had no chance of making the curve going 80. He wouldn't have had a chance on a clear day with a dry road. A black bullet flew past, then we heard…nothing. I expected to hear the screech of tires and a collision, or the engine re-engage if he somehow made the curve, but we didn't hear anything.

I opened the gate for Lacy and walked up the road behind her. A brand new, black Nissan 370Z sat caddywompus in the ditch facing us, headlights shining cockeyed. A guy stood outside the car looking embarrassed. Lacy is a nurse with a bleeding heart, and she made sure the man was okay. I didn't feel much sympathy. You deserved it, buddy. I theorized that the reason we didn't hear a crash was because he became airborne and the fluffy cedars on the fence line caught and cushioned him, then spat him back out.

Every crash I've seen has been a one-car collision, and every driver has been male.

I am a walker and have rambled CR322 for 25 years. Usually, I head to the South Gabriel Cemetery that sits at the end of a half-mile, dead-end road. I can walk in peace there.

The traffic on CR322 has probably quadrupled over the years, especially since the high-end Rio Ancho subdivision was built a few years ago, just at the tip of the road, still in Williamson County. Houses in Rio Ancho run to a million dollars plus. Now I wave at Mercedes and BMWs along with the pickup trucks.

The road has probably become too dangerous to walk, with all the traffic, but it's "my" road, so I keep at it.

A couple of years ago, I was walking the straightaway back toward my house when I saw a big white SUV approaching, maybe a half a mile away. It gradually crossed the center of the road toward my side, and I edged further off the road into the scrub. I figured the driver was talking on a cell phone or texting and would correct his path when he saw me, but he just kept crossing, aiming right at me. I scrambled into the scrub against the fence. When the SUV passed, it was half on the road and half on my shoulder...missed me by a couple of yards. Shaking with anger, I turned to watch it gradually slide back to the right side of the road. For some reason, I looked to identify the model, a Chevy Tahoe, rather than at the license plate. I didn't get a look at the driver either. I stay on the lookout for a white Tahoe but haven't seen it since.

Over the years I have picked up all manner of goods by the side of the road...a 100 foot extension cord, my favorite coffee cup, a brand new decorative metal peacock with rhinestones for a tail (hung on my well house), a man's wallet full of credit cards and family pictures (turned in to the Bertram police), a boy's black suit of clothes hanging on a fence (left as is), a $20 bill, a shovel, two Nerf dart guns (no darts; I had to buy those myself), and countless tools and lumber. One of these days, I'll have enough construction material to build a second house.

One item I chose not to bring home was a giant sex toy, dangling from a fence.

I've seen some disturbing things, too: A young, handsome, dead chocolate Lab, dumped in a drainage ditch near my house. I am a Lab lover, and it made me sick. Occasionally, I'll run across deer carcasses dumped by poachers. Down by the cemetery, I found five of them dumped in a creek, partially dismembered, left to rot. I couldn't tell what, if anything, had been harvested from them.

In the last year, I've "adopted" about a half-mile stretch of CR322 on either side of me and picked up its trash. The litterers in east central Burnet County are prolific; they keep me busy. About two-thirds of their discards are beer cans and bottles. They are almost exclusively domestic light beer drinkers. Bud Light, Natural Light, Coors Light, Miller Light, Keystone Light…lots of Keystone Light. According to the story the trash tells, you'd go broke trying to sell imported beer in Burnet County. I have yet to find a St. Pauli Girl or Guinness bottle.

I'm sure there is a correlation between the beer cans and the car wrecks.

Another encroachment of civilization was the installation of a 40-acre solar farm by the Pedernales Electric Co-Op (PEC) on the Bryson Place next door. I'm all for solar, but right next door? I thought, well, at least I can make a case for a reduction in my skyrocketing property taxes. When I got my tax statement, I filed a protest, complete with pictures and documentation from other parts of the country that indeed, property values do decrease if you live in close proximity to a solar farm.

My protest was summarily denied. I called the Burnet County tax assessor and was told that they had no evidence that my property value would decline. However, if I sold the place for less than the appraised value, then the new owner would see a reduction in *their* taxes.

The construction of the solar farm was a six-month pain in the ass. 18-wheelers rumbled by at all hours, further denting the pot-holed road. Beep-beep-beep blurted the heavy equipment all day long. Worst of all, somebody gave vendors my address, rather than the actual location, so for six months I had all sorts of pallets and packages delivered to my front yard. I called PEC several times, and they never got it straight.

After a few months, I decided I was keeping anything of value. I'd open up their boxes, but never found anything remotely useful.

During the solar farm construction, Mordecai had 11 seizures spread over about three days, his worst episode ever. I ended up staying up for 60 straight hours, trying to take care of him as he literally bounced off the walls. At one point, I lay down and told him, "Buddy, please let me have five minutes of sleep," but he stood over me and barked, out of character for Mordecai. No dice. Desperate, beyond exhaustion, I sat down on the front steps, buried my head in my hands and said out loud, "I am going insane."

Bleary-eyed, I looked up to see a Port-O-Let in the middle of my front yard. Ah, OK, so this is insanity, Port-O-Let hallucinations.

I walked out to the contraption and tapped on it. It was real. It reminded me of the Jazz Fest in New Orleans...the many times I'd used the portable toilets there. But how was it possible that it was in my front yard? I'd been awake. A sizeable truck would have had to enter my yard and drop the thing off. How could I have missed it? Fragile still was my sanity.

The Port-O-Let was intended for the solar farm, of course.

One Sunday afternoon, I walked over to the construction site, just to look around on their day off. I checked out the heavy equipment and climbed onto some sort of earth mover or boulder obliterator whose tires were taller than me. The door was unlocked so I entered the cab and sat in the driver's seat, amazed at the number of knobs and gears. You'd have to be a pretty sharp human to operate one of those things. I looked down and, voila, the key was still in the ignition. I turned the key and the boulder obliterator rumbled to life, chugging like a freight train, bouncing me in the seat.

I remembered Edward Abbey's *The Monkey Wrench Gang*. I hadn't thought of that book in years, about a group of environmental terrorists who sabotage earth-unfriendly construction sites. Why, I could be a monkey-wrencher right here and now, put it to THE MAN, start a revolution against the umm...electric co-op...and their evil, uh, solar power. Maybe not. I switched off the engine and climbed down.

It's been a couple of years now, and I don't mind living next to a solar farm. It's not pretty, but at least it's unobtrusive, makes no noise, and generates clean electricity.

The domicile is holding up well. I painted the exterior of the house one time, said "Never again," and had it rocked with San Saba sandstone, the biggest renovation I have undertaken and worth every cent.

It has turned out to be the dog heaven I hoped for. I've raised five of the happiest dogs you'd ever want to meet. One thing I got a kick out of was that two different handymen who did jobs around the house became friends with Igbert and Mordecai, my yellow Labs. They would stop what they were doing and throw the Frisbee or ball to my dogs. Both men returned later, proud owners of yellow Labs.

I am friendly with several of my far-flung neighbors, but mostly keep to myself. Hermit-hood suits me. Most of my neighborly visits occur when they drive up to me as I'm walking down the road. I avoid talking politics. Burnet is as red a county as they come, and I'm decidedly on the other end of the spectrum.

Lacy and I will be raising a child, a boy, on CR322. Is it a good place to raise a child? I think so. I don't like some things I've seen around here, but the good outweighs the bad. The great outdoors is one step away. Even though civilization is encroaching, we are surrounded by pasture on all sides, so it still feels like country. He'll have two acres to make any kind of field he wants. I'll teach him to honor nature and keep the gate shut so that the dogs don't get out.

I used to think the house was plenty big, but the idea of a teenage boy living in the next room scares the hell out of me. I may need to redouble my tool and lumber collection efforts so I can add on, say, another 100,000 square feet to the house.

He'll go to a small town school. I'm not worried so much about the education he gets--that's on Lacy and me—as I am about the attitudes and ideas he'll encounter. I think of a conversation I overheard in the emergency room at the Burnet hospital, a man telling his wife that if Obama tried to take away their guns, there would be war.

One of my best friends in Bertram is an NRA member and a Trump supporter. His shop TV is tuned to FOX News. I don't take the bait when he goes on a political rant, and we get along fine. He's about my age, close to 60. When I told him I was having a baby boy, the man with the grease-tinted mechanic's hands and dip under his lip said, "Oh, he will melt your heart". His daughter wrecked her life with meth and gave up her son; he and his wife formally adopted the boy and he coaches the kid's baseball team. He undercharges me for car repairs, saying I'll need the money for the baby.

In mutual tolerance, there is hope.

My son will NOT ride his bike on CR322; Cemetery Road, yes, but not Demolition Junction. I think of a scene from *The World According to Garp*, where the father of two young sons sprints after cars speeding through his neighborhood, catches them, and emphatically warns them to slow the hell down. If you happen to be driving down CR322 and see a geezer running down the road, it's probably just me, chasing down a speeder. If you are speeding, slow the hell down.

Author's note: Lacy, Lacy, Lacy…

She Talked to You

On the road on Turkey Day
You got the blood sugar blues
We stopped at a Town and Country
For Reese's and Mountain Dew

Outside, I watched humans
Humpin' a humdrum beat
Pumpin' gas, haulin' ass
Shampoo, rinse, repeat

Then out the door sprang a girl
Aglow from head to toe
A character in color
In a black and white picture show

I wondered what could happen
In an ol' five and dime
To make a gal so happy
To make her beam sunshine

Did she just win the lottery
Was she just plum insane

Had she just found a long-lost friend
Was she on crack cocaine
No, it was something finer
Something righter than the rain
She talked to you
She talked to you

She dashed out mad to tell
Her buddies in the truck
The wondrous thing that happened
Her brilliant stroke of luck

Right away, it hit me
I knew what lit her fuse
I sought you out inside the shop
To prove the thing I knew

I asked if you had met a girl
You said, why yes, that's true
I met her in the ladies' room
Said I loved her shoes

She talked to you
And heard a voice that feels like home
She talked to you
And found a campfire in the cold

Did she just win the lottery

Was she just plain insane
Had she just found a long-lost friend
Was she on crack cocaine
No, it was something finer
Something righter than the rain
She talked to you
She talked to you

Alouicious Buford Clyde

"Mornin', Lacy Ruth."

"Mornin', Jay Scott. What time is it?"

"Fourish."

"Ohhh. How many cups of coffee have you had?"

"Fourish. Did you have any dreams?"

"Umm, yeah, I dreamt about Miss Jolene's cat."

"What's its name."

"It's, um, I can't think of it."

"Is it a he?"

"Yes."

"Alouicious?"

"Ha, no."

"Buford?"

"No."

"Clyde?"

"No, we'll never get it this way."

"Yes, we will. We have to try."

"OK."

"Dar..na..malion?"

"Darnamalion? That's not a name."

"It is now."

"Elspeth?"

"That's not a name either."

"Yeah, this one really is. A lady's name. Elspeth Rostow was a professor at UT. Wife of Walt Rostow, one of LBJ's advisers."

"I never know when to believe you."

"Fledermaus?"

"No."

"Gomer… Homer?

"No."

"I…tasca Tornadoes?"

"Huh?"

"High school football team. You never know. You make me come up with this shit off the top of my head. What do you expect?"

"I make you?"

"It's OK. I'm not mad."

"What a relief."

"Jasper… Kaspar?"

"L…ancelot Link Secret Chimp?"

"No."

"Monroe? Nefertiti?"

"Speaking of titi, I'll be right back."

"Hurry back. This is important."

"…OK, where were we?"

"I love you because you wake up happy."

"I will be happy to go back to sleep very soon."

"Octavius?"

"No."

"Pepe'?"

"That's a skunk's name."

"Queequeg?"

"That's it!"

"Really?"

"No."

"That's cruel, toying with my emotions like that."

"You'll get over it."

"Reginald?"

"Spot?"

"Hmm, the cat's name might start with an "S".

"Sorry, we've used up the "S's" for this round."

"Tigger?"

"U...balla?"

"Vasily?"

"Wallingford?"

"Xerxes?"

"Yo...sarrian?"

"Zeebedee?"

"Nothing? Not even a faint jarring of the memory?"

"Afraid not."

"OK, we'll have to start all over. Agamemnon?"

"No, no, no, please no. I'll think of it in the morning."

"It is morning."

"Real morning."

"OK, I'll go prepare."

"OK, you go prepare. Good night."

"Good night."

Daddy is a Geezer

Your mama passed out on the floor
When she heard the news
Your daddy wrote a million words
Mightily confused

But it's all good, my tiny friend
Can't wait for your debut
We'll throw a big ass party
Don't need anything but you

Grow yourself some body parts
Sit back, relax and chill
Go ahead and kick your mom
She'll reckon it a thrill

Your daddy is a geezer
Your mama is a nun
You got dealt an oddball hand
But doesn't everyone
Life is unpredictable
When all is said and done
You'll be loved profoundly
And we'll have us some fun

Your dad will tease, delightedly

Your fertile infant brain
Maybe just in self-defense
You'll blow mine clear to Spain

Songs and dogs, dogs and songs
The fabric of your day
Mordecai will lick your face
We'll groove to Tenere

As for the changin' of the diapers
Your mom is well-rehearsed
Until you can enunciate
I say she does mine first

Your daddy is a geezer
Your mama is a nun
You got dealt an oddball hand
But doesn't everyone
Life is unpredictable
When all is said and done
You'll be loved profoundly
And we'll have us some fun

Feeding Jesse

Feeding Jesse is like a quarterback throwing to an incompetent, prima donna wide receiver wearing a onesie. Before the game even starts, he yells, "Throw me the ball. Throw me the ball." I throw him the ball, but he plays defense against himself, flailing arms obstructing the passing lane. He knocks down the pass, comes back to the huddle and screams accusingly in my face. Sometimes he'll catch the pass, intentionally throw it on the ground, then shriek at me. Sometimes he'll fall asleep right in the middle of a play.

I try to explain to the little fella that blockading his mouth with his hands when he wants to be fed is illogical, but I gather that logic doesn't register with a four-month-old. When does logic begin to register with a child? When that day arrives, will I have any left to impart?

At first, I took his fits personally and they disturbed me deeply (my son hates me), but I've developed a coping mechanism: I make fun of him. I tell him he's being a baby. Sometimes I scream as loud as he does, which startles him. He'll stop crying for a few seconds and look at me in wonder. "1000 Ways to Ridicule Your Child" will be the title of my daddy manual.

Given the choice between feeding Jesse and changing his diaper, I'd take the diaper every time. Treacly off-yellow baby gunk leaves a sticky sheen on chin, cheeks, lips, hands, bottle, and everything else we touch. Thank god I can't smell. Even the name, Similac

208

Alimentum (Semi-Lack-All-Momentum), is off-putting. Jesse has been through four different formulas, and because of his prematurity and allergies, he requires the most expensive one of all.

Lacy can talk on the phone, crochet, twirl a baton, play ping pong and feed Jesse at the same time, whereas I rigidly hold my one feeding position, with Jesse cradled in my left armpit. I have to use both hands and my body tenses as I assiduously monitor his head angle and intake. Occasionally, I notice that my left hand is clenched on his left calf. Hence, I have developed a golf ball-sized knot at the base of my skull and smaller knots that run in a chain down behind my right shoulder. I am certain that I am creating a permanent deformity and will be a hunchback within six months. I have tried reversing Jesse to my right arm, but it just doesn't feel comfortable. Dexterous in most other endeavors, I am an oaf when it comes to feeding my son.

Jesse sucks. Sometimes he sucks softly, with moans of pleasure so sweet that I want to hug him. Sometimes he sucks so hard he snorts piggishly. His pull on the bottle feels like a fish biting your bait. Tug...tug...tug.

Jesse gets drunk. After scarfing down eight ounces of formula, his eyes glaze over, and his head flops around like a bobble-head doll. Had he words, he'd slur them. If the formula weren't so nasty, I might guzzle a bottle.

After Jesse sucks we play Burp the Twerp. I couldn't make Jesse burp in the NICU to save my life, but I watched the nurses forcefully

209

pound the backs of babies and learned the technique. Now I can get the twerp to burp on my shoulder most of the time, or sometimes just by accident when I'm manhandling him into position. Lacy claims that she can't get him to burp like I can, so she hands him over to me and I think, "Aw, come on, you just have to thump him harder. He actually likes it."

I don't really mind being the designated burper. If Daddy can do something right, he's all in.

Burp the Twerp's unfortunate cousin is Urp the Twerp. Jesse has developed a spit-up problem and sometimes Burp the Twerp goes awry. Recently, Jesse urped a half a bottle right onto Lacy's chest. I would have leapt out of the chair and sprinted to the bathroom like a man on fire, but she sat there calmly, cleaned him up and talked to me for several minutes while puked faux-milk coagulated on her shirt and a stream trickled down her tummy. Mothers.

I'd like to end with some sunny conclusion that it's all going to get better, but I don't see it. I understand he'll move on to gruelish, multi-colored baby food atrocities that get cremated over everything within throwing distance. All I want to do is survive.

Author's note: Baby Leroy was an ill-tempered child who bedeviled W.C. Fields in the movies. Another nickname bestowed by Dave.

Baby Leroy

Baby Leroy dances to Muzak
Baby Leroy wets his own face
Baby Leroy sleeps on the mower
Baby Leroy cries in his cake

Baby Leroy's no help with the ponies
No rocking horse winner is he
Baby Leroy's the infant conductor
Baby Leroy swings from a tree

Baby Leroy abuses his glasses
Bite marks pit lenses and frames
Baby Leroy's an excellent driver
He crashes right where he aims

Baby Leroy loves baths with his Mama
Soap suds splatter the wall
Baby Leroy don't cry when he tumbles
He's fragile as a bowling ball

Baby Leroy sports abs of a gymnast
Earned while learning to crawl

Baby Leroy is missing a dimple
And has no ankles at all

Baby Leroy dances to Muzak

Cutting Cups

In 2021, about a year after Jesse was born, I decided to un-retire and find a part-time job to supplement our incomes. I wasn't going to take just anything; it had to be something I wanted to do. What did I want to do? I wanted to be outdoors at the crack of dawn.

I found a job posting for greens keeper at Horseshoe Bay, a tony golf resort in the hills overlooking Lake LBJ, about 45 miles from home. I had no qualifications and didn't expect to be hired, but what the hell, I gave it a shot, and was offered a job. Golf course superintendents are amenable to hiring retirees, I learned, because of their proven track record of showing up to work every day.

During my interview, I was told that employees were allowed to play golf for free. Holy shit! I would never be able to afford the $180 green fees, yet I would be getting a free pass to play some of the finest golf courses in Texas.

The job hit me right between the eyes. Awake at 3:00 am without the help of an alarm clock, I'd dress in my office, to avoid waking Lacy and Jesse, then make the dark drive in about 5:00. I would come home in the early afternoon, as tired as I'd ever been in my life (a "happy tired" from strenuous outdoor work). I usually needed a nap, but Lacy needed a break from Jesse, too; our competing interests led to occasional friction between us.

It was a work environment I hadn't experience since college summer jobs, lacking the professionalism and political correctness of the corporate world. If you screwed up you might be chewed out in front of the whole crew. I received such a comeuppance once and did not appreciate it. I thought about quitting. My friend Robert, who started work there about a week before me, said it was like working on a construction crew, and I think he was probably right.

I fucked up more in that job than all of my jobs put together the previous 50 years. I crashed a fairway mower into a stone bridge (resulting only in a flat tire, thankfully); I took the wrong mower out and punched holes in a tee box that was supposed to be mowed; I sheared off trailer hitches with a fairway mower. Everybody on the crew, even the most seasoned of hands, told stories of their gaffes, similar or worse...one guy had lost his mower in a pond; another drove his off a six-foot tall retaining wall. Mistakes came with the territory, and on a 3000-pound machine with 10 rotating blades, they always left a mark.

I was a reliable and enthusiastic employee, and over time, became competent mowing fairways, tee boxes, green sides, blowing debris from the course with a pull-behind hydraulic blower, raking bunkers, repairing greens, laying sod...just about everything a greens keeper does besides mowing greens and fertilizing.

The job I prized the most was "cutting cups." Every morning we would set the golf course up anew, and one of the most critical jobs was moving the pin placement on the greens, cutting a new hole and filling up yesterday's hole with the "plug," the cylinder of sod you'd just extracted from the earth for the new hole. Golf is all about putting the ball in the hole; hundreds of golfers, every day, would be aiming at my pin, my hole. I understood that actor Matthew McConaughey and Hall of Fame quarterback Troy Aikman had houses on the course; maybe they sank putts into my holes. One day after cutting cups, I happened to be working around the 18th green. I watched a young man sink a 20-foot putt, and he leapt and hollered, overjoyed; it thrilled me to, as if I had contributed to his elation.

I didn't get to play golf there as much as I hoped, maybe a half a dozen rounds in a year and a half.

I was rusty and never played particularly well, but thoroughly enjoyed it. One day, I played with my friend Freddy after work. He had cut the cups, and I had placed the tee markers...we had set the course up for ourselves.

My last day at work at Horseshoe Bay was July 27th, 2023.

Jesse and I still visit my old work site, where we're treated with the utmost kindness. The superintendent who gave me the public dressing-down has a soft spot for Jesse and me, and gives us the run of the place. Jesse loves mowers and diggers and gets a kick out of sitting on the big machines.

I will be looking for employment again when Jesse goes to kindergarten, and would go back to Horseshoe Bay in a heartbeat, but alas, it's won't be an option...the work day starts too early; I'll be getting Jesse ready for school when I'd need to be driving in to work.

Sunrise on the Bay

They come green from high school
Prison, Mexico
Corporate America
The Rez of the Navajo

Aged eighteen to eighty
Mustered at the slate
Break of day an hour away
They bullshit while they wait

All eyes scan the daily sked
Scrawled in schoolhouse chalk
When the time arrives
Fingers trip the clock

They share an epiphany
God almighty, what a day
Startled by the beauty
Of sunrise on the bay

An armada of machinery
Masses at the gate
Gators putter, mowers drone
Blowers palpitate

The super man he knows his crew
The rig each one should guide
Youngsters do the walking
Geezers get to ride

A snap of cold at morning light
Ribbons stripe the dew
Deer pop wheelies in the sand
The sun says how do you do

They share an epiphany
God almighty, what a day
Startled by the beauty
Of sunrise on the bay

Author's note: Daddy died in 2000; I met Lacy in 2011. They were never going to meet, but that doesn't keep me from aching for their union. Lacy heard many Clyde stories, and didn't approve, rightfully so, of some of the things she heard. I wanted her to know this Clyde: One day, when Carey was eight or so, he came into the room where Daddy and I were, crying. I thought, "Oh no, he's in for it now", knowing Daddy did not tolerate tears over minor injuries. Daddy asked Carey what was wrong, and Carey said, "My girlfriend broke up with me." Daddy put his arm around Carey's shoulder and said, "I'm sorry, buddy. That's rough at any age."

Lacy needed good men in her life. Daddy would have loved and supported Lacy in ways she'd never known, giving her shit, good-naturedly, at every turn because that's what Joneses do with people they love, but siding with Lacy, without fail, in any dispute Lacy and I might have had.

One day, when Lacy was depressed, struggling, I had a heavy heart, wanting to help her in some way, but unsure how. I went out to mow the yard, and wrote the following in my head as I mowed.

Lacy and Clyde

Clyde: "Pull up a chair, sweetheart, and give your old pal a hug."

Lacy and Clyde hug.

Lacy: "I do feel like I almost know you, Mr. Jones, even though we've never met. Jay idolizes you. He talks about you all the time."

Clyde: "As well he should. "

Clyde winks.

Clyde: "And no more of this Mr. Jones crap, Lacy Ruth. Call me Clyde."

Lacy: "OK. I'm sorry...Clyde, but I don't really like bars. Drunk people scare me."

Clyde: "Oh, you'll like this bar, Lacerooni. If you'll notice, the only people in here are dogs. There's Bridget and Igbert and Choctaw and Maggie and old Fig and a host of others. I'll introduce you. And if you'll cast your green-eyed gaze over yonder, you'll see your Lily and my Soul Sister shooting the bull."

Lacy bursts into tears. Her one-time constant companion trots over, tail wagging, brown eyes smiling. Lacy hugs her gentle old friend, and Lily licks Lacy's face. Lily plops down with a grunt beside Lacy's chair.

Lacy, wiping tears from her eyes: "Am I in heaven?"

Clyde: "Oh hell no. You have miles to go before you sleep. I run this joint, my dear, and I call on folks now and then, usually in dreams, but sometimes I deem it necessary to convene a meeting. I know you've been having a rough go, and I thought it was high time we met."

Lacy: "OK."

Clyde: "Tell me, how many people would you say you've saved in your life as a nurse?"

Lacy: "Hmm, I don't know, maybe 50?"

Clyde: "How about you save your own life this time, eh? Put that in your pipe and smoke it."

Lacy: "Yes, sir."

Clyde: "You have several plaques in your apartment with the same saying. What are the words?"

Lacy thinks: "Oh, live, laugh, love."

Clyde: "Righto. I'd say you love your ass off, Arsenic and old Lacy, but could with do a little more laughing and a lot more living."

Lacy: "Sir? Arsenic and...?"

Clyde: "Just farting around with your name until I find the right one. It's a Jones disease."

Lacy: "Oh, right. You remind me of your brother Dave."

Clyde: "Well, Nurse Ratched?"

Lacy: "Yes, Clyde, you're probably right. But there's just so much going on, with my Nanny, with my migraines and seizures, working two jobs.... It doesn't seem like I have the time or energy to do anything."

Clyde: "If there is one thing you've always wanted to do in life but haven't, what would it be?"

Lacy: "I want to ride horses in Montana."

Clyde: "Sounds like a toot. I say do it now. Get Jay up off his lazy butt and go. Now. Hock everything you own if you have to, but get your ass to Montana. Maybe you'll become a dental floss tycoon."

Lacy: "Dental floss, what?"

Clyde: "Oh, just a line from a Frank Zappa song..."

Clyde croons: "...Moving to Montana soon, gonna be a dental floss tycoon..."

Clyde: "It's a very silly song, but I dig it."

Lacy: "You're crazy, Clyde. You remind me of Jay... or Jay reminds me of you."

Clyde: "I'm not shittin' you, Nurse Ratched. Get the hell to Montana. Maybe you'll discover something that changes your life. Have some fun...throw Jay on the wildest bronco you can find. And when you get back, I want you to tell me all about it."

Lacy: "OK, Clyde, it's a deal."

Clyde: "Now, about Jay… if he gets out of line, pop him. A forearm shiver to the chin will straighten him out."

Clyde slaps his elbow into his palm, making a popping noise.

Clyde: "Come on, sister, give it a shot. Let me feel your forearm shiver, right on my magnificent mandible."

Clyde closes his eyes and offers his chin as a target.

Lacy giggles, feebly mimics Clyde's forearm shiver, then collapses in laughter, her arm sliding around Clyde's shoulder.

Lacy: "I can't do it, Clyde."

Clyde: "Jay's odd as a nine-dollar bill, you know that by now. I can't give you any advice on his hermit mentality. He got that from me, and there ain't no cure. If it's any consolation, he probably spends a lot of his alone time thinking of you. I know I was away from Queen more often than she would have liked, but she was always on my mind."

Lacy: "Thanks, Clyde, that's good of you to say."

Lacy: "I loved Beverly. I wanted to take her home with me."

Clyde: "Queen loves you too, Lacy, more than you can imagine. She watches over you."

Clyde: "I know some of the men in your life haven't treated you well. You need to ignore those horse's asses. Walk out the door. They don't deserve your company."

Lacy: "Yes, sir."

Clyde: "And you know Jay would never hurt a hair on your pretty little dented head, right?"

Lacy: "I know that, Clyde."

Clyde: "All right. Enough of this serious shit. May I have this dance?"

Clyde offers his hand, and Lacy takes it. The jukebox begins playing "Shenandoah," sung by Tennessee Ernie Ford. Lacy doesn't know if she can dance to such a slow song, but she feels safe in Clyde's strong, warm arms. It feels right after all. Clyde sings softly as they sway, his deep voice radiating through her body and into her heart, soothing her like a lullaby.

Somebody

Somebody else is thinking these thoughts
Somebody else, not me
Somebody envisions it clearly
Waste the motherfucker with a Louisville Slugger
First, I shatter his knee

Somebody's baby is motherless
Somebody's baby, not mine
Somebody says to his blue-eyed boy
Your Mommy's in heaven with Nanny and Dave
As for me, whoa, I'm doing fine

Somebody died unspeakably
Somebody died, not her
Somebody tragic unlucky
To chance on that drunk on the road
Somebody, please, not her, not her
Somebody, please not her

Waiting for Mommy

"Waiting for Mommy" was a listening game, I explained to three-year-old Jesse. When Lacy was due to arrive, I'd take Jesse out to the front porch rocker and we'd watch and listen to the traffic, on the lookout for Mommy's car.

It's quiet out here in the country, 40 miles northwest of Austin; traffic is sparse. We could hear a vehicle (pronounced "vickle" by Jesse) approaching from half a mile away. My house is perched on a small rise about half a football field from County Road 322. Cedar, cedar elm, and mesquite trees block our view in each direction, east and west, so we don't see cars approaching; we hear them. I'd bullshit with Jesse about what kind of jalopy or chariot was coming by next, by the sound it made. Silly Dad. Rocking gently to my beat (his feet don't touch the ground) in the twin swing, we enjoyed the sense of anticipation, waiting for Mommy.

I told Jesse to listen for a car slowing down, breaking, and for the muffled blare of music. Lacy cranked up her stereo to the max if she wasn't talking on the phone. She might be rapping, weeping to country, or rocking out, depending on her state of mind. Jesse didn't really understand the nuances of listening for Mommy, but he would light up when her grey Kia Sorento, blinker on, turned into the open gate and crunched up our gravel driveway. Lacy's arrival meant Jesse got to drive.

Jesse would shout "Mommy" delightedly and run down the ramp to her car. Lacy would hug him, sit him in her lap and let him steer back down and up the drive. I usually went back in the house because I didn't like Jesse driving, afraid he'd try it on his own sometime. Every once in a while Jesse would get hold of the keys and press every button, setting off the alarm, turning on the lights, locking the doors. He'd locked himself inside the car more than once. Lacy's dad had let her "drive" when she was young, and she was sustaining a family tradition. I understood. Lacy and I had discussed it and agreed to disagree; no hard feelings.

I waited alone for Mommy that night.

Jesse had crashed early and was asleep in our bed. Lacy had worked two three-hour shifts for Visiting Angels that day. She'd gotten home from work before dark, gushing about her "precious" new patient in Liberty Hill, Mr. Mondragon. "You would love him", Lacy said. She said that Mr. Mondragon's favorite place to eat was Jardin Corona in Liberty Hill, and she'd promised him that we would all eat there some time.

It was a scene I knew well, Lacy coming home, excited to tell me about her time with an elderly patient. She always told me I would love them. It made me think that, in her love for you, Lacy would bestow on you admirable qualities of character you didn't know you had or adopted because she believed you did. At different times Lacy had told me I was the smartest person she'd ever known, the most honest. I felt a little smarter and a little more honest because Lacy told me so. In saying "you would love them," she assumed that I had her gift of immediate love for another human, and it touched me that she believed such innate goodness resided in me.

Lacy hadn't gotten settled in yet and was still in her scrubs when I mentioned I was paying bills, and she said, "I'll go get you some money." I said, "No, no, no, you don't need to do that. I've got it covered." We went back and forth about it, Lacy saying that she would go hit an ATM, me saying, please don't. Lacy was in high spirits, feeling good, and excited to run the errand.

I did not understand then why Lacy was so insistent on running to the ATM.

I understand now.

I let her go.

My sister, Junie, had stayed with Lacy and Jesse the week before, when I took my yearly Saratoga trip and said later that Lacy was as happy as she'd ever been. I think Junie was right. Lacy had settled into her life. She'd lost weight and found a hairstyle she liked; she wore glasses now and looked as cute in them as without.

Several men in Lacy's life, starting with her father, had abused her mentally and physically, leaving her scarred, mistrustful and in need of continual reassurance. I wasn't as demonstrative in my love as she would have liked, but I think she'd finally come to trust that I loved her and was committed to us as a family evermore. After I told her I loved her on a call from Saratoga, she told Junie how good that made her feel.

Above all, her miracle baby, Jesse, was thriving, a joy to us all.

A couple of months before, Junie had taken a picture of Lacy, Jesse and me standing on a bridge spanning the Arkansas River in Buena Vista, Colorado, that captured Lacy in full bloom. Big smile on her face, one hand holding Jesse's and the other resting on his head; Lacy leans in to me, my arm draped over her shoulder. The only flaw in the picture is that she is squinting into the sun, so you don't see her beautiful light green eyes. Most telling of all about her state of mind...Lacy wore shorts! Lacy never wore shorts, even on the hottest Texas summer day. Embarrassed about varicose veins in her legs, she lacked the confidence to bare them. She had the confidence now.

I waited for Mommy.

Lacy was gone too long. The thing is, Lacy would go off driving on a whim sometimes. Once, she told Junie and me that she was going up to Dollar General, five minutes away, and she was gone for two hours. She'd been thinking about her Nanny and driven out to Kingsland, to the Slab, revisiting childhood memories.

As I sat on the front porch the traffic in front of me became a flood. Oh shit. I'd seen it several times in the 28 years I've lived here. When there was a wreck on a certain stretch of Highway 29 outside of Bertram the police would divert traffic down our county road.

I thought perhaps Lacy was stuck in a traffic jam from the wreck. I wanted to tell her to be very careful turning into our driveway... too many cars going too fast on a winding, narrow road.

228

I couldn't call her because Dumb Ass Daddy had lost his cell phone a couple of days before. Lacy and I had looked everywhere for it, and called it repeatedly, no luck. At one point, Lacy said, "You're not as worried about your phone as I am." I said, "Oh yes, I am," not for the loss of the phone, but for my sanity. This was the second phone I'd lost in the span of a couple of years. I'm 63, is this when I lose my fucking mind? I didn't lose things before.

Another thought was that Lacy was treating victims of the wreck. She was a Registered Nurse and required by law to lend assistance if she came upon a wreck before an ambulance arrived. "Required by law" didn't matter to Lacy; were she a farrier, an astronaut or a lumberjack, Lacy would have been helping people in crisis.

I thought about our first trip together to New Orleans one Thanksgiving week...what happened on the Lake Ponchartrain bridge outside the Big Easy. I had vivid memories of the bridge already from a trip 40 years ago when my friend Kevin and I had gone on a whirlwind trip to New Orleans. On the way back out of town after midnight, Kevin nodded off at the wheel of his white Camaro. We rode with the windows down, and my arm lolled out the passenger side window. Just after I lifted my arm back inside, we bounced off the bridge railing.

I drove Miss Lacy on our trip, and as we caught sight of New Orleans in the distance, brake lights lit up the lanes, and we got stopped dead on the bridge, a few cars behind a wreck. Just one police car was there, lights flashing, blocking traffic. Lacy explained to me her duty as a nurse and said she had to help. She told me to stay there, and I didn't argue; I didn't have any heroic instinct at that moment...she knew what she was doing, and I didn't. It was a side of Lacy I'd never seen before like a switch flipped inside her, and she took command. She strode in her flip-flops through glass shards and demolition derby debris, talked to the cop, then attended to the injured in both cars. Emergency vehicles arrived in a blitz of flashes and wails.

A helmeted fireman took charge. He and Lacy found each other, and the scene was almost comical, this little girl no taller than Yosemite Sam schooling a giant fireman in his big black boots, bulky Kevlar suit and towering headgear.

Lacy returned to the car and filled me in. The guy in the car that had flipped said he was okay. He had a cut on his forehead, but what worried Lacy the most was that he might be bleeding internally. She wasn't sure if he was drunk but thought he was "on something." Lacy's heart hurt for the two elderly ladies in the other car. They were dazed and battered, and she feared that one of them had a broken hip.

I think about heroism, how little I've seen of it in my life, and how often I saw it in Lacy. I saw it that night; I saw it when she was pregnant...a 35-year-old Type 1 diabetic who threw up every day for eight months, whose dreaded seizures had returned...reducing her blood sugar level to the lowest it had ever been so she would bear a healthy baby; I saw it when she ministered a non-compliant, drug-seeking, loveable amputee for nine months in her own home...she quite literally saved my uncle Dave's life; I saw it in the decade she cared for her Nanny, who was afflicted with Lewy Body Dementia…how, after a few years you might start going through the motions, give yourself a break. Lacy never slacked; she was all in, all the time.

And, like any hero I'd want to know, Lacy's heroism could take a comical turn. Lacy once managed an apartment complex for senior citizens. She knew intimately every resident and cared for them all. One day she walked by the apartment of Miss Jolene, who was outside, panic-stricken. Lacy asked Miss Jolene what was wrong, and Miss Jolene said that her cat, Shadow, had escaped. Shadow was strictly an inside cat, never allowed outside. Lacy said, "I'll help you, Miss Jolene." Shadow had run out the door and hidden under a parked car. Lacy crouched down and spotted black Shadow but didn't know what to do. She wasn't a cat person and had no idea how to beckon a cat. Lacy did the first thing that came to mind, which was to start singing "Jesus Loves the Little Children." Lacy had a sweet, soft, soothing singing voice, and Shadow responded.

Shadow ran out from under the car and jumped into Lacy's arms.

Lacy whispered in Shadow's ear, "If you scratch me, I will throw you."

Part of what made Lacy heroic was her radical selflessness. In her mind, *everyone* else came first. She felt guilty if she spent any money on herself; it should go to someone needier. When Lacy was a teenager, she had four brain surgeries to treat debilitating epilepsy. A left temporal lobe "hemispherectomy" was performed, and a significant portion of her brain was removed. It was like any trace of selfishness was removed along with her hippocampus. Her family says she was just born that way.

I'd waited for Mommy long enough.

I smoked one last cigarette on the front porch, trying to will Lacy's car into our driveway, but it never came. It was well past dark now. Headlit cars streamed past.

As bad as I hated to wake Jesse up, I had to. I had to do something. I carried my groggy little boy out to my Mini Countryman and put him in his car seat. I hoped he would fall back to sleep, but he was up for good.

I drove the two miles east on the county road, and sure enough, police cars had blockaded Highway 29. I pulled up to the policeman directing traffic, told him that my girlfriend had been gone too long, and I was worried about her. He said there had been a wreck down the road that I should pull up parallel to his car, and he would radio ahead.

Window rolled down, I listened to the squawk of police radios and heard something about "a lady in a white Cadillac," a "Mini Cooper"... Lacy's Kia was in the shop, so she was driving a rental car, a Mini Countryman, the same color as mine, but with a white roof. I'd told Lacy we should race. Because the squawk said "Cooper," not "Countryman," I wasn't too alarmed.

I was parked diagonally on 29 in front of the cop's car. The road rises to the east…westbound traffic is blind to the intersection until it tops the hill. If a car was going too fast, Jesse and I could be broadsided. Where the cop had told me to park was just plain stupid. I hollered over to him and told him I was going to pull off the road. He said, "Yeah, seeing as you have a little one, that's probably the thing to do." Ah. Saved by the little one.

I pulled well off the shoulder and felt something crunch under my car. I talked to Jesse and told him everything was okay; we were just trying to find Mommy. He has this high-pitched fake laugh that he'll produce when he's nervous or in trouble. That's how he laughed then.

A few minutes later, the policeman came over and told me to follow him. A state trooper wanted to speak to me. He didn't betray any news, good or bad, just that I needed to talk to the trooper.

I pulled out behind the cop and realized I was still dragging whatever I'd run over on the side of the road. Every other time in my life, I would have pulled over and dislodged it, but I was following a police car, taking me to meet someone who could give me news about Lacy, my love. It lent a sense of unreality to the scene that this object was stuck under my car, probably doing some kind of damage, yet I grinded on down the road.

Even then, I was hopeful. Worst case, Lacy had been hurt in the wreck and was being taken to the hospital. Maybe he was going to tell me that Lacy was still treating patients and wanted to get word to me that she was okay.

We pulled onto a side road off 29. The trooper was already there, standing outside his black and white patrol car, red and white lights flashing. I told Jesse I'd be right back.

"What is your name and address?"

"Jay Jones…1032 County Road 322."

"What is your relationship to Lacy Van Zandt?"

"I'm her boyfriend."

"Mr. Jones, I regret to inform you that Ms. Van Zandt was killed in a collision tonight on Highway 29."

That sentence sent me careening into another universe.

"No! No! No! No!"

"Not Lacy…No No No Not Lacy…It's not fair…She did not deserve this…No No No Not Lacy….No No No Not Lacy…"

I know I paced back and forth. I know I bleated words of denial, shock, heartbreak. It flashed through my mind, "What is Jesse thinking?" sitting in his car seat, watching a policeman wearing a brown cowboy hat talking to his Daddy and his Daddy walking around in circles, shouting.

As if it mattered, I finally asked the trooper, in a crackly, meek voice, "What happened?"

"A red Ford F150 crossed the center line and hit her head-on. She died instantly."

I nodded.

"Do you know why Ms. Van Zandt might have been going to Liberty Hill?"

Lacy was going to Liberty Hill? Nothing made sense anymore.

"No, no, I have no idea. She was just running into Bertram to hit an ATM."

I told the trooper I'd lost my cell phone and asked if I could use his to call my sister. He handed it over, but my brain was scrambled, and I couldn't remember either of her phone numbers. I got wrong numbers twice before I reached her home phone answering machine, which she might or might not check. The trooper said he would come by my house later to ask some questions.

A plastic yellow paint bucket was lodged under the oil pan of the Mini. I jerked it out, then drove back down the deserted highway, desperately lost. I think I kept a stream of conversation going with Jesse to reassure him, but what was I going to do...now and for the rest of my life? Vibrant, loving Lacy, who I'd held in my arms two hours ago, "died instantly," gone from us forever? Impossible.

A cascade of thoughts...What did Lacy see, think and feel in her last moment? Why was she going to Liberty Hill? Was there an emergency with Mr. Mondragon?

I hate goddamned cell phones for their distraction and the perfunctory rudeness they engender, now ingrained in our culture. And I was desperate for one. I needed help. I needed to let people know. I didn't know what to do. Should I stop at a neighbor's and ask to use their phone? I pulled up at my house, took Jesse inside and sent a couple of hopeless emails to Junie and Murphy. "I need help."

I needed Junie most. I needed her good sense, her calm in crisis, her way with words. I needed her for Jesse. Their love for each other is boundless.

Impotent at home, I tried to think of where I should go and which of my friend's houses was nearest. I don't have any close friends in Bertram. Finally, I decided to head to my cousin Jeffrey's house in Round Rock, but I wasn't even sure I could find it, as addled as I was. Lost emotionally, I didn't want to be lost in space as well. I grabbed my obsolete Franklin Planner, which still might have a few viable phone numbers in it.

As I drove east, I made my best decision of the night...I would stop at Erika's house in Liberty Hill. Erika is Jeffrey's sister-in-law, and their whole family has always made me feel welcome.

I rang Erika's doorbell. No one answered, no one came to the door. Erika's dog barked. Just as I was about to leave, I heard Erika's disembodied voice. "Jay, it's Erika and Nicole. We just got out of a movie. What's up?" (Technology today…her cell phone is connected to her doorbell.) I told the doorbell the news. Nicole is Jeffrey's wife, and I knew she, especially, would take it hard because she and Lacy were very close. Nicole had been the one to find my uncle Dave dead in his wheelchair seven months ago. Now, she had to take another unspeakably tragic blow. Crying, Nicole said they'd get there as fast as they could.

I sat on the curb and waited. I tried to keep Jesse occupied. Erika's neighbor appeared, and I told him what happened. He seemed genuinely moved, and offered his cell phone for me to make calls. Erika and Nicole arrived shortly after, and Nicole gave me her phone to use for the rest of the night.

Jesse clung to me as I called Junie, so I couldn't tell her exactly what happened.

I said, "I need you to get here safely, as fast as you can."

"Are you and Jesse and Lacy OK?" she asked, alarmed.

I said, "Jesse's OK, I'm OK."

"Oh no. I'll get there as soon as I can."

Later, when Jesse was distracted, I called Junie back, apologized for the cryptic message, and told her what happened. I ached for my sister, making the saddest, loneliest drive of her life. She and Lacy were "sisters."

I sat on the curb most of the night, inexpressibly grateful for the love, support, and shared suffering of Jeffrey and Nicole, their daughter Audrey, and Nicole's entire family.

The first person I reached in Lacy's family was her uncle Willie, who spread the news. I'd called Lacy's mom, Terri, first but got voicemail. I didn't leave a message. Terri called back in agony.

"Oh, Jay, what are we going to do without our sweet little girl?"

"I know, Terri. I don't know."

I would not speak of Lacy in the past tense that night or for days to come.

Junie arrived about 4:00 am, after her four-hour drive from Plano. It seemed like one minute I called, and the next minute, she was there. Of all the thoughts spinning through my brain that night, foremost was that I had to tell Jesse, somehow...not what happened, but that his Mommy was gone. I had to tell him that night. I had to be honest with my child. Junie agreed.

How do you tell a three-year-old child that his Mommy died? How would he react? I didn't have the faintest instinct. I assumed he would cry and be as upset as all of us were, but my biggest fear was that he would become an angry, sullen child. Junie said that he would probably get distracted in the moment and need to take it in over time. She was right.

Junie took the initiative to round Jesse up and sit him down between us on the front porch.

I said, "Jesse, we have something very sad to tell you."

"OK."

Junie said, "Your Mommy has gone to heaven with Nanny and Dave."

"I love my Mommy."

I said, "We love your Mommy, too, buddy, with all our hearts, but she's gone away and isn't coming back."

"Can I go play?"

Later, I took Jesse to bed in a spare bedroom of Erika's and got him to sleep. I may have dozed for 30 minutes. I got back up, still before dawn. The house was quiet. I decided to go get donuts for everyone. When I got behind the wheel of my car, I felt fragile, brittle. As I pulled out of the driveway, I noticed a puddle of oil where my car had been parked.

I drove slowly the mile up to the highway. Liberty Hill rush hour was just beginning, so there was a fair amount of traffic, and it scared the shit out of me...cars zoomed by... they were going so fast. My god, what would happen if you were hit by a car going that fast?

I didn't cry much that night, then every day after for two months, I would burst into tears randomly, telling Lacy how much I loved her, apologizing for not being a better mate, for letting her take the load with Jesse, for never kneeling and asking for her hand.

239

Lacy had been right beside me for some of the saddest, hardest moments of my life...when my mother died and when my beloved dogs Dakota and Mordecai died. I would fight back the tears, and she would hold me and tell me it's okay to cry. "Let it go," she whispered, "Just let it go."

I let it go. I let it go.

Over the months since the wreck, we've learned that the other driver, Alejandro Molina, a 22-year-old kid from Burnet with two cocaine busts and two DWIs in the last year, was drunk. He blew three times the legal limit on the breathalyzer that night. Despite the recent DWIs he has a valid driver's license to this day.

How is that possible? He was not arrested after the wreck because he spent the night in the hospital. He flaunts a gangsta persona on social media and grins for mugshots.

I avoid the wreck site, just a couple of miles from my house. I think about moving away. I don't want to see Lacy's demolished car or crime scene pictures. I have no desire to read the autopsy. When the trial comes, I will leave the courtroom before any crash photos are displayed. I decide for Jesse, and he won't see them either, unless he chooses to sometime in the far distant future. I have my precious memories of Lacy, and that's enough for me. I don't want some ghastly image planted in my mind. You can't "unlook" at something.

I understand why others want all the details. Lacy would too.

This new universe features insurance companies, lawyers, state troopers, state agencies, red tape, and waiting, waiting, waiting for some kind of justice. Black-and-white answers are hard to come by.

In my former universe, I cuddled with Lacy in bed every night...in the new universe, the only human touch I have is with my son; in the old universe, I relied on a born mother to educate me on the trajectory of a child's development, to do most of the dirty work...in the new universe it's all on me, and I operate on instinct and what Lacy taught me; in the old universe I went to work every day...in the new universe I'm jobless, home with Jesse; in the old universe we were comfortable enough financially...in the new universe I have the financial footing of a broke college student, but with 100 times the complexity and responsibility, without the prospects of youth; in the old universe I had an idea what the next five years would look like...the next five years are a mystery in the new universe; in the old universe I felt like I had most of the answers...my answer to every question in this universe is "I don't know."

The most gratifying thing about the new universe is that my friends, my family and Lacy's family are still here, more present than ever. Every single one of them has stepped up to help Jesse and me in ways that leave me humbled. My new hero is Junie, who has sacrificed life as she knew it to take a major part of the load with Jesse, who, given the choice of who to sleep with at night, chooses Junie every time.

One of Junie's greatest gifts to me is helping me remember and understand Lacy. When Jesse is occupied or asleep, Junie and I will sit out on the front porch and bullshit. Our conversations almost always turn to Lacy. One memory stirs another, and we're off, remembering things we never thought we would free to talk about disagreements we had with Lacy, her quirks…

I share the same gift with Terri and Lacy's sisters Zana and Christi. One night, a few days after the wreck, Zana, her husband, Sam, and I sat on the front porch and talked about Lacy all night. Zana is closest in age to Lacy of her siblings, her only little sister. They shared a bedroom for most of their childhood and had a bond "like no other," as Lacy would say. Zana told me stories from Lacy's childhood that I never knew, which helped me understand the dynamic between Lacy and her father, Vincent, who they loved deeply and, when he was drunk, feared desperately. I understood Lacy better after the all-nighter.

Jesse was a bright, happy child before Lacy died, and Jesse remains a bright, happy child. He says, "I miss Mommy". I tell him I miss her too and love her. We'll look at pictures of Lacy and talk about what a great Mommy she was, what a great smile she had. Every once in a while he'll say something that astonishes me. One night, I was making supper, in a sour mood, and I thought I heard Jesse say, "Daddy's hurting." I said, "What did you say, buddy?" He said, "Daddy's hurting because he misses Mommy." Oh man, all I could do was hug him. Later he told Junie, "Daddy and I are hurting because we miss Mommy."

For a while, he called Lacy on his "hand phone" and talked to her. I had no problem with that; I encouraged him. One time, I asked him what Mommy said, and he looked at me real seriously and said, "Mommy is crying."

He says he dreams about Mommy sometimes, but I don't have a feel for their texture. He dreams of scary "ghostes," but I don't think they're related to Mommy.

What will Jesse remember of Lacy? Will he remember their joyous baths? Will he remember driving with Mommy? When he was younger, and Lacy would tickle him to hysteria, she would say, "I'm gonna git you," when Jesse got older and was in trouble, the phrase became a threat. Will Jesse remember, "I'm gonna git you."?

At first, I thought that he couldn't possibly forget her, but now I worry. I've learned that a child's memory begins at about three and a half years of age, maybe a little earlier for girls. Jesse was three years and two months old when Lacy died. Wanting to preserve his memories, I tried to get into a routine of telling a Mommy story every night before we go to sleep, but he gets distracted. I'll try again.

The person most affected by the tragedy comprehends it least. Lacy's death devastated us all, but Jesse's life was irretrievably altered at age three, and the repercussions will shape the person he becomes. Instead of being raised by Lacy and me, Jesse will be raised by me and a village of Joneses, Van Zandts, and friends.

Lacy dreamed of having a little boy who would still sit in her lap when he was 18. When she was pregnant she would unabashedly say

243

she wanted a boy. She was nervous before the first ultrasound when we would find out the gender, and when the doctor told us the news, Lacy was over the moon. I was thrilled for her and for us.

Had it been up to me alone, our son would have been named Clyde, after my father. Junie and my brother, Carey, don't have children, so my son would be the only Jones offspring among us. I felt strongly about it, but Lacy hated the name Clyde. It hurt. We went round and round on names and finally settled on Jesse, another Jones family name, and Clyde as the middle name. So be it...Jesse Clyde Jones.

Jesse didn't come easy. Lacy and I had been through all the birthing classes, and we might as well have been playing croquet...nothing went according to plan. Lacy's pregnancy came at the height of the Covid outbreak. When we'd drive to doctor appointments in Austin at rush hour, the roads were eerily devoid of cars. Jesse wouldn't see an unmasked human face for almost the entire first month of his life.

Lacy's doctor decided to induce labor almost a month ahead of schedule, fearing that her and Jesse's health might deteriorate with the difficulty of her pregnancy. Because of Covid restrictions, only one person could be in the hospital room with Lacy for the birthing. Terri, Christi and Zana had seen it all as mothers; Zana was formally trained as a doula. Then there was me, a man who'd never been within cannon shot of a birth. It was like having a choice between Mother Teresa, Florence Nightingale, Marie Curie, or Pee Wee Herman. Lacy and I agreed... it had to be Pee Wee.

"To make a long story short," as Lacy would say, then talk for a while longer, Lacy tried her guts out to give birth naturally, but things went south, and she had to have an emergency C-Section. We were taught that Lacy would be conscious during the C-Section; she was out cold the entire time. Donned in ER gear, I comforted my unconscious sweetheart until Jesse arrived, silent. He was supposed to cry. As I walked from Lacy to my newborn, I glanced back at the operating table and saw a flash of a white internal organ amidst the blood from her midsection. Yikes. When I described it to Lacy later, she laughed and laughed.

Purple Jesse wasn't crying or breathing properly; the nurses laid him down on a table and performed Apgar testing. He failed all five counts. The calmness of the nurses reassured me as I sat right beside them and watched them bring our baby to life.

Jesse was supposed to be presented to Lacy and me in the recovery room. No Jesse. Lacy was one wacked-out girl.

Jesse ended up spending 22 days in the NICU, but we finally got him home, and he thrived under Lacy's indefatigable care.

Lacy and Jesse: A mother and child in all their glory. Sometimes I would step in on Lacy giving Jesse a bath and marvel at the laughter and unbridled glee emanating from both of them. As I wrote in Lacy's obituary, I witnessed the most joyful event on the planet. I feel honored to have shared in their union.

Why was Lacy going to Liberty Hill that night? I thought I might never know. Lacy's cell phone hadn't been found, but about a month after the wreck, Terri accessed Lacy's phone records. A couple of minutes before the wreck, Lacy had called Jardin Corona, where I'd order frozen margaritas, take-out; Jesse's favorite meal was their cheese enchiladas.

Now, I understand. The errand to the ATM was a ruse. The real reason for her trip was to surprise Jesse and me with a treat.

Lacy's last act was an act of love.

One Second

A car moving at a rate of 55 miles per hour, as Lacy's was the night of 7/27/23, travels about 80 feet per second. Had she arrived at the fateful intersection one second earlier or one second later, she would have been clear of the red Ford 150 pickup truck that swerved into her lane and hit her head-on. Had she scratched her nose, adjusted her seat belt, turned up the volume on the radio, or performed any of infinite one-second actions, she would be alive today; or conversely, did she scratch her nose, adjust her seat belt, or turn up the volume on the radio, putting her in the crosshairs of a blind drunk on the road? Of the 86,400 seconds of that day...of the 31 million seconds of that year...of the 1.8 billion seconds of her life...why did she have to be there at the only instant that would kill her?

Baby, I Rub My Head

When you say
Let's ride horses at midnight (1)
Baby, I rub my head

When you ask
Wanna go to a wedding in Muleshoe? (2)
Baby, I rub my head

When you give
The panhandler your last twenty (3)
Baby, I rub my head

When you ask
Babe, can you fix the deal on the thing? (4)
Baby, I rub my head

When you call
Four times from the grocery store (5)
Baby, I rub my head

When you make
Jesse laugh till he cries (6)
Baby, I rub my head

When you say

We need to talk

Baby, I rub my head (7)

When you say

I know you, you rub your head when the answer is no (8)

Baby, I rub my head

When you say

I save every petal from every rose you ever gave me (9)

Baby, I rub my head

Baby, I rub my head

And I'd do it all over again.

(A poem with footnotes...I think I've stumbled upon the most obtuse, least reader-friendly format ever invented. I give myself a pass. An exercise in remembering Lacy can't be all wrong.)

1--The day of our first date, Lacy called and proposed that we ride horses after dinner and a movie. The romanticism of the idea floored me, but what are the logistics, I wondered. I'd never fallen off a horse on a first date before. (A good example of our contrasting thought processes: Lacy, sentimental and romantic; me, practical and detail-oriented.) Giddy, I called Murphy just to tell somebody about this amazing girl. I think I fell in love with Lacy then.

2--I attended a wedding some years back where I had a fake smile plastered to my face for hours. Miserable, I said to myself, "Never again." As you age, you learn what you like and don't like, and I think you earn the right to say no. Lacy argued, "If you loved me, you would go." I would say, "If you loved me, you wouldn't ask." Those words sound harsh now...of course, we loved each other...but Lacy tended to express herself in dramatic extremes, and I never learned how not to respond in kind.

3--On the Riverwalk in San Antonio...Lacy's lifelong financial disposition captured in one act.

4--At Carey's house in Colorado. The deal was the antenna, and the thing was the car. One of the consequences of Lacy's brain surgeries, besides the memory loss, was an inability to find the right word at times. "Whatchamacallit" was another fallback word for Lacy.

5--If something came to Lacy's mind, she had to tell you then, and I guess the grocery store goosed her synapses.

6--Lacy would make Jesse laugh till he was breathless. He squealed and laughed to exhaustion, then would finally yell, "no, no, no." She would pause for a dramatic moment, then dive back in on top of him, face under his shirt, blubbering on his belly, and he was in hysterics all over again.

7--When I say I rub my head, what I do is muss my hair back and forth, circularly...the intensity depending upon my wonderment or consternation.

8--I never really thought about rubbing my head until Lacy called me out on it. (A new argument comes to mind: Maybe, babe, I didn't rub my head until I met you.) She should have made more fun of me than she did. She didn't have the Jones cruel humor gene... My answer was usually not no, and it was more like, I'm not sure I like that idea, re: wedding in Muleshoe.

9--Man alive, to be loved by Lacy...

Geezer Daddy and baby Jesse in their angles of repose. Photo taken by Mommy (Lacy Van Zandt).

1932 Sweetwater Mustangs. Courtesy of the Pioneer City County Museum in Sweetwater, Texas.

Little girl Lacy. My favorite picture of her.

Love

Jesse, wearing chocolate pudding

Left to right, Lacy, Jay (toting Jesse like a sack of potatoes), Faye and Junie at Lone Star Park.

Lacy, Lacy, Lacy...what a smile

Lacy, Jesse, and Jay in Buena Vista, Colorado. Our last picture together.

Jesse and Jay in Colorado

Junie, her dog, Gus, and Jesse. in Colorado

Emptying Out

I miss your walk
Your sweet-swinging gait
A tip-toey prance with a swish
I practice in the morning dark
Here, let me demonstrate

A stanza of a poem I couldn't make work. When all of the family was here, sleeping on couches and pallets, in the wake of the event, at 3:00 am, I would practice Lacy's walk, silently, through the prone and splayed bodies. I think I got it, mostly, though my butt doesn't swing as carefree as Lacy's did. I think Lacy's walk said a lot about her...to me, it was a happy walk, exquisitely feminine, eager to please.

The trap is to lionize a loved one who died young and suddenly, so they don't sound human. Lacy had maddening, gaping flaws like all of us. Simple in her dreams and desires, yet the most confoundingly complicated person I have ever known. She deserves to be remembered in all her pain and glory.

I find that writing about Lacy and our relationship is the hardest thing I've ever attempted to put on paper. What stories do I tell, and what do I leave out? The leaving out is the challenge because I want to tell you everything about her, to help you understand her, to help me understand her. I crave to tell Lacy's story in some logical and orderly way, but Lacy defied logic and order; my subject will not cooperate.

Sometimes, my memories of Lacy are so strong...I can see her and hear her voice so clearly that I think, if I'm quick enough, I can snatch her back before...from...what?

I met Lacy on a cool December day in 2011. I needed a dental procedure done where you're drugged and can't drive. I called a medical service that could provide a ride. I'd settled into my hermit-hood and didn't have a friend handy who could ferry me.

Lacy pulled up at the gate in her blue Ford pickup truck. My yellow labs, Mordecai and Dakota, overjoyed to have a visitor, bounded to her, grinning and leaping. Unintimidated by the big galoots, she loved them right back.

I can still see this smiling, blond-haired, cherub-cheeked girl standing in my kitchen doorway, dressed in tan corduroy jeans, a blue jacket, and dark brown, fleece-lined boots, and I felt an uncommon urge...I wanted to hug a stranger.

When I meet someone new, the first thing I notice about them is their hands. I think they tell a story. I have a visceral reaction, too; I will swoon over beautiful hands. Lacy's hands were petite, exceedingly pink (from habitual handwashing, I learned later), with short, unworried fingernails. Her thumbnails were elongated, slightly disproportionate to the rest of her nails; if she were anxious, she would chew on a thumbnail. She wore no rings. Lacy's hands spoke to me of innocence. I thought of them as "little girl hands" and would tell her so later.

We sat at my kitchen table and Lacy produced a questionnaire with many more pages than I wanted to see. I was busy at work and thought we could wrap it up in fifteen minutes. The questions were the most personal, intimate details of my medical history, and I felt, at turns, sheepish and impatient. I kept saying, "Look, I just need a ride to the dentist," but she sweetly persisted. She called me Mr. Jones, though I told her to call me Jay. If it had been anyone but Lacy, I might have said, "Ma'am, I'm sorry to waste your time, but I have work to do and don't have time for this." But she had this big ol' smile and was so easy to talk to.

Amid the medical questions, we talked about dogs, horses, West Texas...I led her into my bedroom to show her a picture of the 1932 Sweetwater Mustangs football team and pointed out my grandfather, Sam L. Jones, "Daddy Sam," and Sammy Baugh, who went on to become a Hall of Fame quarterback in the NFL. Daddy Sam was 6'2", the tallest boy on the team and his American Indian features leaped off the picture (he was one-quarter Cherokee). Lacy remarked how handsome he was. I told her that I'd asked him why he didn't play pro football, and he said, "There was no money in it back then. I needed a good job."

I think the 80-year old black and white picture and the pride I expressed in my grandfather clicked with Lacy.

After our three-hour interview, I knew I had to see her again, but how would I ask? I had always been awkward about asking for a date, hadn't had one in years, and was 20-odd years older than her. I might sound like an idiot. I called her the next day and told her I would like to see her outside of work. She happily accepted.

Lacy called me six times the next day.

I don't particularly enjoy talking on the phone. After about the third call, I thought, "What the hell am I getting into?" That was just Lacy, I would learn.

I've written elsewhere about our first date. We went to a movie, then to the Bluebonnet Café in Marble Falls. We didn't end up riding horses at midnight, as she'd proposed, but we talked happily for hours. Awkward conversational pauses didn't exist with Lacy.

I met Lacy when I was 51; she was 26. My last significant relationship had ended 18 years ago.

Susan and I were together for four years. At one point, I was certain we would marry; I know she felt the same way at another time, but our intentions never jived, and we eventually split up, painfully for me.

I told myself, "Learn to be happy on your own," and that's what I set about doing. It came pretty easy, being a born loner. I bought my house, paid it off in 11 years, worked my ass off as a Project Manager with Verizon, raised some great dogs, learned to like yardwork, wrote, played golf and the horses, and traveled as I pleased. I quit drinking and smoking dope when I was 50 (and would start back, in much greater moderation, when I was 62).

You could count on one hand the number of dates I had in the 18 years before I met Lacy. The idea of getting married and having kids, something that I'd always imagined I would do, evaporated. It's not that I didn't want that life; it just became inconceivable.

I told Lacy much of my story on our first date. I remember being confident, clear-headed, completely honest. The contrast between the clarity I felt at age 51 and the confusion and uncertainty I feel now, at 64, leaves me dumbfounded.

On the night of the crash that ended her life, Lacy had mapped the location of Jardin Corona, her intended destination, into her cell phone. The restaurant is about seven miles from our house, right on the highway. You can't miss it. She'd been there dozens of times, yet she couldn't be certain she could find it. After her hippocampus was removed, Lacy faced such challenges for every second of her waking life. Every second.

Can you imagine how hard she had to try to live a normal life?

Known many people who've had their hippocampus removed? It's a condition that 99.99% of human beings cannot fathom. The hippocampus regulates motivation, emotion, learning, and memory. Can you imagine your basic skills for life scrambled forever at age

261

15? Never mind that you've had to manage Type 1 diabetes since you were two years old, are partially blind in your left eye, suffer from migraines, bipolarity, depression, have a foot-long scar down your spine from another surgery, face agonizing bouts of CRPS...

Of the eight billion people inhabiting the earth, how many fit a similar profile?

Can you imagine...you are a vulnerable, tender-hearted teenager...at the beauty shop, your hairstylist recoils at the touch of the four-inch long arroyo in your skull and refuses to give you a hairdo?

Can you imagine, after a decade and a half of relative stability, the epileptic seizures that led to four brain surgeries return to haunt you again? The dreaded "aura" that tells you another seizure is imminent...the lost-in-space, hallucinatory seizure itself...the post-seizure confusion and fatigue.

Can you imagine the horror she must have felt once the seizures returned?

Levothyroxin, Propanolol, Rybelsus, Hydroxyzine, Zonisamide, Citalopram, Synthroid, BusPIRone, Amytriptylin, Humalog, Lantus...these were the medicines coursing through her brain and body during her last years. Can you imagine how they might have affected her?

Lacy would not want me to feature her medical challenges in a story about her. She did not advertise them, nor did they define her.

A few weeks after we met, she told me about her hemispherectomy. I traced with my finger the scar on her skull and did not recoil, and I think my equanimity relieved her. I found a study that followed 24 people who'd had hemispherectomies similar to Lacy's...only seven were able to hold down jobs. Lacy was an RN and a licensed counselor.

Can you imagine being in a relationship with a person with whom you don't have shared memories? I know that everybody remembers things to their own tune, but if a vinyl phonograph record represented Lacy's memory, it would be marred with scratches and skips. She didn't remember trips we took, concerts we'd attended, people we'd met. It was a wildcard in our relationship, what she remembered and how she remembered it. My memory is fallible, too, but some things I know.

She misremembered two things that disturbed me. A couple of years after we'd met, I suggested that I give her the money to pay off what she owed on her Toyota Camry. She was paying substantial interest, I was riding high...it was the thing to do. "Only if it's a loan, and I want to write up an agreement," she said. OK, OK, I said. I didn't worry about it; Lacy worried to the point that I wished we'd never done it.

One of the lessons Daddy tried to teach me was what he called "grace with money." "If you have money, don't flaunt it. If you pay the tab, don't advertise it. If you loan money to somebody, don't ask

263

for it back. You'll find out who your true friends are." In my life, I've loaned money to several people, never asked for it back, and found out who my true friends were.

A couple of years after we settled up, Lacy told me that one thing I did that hurt her was making her sign a loan agreement. I'm sure she was "struggling" at the time... "struggling" was a term she used to describe her bouts of depression. Maybe her mind was clouded by the depression, I don't know, but I felt like I behaved honorably. Why would she misremember me in such a negative light?

The second misremembrance involved Lacy's dog (now my dog), Lola, a silver Labrador retriever given to Lacy by her brother, Cody, for protection and companionship when Lola was about two years old. When Lacy told me about it, I was excited for her...I come from a Lab family and have loved about a dozen of them with all my heart. My only misgivings were that I had no experience with silver Labs, didn't even know there was such a thing, and am somewhat skeptical of "designer" breeds. My other qualm was that a young Lab in a small apartment like Lacy's would be a challenge. Labs need room to run and play. Lacy said that Lola had been abused when she was a puppy and had some "issues."

My reaction when I met Lola was, "Whoa". Lola ran and hid in the corner of the room when I arrived and shivered almost uncontrollably the entire visit. I asked Lacy about it, and she said Lola shivered constantly. Lola refused to go outside during daylight and had to be dragged out at night. If she saw any creature, she would bolt immediately back to the house. She was compact and strong and Lacy could not hold her on the leash when Lola ran. Housetraining was not going well because of Lola's fear of the outdoors.

I'd housetrained half a dozen dogs in my life, and they all got it within a week. Not Lola. To this day, if Lola wants to do her business in the house, she does. After about a week, I told Lacy, "Man, I don't see how it's going to work. I think you need to give Lola back to your brother." I said that taking on a dog is a 10-year-plus commitment, and she was looking at some tough years. Lacy agreed but was afraid of asking her brother. Lola stayed. We looked into dog training school, but loading Lola in a car was a wrestling match, and the class was expensive.

I don't think it would have mattered.

Lacy became convinced that Lola was autistic.

The thing that terrifies Lola most is riding in a car. We soon learned that loading her with a leash was impossible, so I ordered a body-length halter that sometimes worked if you manhandled her. Lola escaped from Lacy more often than not, and several trips had to be canceled because Lola fled and hid. If you got Lola in the car, she shivered and drooled the entire trip; she still does to this day. Lola has peed and shat in every car that Lacy and I have owned since she's been here. Every trip where Lola has to go starts out with the nightmare of wrestling her into the car.

Lacy loved Lola, but Lola brought Lacy to tears dozens of times with the loading episodes, canceled trips, and soiling of the car. One day, Lacy called, crying over the ordeal she'd gone through to get Lola loaded. She was still crying when she arrived at my house forty minutes later. Lola had defecated in the car.

It killed me to see Lacy distraught, and after anguished thought, I said, "Lacy, if you want me to have Lola put down, I will. She is not a happy dog, and she is making our lives miserable." The last thing I wanted to do was put a dog down; I've had to do it with all of my beloved dogs and been devastated every time. It is the single hardest thing I've ever done in my life.

During another one of Lacy's struggles, she said she was hurt that I wanted to put Lola down.

How do you process the misremembrances and factor them into your behavior in a relationship? What other memories did she have that were similarly tainted?

Lacy's fraught relationship with her father, Vincent, acted upon her in ways we could not know.

When sober, he was a kind, gentle, soft-spoken man, Lacy said, who played the guitar and harmonica, took his kids and grandkids fishing, mowed the lawn with a grandkid seated in his lap, bestowed them with endearing nicknames....

When drunk, he could be a monster, physically and verbally abusive to everyone in range. Lacy said that one time, when he was in a drunken rage, she fired a pistol shot through the ceiling of the house to try to stop the rampage.

He said unforgivable things to Lacy that I won't repeat. Several times, early in our relationship, Lacy would hang up the phone, sobbing, after he hurt her feelings. I would say, "Just don't talk to him".

I associated with Vincent maybe half a dozen times at family gatherings, on my guard, predisposed to dislike him. He was quiet, I am quiet...we never had more than a minute's conversation about anything. I can't say I knew him at all.

Vincent died unexpectedly in 2017. In the following years, Lacy seemed to rewrite their history in her head, hardly acknowledging the damage he'd done, the scars he'd left.

In 95% of the dreams Lacy had about me, I was cruel or unfaithful. I was never unfaithful, and I don't believe I was cruel. I think Lacy had a deep-seated mistrust of men because of what her father and other men had done to her, and it evinced itself in her dreams.

Lacy referred to herself and others of German descent as "squares," as in square heads. Lacy's grandfather on her father's side, Pato, had emigrated from Germany. He taught Lacy German, which she spoke fluently. Despite her mental challenges, she had a facility with languages...she became conversant in Spanish in a matter of weeks...she wanted me to teach her French, but my accent had always been atrocious, and what I'd learned in high school had long since atrophied, so I could only manage a few dozen words. She wanted to learn Swahili.

Lacy believed that Pato's wife, her grandmother, Ma Ruth, from Louisiana, was of African-American descent, but there is some dispute in her family about that. Lacy claimed that it was from Ma Ruth that she got her prominent be-hind and kinky hair.

Lacy had been "banking it," she said, as an RN in Lubbock before she moved to Kingsland to take care of her Nanny. She told me she was spending about $10,000 a year on medicine and groceries for Nanny. Nanny's husband, Lacy's step-grandfather, had the money to cover the expenses but gave Lacy such grief that Lacy covered them to avoid a cussing-out.

I told Lacy, "You can't keep doing this, or you're going to wreck yourself financially." She said, "I know, I know, I'll make him pay." And Lacy really did try, but she did end up wrecking herself financially, with repercussions for both of us.

"Let me put a pencil to it" was Lacy's term for working out a budget, and I came to cringe every time I heard it. "Let me put a pencil to it" meant that Lacy would rattle off the top of her head the expenses she could think of and have me add them up in my head...

"You're good with math," she would say. I'd add them up and she would conclude she had it all covered.

For 20 years or so, I'd kept my budget on a simple Excel spreadsheet, and it worked for me. I urged her to do the same and created one for her. Lacy and computers did not get along, and she never touched it. She did show me notebooks full of pencil-written debits and credits.

A few weeks before she died, we took out a loan to consolidate and pay off Lacy's debt. I learned later that half of the loan was earmarked to give to a needy family member.

I said to Junie, "I'm sorry, but that's not even in the realm of sanity."

Junie said, "I don't think Lacy had any boundaries."

I think Junie was right. Lacy didn't have any boundaries with the money she would give away, to her own detriment, nor the number of Diet Dr. Pepper's she drank in a day, nor the Christmas gifts she wanted to buy in May because she thought of somebody, nor the number of hours she might talk on the phone in a day, nor the elderly strangers she might adopt, nor the limits of her love.

I think of some of Lacy's stock phrases and what they said about her.

"Let me read this to you…" was another one that made me cringe after a while because Lacy did not have the ability to summarize, to put anything into shorthand. If she happened to see an article that interested her, she would read the entire article from start to finish, out loud, even if it turned out to be a bore.

One time, we had an argument about watering the new flowers we planted. We are on a water well, so we aren't under the mandate of neighborhood water restrictions. I said that we were in a drought and needed to be responsible with water usage; she wanted to water every day. Lacy got upset and googled what counties had watering restrictions and read down the list one by one. If a county was listed five times, she read it five times. She got to Kerr County, which had 19 entries, and she read out Kerr County, Kerr County, Kerr County. She would have read Kerr County 19 times, but Junie and I started laughing. Lacy realized the absurdity of her repetition, and that broke the tension.

Junie remembers the event poignantly…it was the last night she ever spent with Lacy.

"I'm gonna throat punch you…" Lacy never did throat punch me or anybody else, although I'm sure I deserved it. I don't know where she got the phrase, but hearing it from the mouth of the sweetest, most innocent girl you ever wanted to meet rendered it comical.

"Mary Mother of God…" Lacy latched on this one in her last couple of years as an exclamation about anything. I thought it represented the drama that she imbued on daily events. "Mary

Mother of God, the tire is low." There was no blasé' with Lacy, everything was over the top.

"S-H-one-T"... Lacy's version of cursing.

"You need to tell your brother..." Junie said she heard this one a lot. "You need to tell your brother to get rid of that ratty old t-shirt he's wearing." "You need to tell your brother to go to the doctor."

"My heart hurt..." I think she said this every day of her life in reference to a lonely or unfortunate soul she encountered, and I think she felt palpable pain every time.

"Can you imagine..." Most often used in awe of mothers who had many children or children who were born close together. Junie and I were born 11 months apart, and Lacy marveled at how Mother could have handled two babies at once.

Lacy worried about an obese child she saw at the store; she worried about an old man walking down the street; she worried that I was mad at her; she worried about how we would fund Jesse's college; she worried that her dress showed the scar on her back....I can't think of anything Lacy *didn't* worry about.

Early in our relationship Lacy worried that I was uncomfortable being seen in public with her, at a restaurant, say, because of our age difference. I promised her over and over that it did not bother me in the least, that I was proud to be seen with her...here I am, a geezer out with this vivacious young lady.

271

I wondered why Lacy was so plagued with worry. Part of it was just built-in, stemming from her intense care for her fellow human beings. I think the radical health problems she encountered her entire life must have contributed in some way, too.

A couple of months before she died, Lacy was on her way to her 20-year high school reunion. She was about an hour into the trip when she saw an elderly couple stranded by the side of the road in a broken-down car. Hundreds of cars whizzed past, but not the one driven by Lacy Van Zandt. She stopped to help, even though she had someplace she needed to be. She comforted the frightened old folks and invited them to sit in her car with Jesse while she changed their flat tire. Lacy had never changed a tire in her life, but she worked away in the 105-degree heat, got it done, and sent the grateful couple on their way. She ruined her reunion outfit in the heat, drove the hour back home, showered, changed clothes, and resumed her trek.

When Lacy told me the story, I shrugged it off, I regret to say. She told me similar stories so often that I began to take them for granted.

Often, when I visited her apartment in Kingsland or when I came home from work when we were living together, the minute I walked in the door, Lacy would hit me with a barrage of worries or crises. She needed to tell you now…. Frustrated, I would talk to her

272

about her attitude, then say, "OK, let's deal with the most important thing first..."

I wish I'd kept my mouth shut and hugged her and held her tight.

I did not do a good job handling her struggles. I'd never been in close quarters with someone who was clinically depressed. I would get depressed, too, and defensive.

I wish I'd hugged her and held her tight.

I didn't realize it until the last couple of years, but Lacy's "we need to talk" moments came cyclically, about every two weeks. Her mother said she noticed the cycles, too. Everything would come to a head a couple of times a month, and Lacy needed to have a heart-to-heart, knock-down-drag-out talk.

She would express things in absolutes... "You never talk"... "You never say you love me,"...and that would anger me, right off the bat, because it just wasn't true. I didn't talk or express my love for her as often as she liked, but "never," no. I came to dread our talks because it never seemed like we resolved anything; we just ended up with hurt feelings.

An hour or so after one of our talks, no matter what was said, Lacy would feel much better like all the steam had escaped, and we'd reconcile.

We still had some hard times after Jesse was born, and once or twice, during one of our talks, Lacy would say, "Maybe we need to live apart. I'll get an apartment and take Jesse." I would say, "I don't want that. I love you. Your place is here. We are a family."

Lacy's addendum to "Maybe we need to live apart" was, "But no matter what happens, I will always be there to take care of you."

In our 12 years together, Lacy got pulled over by the police about once a year, on average, for minor violations. She did like to drive fast on occasion, but she was a good driver. I trusted her behind the wheel, and my trust in other drivers is hard-won. My only beef was that she drove in the left lane more than I would have liked. She said she drove there to compensate for her partial blindness.

Lacy never got one ticket. Not one. I wish I could find another word, but the "sweetness" Lacy exuded was so palpable that cops could not bring themselves to ticket her. If she felt that a policeman was rude or disrespectful, she would call him out and give him a scolding. Even the cops whom she dressed down did not ticket her. I vowed that if I ever got stopped with Lacy in the car with me, she would do the talking.

Over the years, I wrote down several conversations I had with Lacy, verbatim, and I'm so glad I did. I hear her voice all over again. I had fun with this one:

Person A: I turned off the AC in the car last night before I came in, and now I can't get it to work right.

Person B: Why did you turn off the AC?

Person A: Because, Babe, you didn't tell me not to.

From the tone of Person A's voice, it is apparent that Person B fucked up by NOT telling Person A NOT to turn off the AC. It goes without saying that Person A's inability to work the AC is Person B's fault.

Obviously, Person B needs to imagine all of the things that Person A might do in a car and alert them NOT to do them.

Person B suggests...

...Do not deflate the tires.

...Do not not put gas in the car when it is close to empty.

...Do not pour sugar in the gas tank.

...Do not throw the car key in the lake.

...Do not remove the oil plug.

...Do not drive the car into another car.

...Do not drive the car with the hood up.

...Do not drive with your eyes closed.

Person B fears that he still may have missed some "do-nots" and will be held accountable.

I don't know what era Lacy's taste in clothes came from, but it wasn't any of the last half-century. Lacy loved the color purple. So many of her clothes featured purple frills, ruffles, flounces, bangles... Lacy was old, old, old school when it came to dress and so many other things.

I wasn't a big fan of some of her sartorial flourishes, but I never told her that. One year, for Christmas, I took her to a women's clothing boutique in Austin called Anthropologie and told her to buy out the store. I didn't know squat about women's clothing stores, but it was right next to REI, where I do shop, and I had an inkling it might be all right. Junie may have suggested the place. Lacy argued with me about it, did not want me to spend a lot of money on her (a recurrent theme), but I won out, and we had a blast. I sat on a settee near the fitting room and watched her model a dozen different outfits. She'd model each one, we'd talk about how they fit...and decide yea or nay. We ended up with several blouses, including one that became both of our favorites, a red and black flannel number with a white lace backing. I know, flannel and lace sounds funky, but it's lovely and I treasure it to this day.

An "it's a small world" coincidence: When she was twenty, Lacy was engaged to a man from Carmine, near Giddings, where she went to high school. She told me he'd bought her engagement ring at a pawn shop. They'd planned the wedding, and all the myriad details had been settled, but Lacy didn't feel right about it and broke off the engagement. When she told her Nanny about it, Nanny said "Hallelujah" because she knew it wasn't right either.

The man proposed to Lacy at the 4th of July parade in Round Top, Texas, in 2005.

I was there.

I had to have been within a couple of hundred yards away from them, at most. I was there because my friend Paul Saustrup decided he wanted to enter a float in the Round Top 4th of July parade, the longest-running 4th of July celebration west of the Mississippi. His idea was to grill hot dogs on the back of his flatbed trailer and toss them to the crowd. And that's what we did for a couple of years, although early on, we realized that a fired-up grill on top of a rickety flatbed might be a little dangerous, so we grilled them before the parade. The first year, our float was themed "Dressed to Grill" (other nominees were "Grillers in the Mist" and "Monty Python and the Holy Grill"), and we were awarded a 2nd place ribbon, mostly because Paul charmed the pants off the four lady judges, loopy from the Mimosas they were drinking, who inspected the floats from their Cadillac convertible.

Six or eight of us manned the grill, stuffing the hotdogs into buns, adding our condiment of choice, mustard or ketchup (ketchup? No way...mine were strictly mustard), then placing them in sandwich bags and tossing them to the crowd.

Lacy may have caught one of my hot dogs six years before we met.

One of Jesse's favorite Mommy stories is the one about the turtle.

One day, Lacy and I pulled into her apartment complex in Kingsland and saw a giant snapping turtle clomping across the parking lot. Lacy said, "That thing shouldn't be here. We need to get it to the Slab." I was thinking the same thing, weighing it over in my mind, but with Lacy involved, the decision was already made. The Slab was a low-water crossing of the Llano River, a football field wide, strewn with boulders. Lacy loved the Slab from childhood summers at her Nanny's.

Taking charge, I said, "OK, we'll get a box from inside, drop the turtle in and be off."

We marveled at the size of the turtle, almost the width of a manhole cover, and its nasty, ripping claws. I'd always thought of turtles as harmless creatures, but this one could do damage.

I squatted down behind it, and as I placed my hands under the sides of its shell, the damn thing hissed and jumped.

I stepped back. "Dang, I didn't know these suckers could jump."

I squatted and began to lift it again, and it jumped right out of my hands.

Lacy elbowed me aside, grabbed the turtle and dropped it in the box.

As I was lugging the boxed turtle to water at the Slab, Lacy slipped in her flip-flops and fell painfully on her butt in the middle of the road. An injustice, I felt.

Lacy was hypernosmic, and I am anosmic...Lacy had an otherworldly sense of smell, and I have none. She said she could smell water...not only foul or contaminated water...plain old water. Maybe it was a function of her brain trauma when one sense is heightened as others diminish. To me, it seemed more of a curse than a blessing because she was offended by smells throughout each day.

As many differences as Lacy and I had, we had our commonalities, too. We were both dog lovers, both mannerly "yes sir, no sir" people.

Lacy was a "driver" like me. We both enjoyed driving long distances. I think the love of driving is a Texan thing; everything is spread so far apart that you have to do a lot of driving. Some of us learn to love it. When Lacy was pregnant and we were holed up in the house, our main source of entertainment was going for drives out in the country, trying to get lost.

Love of music was ingrained in our souls, though our tastes were different. Lacy loved country and rap the most, but she liked some rock'n'roll too. She found Pearl Jam in the last couple of years and loved them. I like just about everything in the world except country. Because I didn't like country, Lacy decided that she was more open-minded about music than I was and would tell people that.

One of the first things that charmed me about Lacy was watching her rap. Country girl to her bones would rap unabashedly, enthusiastically, with an attitude, no diggity... then apologize... her Nanny (Lacy always referred to her grandmother as "my Nanny") would never approve of the verse she just laid. It was one of Lacy's lovable surprises.

Lacy had a beautiful singing voice, soft and tender. I told her she should try out for one of those TV "talent" shows. She sang "Amazing Grace" angelically at Mother's memorial service.

One of my heroes is the American songwriter John Prine. You know how it is, you want your loved ones to love your heroes like you do. I should have known that it doesn't happen that way. Everyone has their own heroes for their own intimately personal reasons...nobody else loves your dog as much as you love your dog.

John Prine wrote a song called "Hello in There" about taking the time to talk to lonesome old people. This is the last stanza:

"So if you're walking down the street sometime
And spot some hollow, ancient eyes
Please don't just pass them by and stare
As if you didn't care
Say hello in there, hello."

I couldn't wait for Lacy to hear the song, because it represented what she did in life. Lacy not only said hello, she wanted to take them home.

The song did nothing for Lacy; it didn't mean a thing.

I made Lacy a John Prine playlist, and she ignored it. I made Nanny one, too, and Nanny loved it and thanked me for it every time I saw her.

One time, I was watching John Prine on Austin City Limits, and he sang a slightly risque' song called "In Spite of Ourselves." Lacy watched part of it, then walked into the other room and asked Junie if she thought John Prine was a pervert.

In my first draft, I wrote that I never understood why she was so openly disrespectful of my hero, but I think I know. I think maybe I came across as a music snob to Lacy, talking about going to Jazz Fest 25 years straight, telling her about all the live shows I saw in Austin for 20 years, expressing love and hate for what I heard, that I cannot abide most "country" music, that I don't much like the twang, in voice and instrument, nor cliché-ridden lyrics.

I was just a listener, though. The only musical bone I have in my body is my ear.

Music ran through Lacy's veins. A distant relative of Townes Van Zandt, Lacy and her whole family *played* music. Lacy depended on music to help get her through struggles. She would feel a seizure aura to some songs. She loved her traditional country music.

I think we touched nerves, and Lacy took a stand.

Maybe that's a component of love: Taking a stand inexplicable to everybody else in the world except your love.

Early in our relationship, Lacy felt intimidated by my relationship with Junie. I'd told Lacy how close we were, and I think she worried that Junie would always be the one I confided in the most. Like Mother, I knew that Junie would love Lacy with all her heart, and she did. As I've said, they became sisters.

Lacy worried that Junie didn't like her. I told her over and over that Junie loved her. Junie did, too.

One November day, Lacy pulled up in the driveway and got out of her car, bawling. I'd been waiting for her and met her on the sidewalk.

I said, "What's wrong?"

Lacy said, "Thanksgiving is ruined."

I asked her why and she said that she and Junie had an argument and Junie had said "mean things" to her. I was flabbergasted. I'd never known Junie to say a mean thing to anybody in my life.

I talked to Junie, who was as upset as Lacy was, and didn't know what to do.

I think part of the problem had arisen when Lacy laid one of her "brain dumps" on Junie, and Junie tried to address each of the ten crises she was presented with and somehow said something that didn't sit right with Lacy. Junie wasn't as familiar with Lacy's ways of expression as I was.

This was during the time after my uncle Dave had his leg amputated and lived with Lacy, Jesse and me for nine months. The stress on all of us was enormous. Managing a one-year-old was a cakewalk compared to Dave, who Lacy came to love deeply, but who could be tactless and cruel, questioning Lacy about her weight, why we weren't married...

The frost between Junie and Lacy lasted a few weeks, and it made me as depressed as I'd ever been in my life...the two people on earth I was closest to could not get along, it seemed. How would we live life?

Lacy and Junie reconciled, but it was a rough stretch.

When Lacy was 30ish, about five years into our relationship, she lapsed into a gradual downward spiral that lasted for a couple of years. I see the progression now, in retrospect, but in the moment, I felt bewildered. Over the two years, her struggles became more frequent, and she went through at least a dozen jobs, each progressively worse than the last. She had conflicts with her bosses, which wasn't like her, and she had trouble learning a new computer. She was repetitively late for work, which angered me. I told her that 50% of success at a job is just showing up every day on time.

Later, she would say that I hurt her by allowing her to be a clerk at 7-Eleven or for the two-week stint where she picked up trash by the side of the road for the county. I would say that I didn't make her take those jobs and that if she had shown up on time at her last job, she wouldn't be in this predicament. I hated it for her, but I believe in personal responsibility. Right or wrong, I wanted her to prove to both of us that she could hold a job.

Lacy still lived in her apartment in Kingsland to be near her Nanny and I was in Bertram, 40 miles away. Lacy wanted to get married, but I still had doubts and resisted.

She hit rock bottom financially, and I began supporting her to some extent from then on.

Dark days.

We were not getting along, and I suggested that we take a break from each other for a little while. It was at this point that Lacy threatened suicide twice. One day, during our "break" she called and asked me to bring her a Diet Dr. Pepper at her roadside job. Exasperated that she wasn't abiding by our agreement, I arrived with her drink, and she said, "Maybe I'll just walk out into traffic and end it." Another time, she said, "I might as well shoot myself."

Our separation ended there. I thought...I hoped... that I had talked her down from the suicidal thoughts. She said she'd had them before. Zana concurred. I talked to Junie, who, as a high school counselor, had seen it up close far too many times. Lacy began seeing a counselor. We resumed our relationship as we knew it, and her outlook gradually improved.

I don't know what caused Lacy's malaise...maybe the cocktail of drugs in her system didn't jive...a by-product of the brain surgeries...my reluctance to marry...her financial straits...Lola's challenges...a combination of everything, I suppose, but I'll never know.

Another way of looking at it is that Lacy had every right to be a sad, tormented soul...those two years could have been her life's condition, but her indomitable spirit won out.

For a long time, I think I disbelieved in the love Lacy had for me...not from an "I'm not worthy" perspective but in the sense of "I've never experienced anything like this before."

285

I've written about Lacy saving the petals off of every rose I ever gave her. Junie was there when Lacy said it, and we looked at each other, not speaking, both thinking, "Wow."

Lacy thought I was extremely good-looking. She told me that all the time. If a friend of hers had something complimentary to say about me, she couldn't wait to tell me. I'd never thought of myself as handsome; it wasn't in the scope of my self-perception. None of my previous girlfriends raved about my looks as Lacy did. It was like she gave me a preposterous surprise.

Of all the things I miss about Lacy, the one I might miss the most is a gift I received every day. Lacy called me "Babe." Nobody had ever called me "Babe" before. It lit me up, I'm not sure why. It made me feel loved, perhaps. I treasure words, and "Babe" just sends me. It reminds me of a time in New Orleans...Steffen and I went to a bar next to our hotel and the barmaid, in her distinct Nahlins accent would call us "Baa-by." We returned to that bar time after time just to be called "Baa-by."

To be Lacy's babe...I can't think of anything finer in the world. Oh, to be "Babe" just once more.

One day, I went over to Lacy's apartment after shooting par for a round of golf for the first time in my life. It was very important to me like I would be a failure in life, a loser, a choker, if I went to my grave without shooting par, as hard as I'd tried. Lacy didn't know anything about golf, hated it actually, didn't even know what par meant, but she knew how important it was to me, and when I told

286

her, she lit up, as excited as I was. Her mom was there, and she bubbled, "Mom, did you hear that? Jay shot par! Isn't that great."

One year, Lacy's Christmas gift to me was a compilation of my writing in a notebook. She had loftier goals...unbeknownst to me, she took a sheaf of my material to "a lady in Austin," I don't know who, and tried to get it published. Lacy said the lady complimented the work, but publication was another matter. I couldn't have had a better saleswoman than Lacy...you couldn't turn her down. I thought, "Whew, if Lacy can't get me published, then it must really be crap."

Diet Dr. Pepper was Lacy's soft drink of choice for as long as I knew her...it was common knowledge among family in friends...if you were ordering a drink for Lacy in a restaurant, it was Diet Dr. Pepper.

On the last day of her life, I'd mentioned to Lacy that I'd drunk a Diet Dr. Pepper out of a machine at work and liked it even better than my usual Diet Coke. We had both in the refrigerator at home.

Before she drove out of our driveway for the last time, Lacy said, "Oh, I'm leaving the Diet Dr. Peppers for you. I'll drink the Cokes."

One year, prior to her birthday, Lacy told me she didn't want flowers or gifts...she wanted me to write something for her. I'd written several stories and poems *about* Lacy already, but she wanted me to express how I felt about her. For whatever reason, I do not express my emotions well verbally, and left Lacy wanting. I would tell her that my actions told my story, and I believe my actions, for the most part, proved my depth of love for her.

Lacy's one criticism of my writing was that I "use too many big words." She may have been right when it comes to songs or poems, but prose, no. It's the reader's responsibility to know or look up words they might not be familiar with. I need a dictionary handy when I read Martin Amis. Lacy didn't value vocabulary like I do.

So, I had to write something that spoke to Lacy and stay true to myself. What I came up with was this, printed on a card in a large, flowery, purple font:

I love you cuz you bust a rhyme
I love the sunshine that you spread
I love you cuz you rise with joy
When you (finally) get up out of bed

I love you for your tolerance
I love you for your smile
I love you for your open heart
I love you a country mile

I believe it did speak to Lacy. She cried and said she loved it.

On a late October day in 2019, Lacy and I met for lunch at Boat Town in Kingsland. Lacy seemed distracted, disturbed; something was off. When Lacy was struggling, you heard the hurt in her voice and saw the pain in her eyes. She drank water instead of her usual Diet Dr. Pepper. She would only say that she was struggling. We parted for the day.

The next day, she called and said we needed to talk. By then, I had figured it out.

Reminiscent of the day we met, I met her at my front gate. This time, I did the talking.

I said, "Are you pregnant?"

She nodded through tears.

I said, "I'm all in."

Her teardrops dappled my neck as we hugged, then walked up my driveway, my arm around her shoulder. We sat at my kitchen table and talked about the future, closer then than we'd ever been.

I think of us as "married" at that moment. "I'm all in" was my vow, and I think I held up to it. I want to say that in some universe, Lacy would have understood and accepted my pledge and that would have made her happy, but I know that's not true. In every conceivable universe, Lacy would want to be married.

Lacy wanted a formal wedding. She had the preacher picked out and a thousand ideas about the ceremony. I believe to this day that if we could have just gone to a Justice of the Peace (like Murphy and

Sharon did), we would have been married, but it wasn't going to be that easy.

One time at a business meeting, a team-building event in Colorado during my WorldCon years, we took a Meyers-Briggs personality test. All of us employees sat around a conference table, and the lady who administered the test reviewed our scores. She came to mine and said, "Jay, you scored a 59 out of a possible 60 on the introversion scale. I don't think I've ever seen one that high. I bet that being in a meeting like this makes you feel very uncomfortable."

"Hallelujah, somebody finally understands," I thought.

I've learned to function in large groups, but I still feel uneasy and often escape for quiet time. I can talk to anybody one-on-one, but the more faces and voices that present themselves; the more dissonance I feel, the more uncomfortable I become.

The idea of being the centerpiece in a large wedding left me with a sense of dread.

I know...it doesn't matter. Lacy deserved the wedding she wanted and I should have made it happen, some way, somehow.

A few months before Lacy died, I had a pearl engagement ring made for her...just what she wanted. I hadn't yet found or created the moment to give it to her. I think she would have loved it.

The bizarre term of Lacy's pregnancy reminds me of the months before Daddy died in Colorado, when Mother, Junie, Carey and I teamed up to take care of a man whose inoperable pancreatic cancer had probably spread to his brain. Junie and I traveled from Texas every other week or so, taking turns and giving each other breaks. I think of it as the saddest time of my life (up till then), but also the most beautiful, the way we came together as a family, lifting up Daddy and each other.

Lacy and I...first-time parents, with all of her physical challenges....at the height of the Covid outbreak, which lent a surreal aura to everything... canceled baby showers...holed up inside our house, alone, not seeing family for months at a time...doctor appointments when we drove into the ghost town of two million people...then the premature, calamitous birth of Jesse...the 22 days in the NICU, taking turns with Lacy (because only one parent was allowed in at a time) to visit our struggling little boy...then the last night in the hospital when Lacy and I saw Jesse together for the first time since his birth...

Lacy and I saw it through. It was beautiful.

Lacy faith in God was total and unwavering. She didn't harbor one scintilla of doubt.

I am more skeptical, but if anyone on earth could convince me of His existence it would have been Lacy, by the example she set. Had Lacy somehow survived the crash, she would have been the first

291

one at the drunk driver's hospital bedside, forgiving and comforting him. She would have us forgive him today.

Lacy and I had many discussions about faith, and she worried about my salvation. To her credit, she did not proselytize; her actions showed the way.

I told her of my distaste for organized religion.

A turning point for me came when I was in my teens. Somehow, the subject came up whether Daddy Sam went to church, whether he was "saved." The idea that Daddy Sam might go to hell because he didn't accept Jesus as his savior struck me as complete bullshit. There was no finer man on earth than Daddy Sam; if he didn't go to heaven, then nobody should. I've known my share of churchgoers who were sorry sons of bitches, and the idea that they would go to heaven and Daddy Sam would not made make me angry. I would have no part of any religion that would consign my grandfather to hell.

Another thing that doesn't ring true to me is the copout, non-answer, "God works in mysterious ways" when something inexplicably evil or unfair happens, but if a "miraculous" event occurs, it's "a God thing." You can't have it both ways.

Murder in the name of religion throughout history that continues to this day...blatant hypocrisy...discrimination.... Organized religion is not for me.

One morning, a few weeks after Lacy died, I glanced over at Lacy's desk, at the plaque that reads "God is good, y'all," which ignited the following screed:

Well, what the fuck, god?
Lacy, as loyal and faithful a servant as you might have
Needed to be obliterated by some drunk on the road?
God is good, how?

Lacy didn't get to do the one thing she most wanted
To raise her beloved son
Jesse's better off without her? Well?
God is good, how?

Oh, you work in mysterious ways
Well, goddamn, that's right
Lacy is dead and gone to all of us
Not much mystery in that
God is good, how?

All the lives Lacy lit up, now bereft
That's a cool little wrinkle
Everybody's life gets a little or a lot shittier
God is good, how?

Some new cruelty befalls me every week since Lacy died
God likes to fuck with the survivors?
They don't have enough grief

293

God is good, how?

So God has some master plan none of us can imagine
We eat shit in the meantime, but God's plan is gonna be something
Man, I can't wait
God is good, how?

Or you're a hands-off God who doesn't touch daily life?
Lacy's accident was unfortunate, just a matter of timing
Nothing God could do
God is good, how?

OK, OK, I get it
You're not there
I'm screaming into a void
Ain't nobody listening

With all my heart, I want to believe that Lacy is in heaven, walking her walk. I tell Jesse Mommy is in heaven. I can picture her there, reunited with Nanny and Dave and Mother...finally meeting Daddy. Because I can picture it, does that mean I believe it?

Even in death, Lacy wanted to help people. Because of all of the physical trauma and illnesses Lacy survived, she wanted her body donated to science for research after she died. She didn't want her loved ones to bear the cost of a funeral either...that's how Lacy thought.

I promised her that I'd see to it, certain in the knowledge that I would die before her and would never have to fulfill my pledge.

Lacy had been right about her body being useful for science. After the tragedy, we contacted UT Southwestern Medical Center, who did indeed want her body for research. After they discovered how annihilated Lacy's body had been by the wreck, however, they had to decline. Lacy's dying wish went unfulfilled.

I thought I had finished "emptying out," but there's more to tell, it turns out.

I wrote about Lacy being an RN and a licensed counselor, which, for the entirety of our relationship, she avowed, and I believed to be true. According to her mother, Terri, and other members of her family, Lacy never completed her Masters; she came close but never graduated. Lacy was neither an RN nor a licensed counselor. Terri had mentioned it not long after Lacy died, but I suppose I couldn't process it mentally as I tried to get a handle on the grief and the life ahead for Jesse and me...my mind had already been blown.

So, the woman I loved, who bore my child...whom I had supported for years, whom I had beat myself up for not marrying, had lied to me since day one about one of the most basic aspects of her life...her career. She had pulled off the lie on me for 12 years.

Did it reframe how I looked at our relationship?

The answer is no. I knew Lacy. Lacy believed she was a nurse and a counselor, and what's more, she lived it. I don't know what her actual nursing accreditation was, but I saw her in action on nursing jobs, and she was wonderful, more caring and solicitous than any nurse I've ever seen. As I've said, I watched her nurse my uncle Dave in our house for nine months after he'd had his leg amputated. I watched her save his life.

I saw Lacy interact with other experienced nurses, and in every case, she was treated with respect and admiration. She taught many young CNAs how to do their jobs, encouraged them and helped them pursue nursing careers.

Lacy worried, as only Lacy could, about losing her nursing license. If she saw any irregularity with the dispensation of medication, for example, she would put her foot down and say, "No, we don't do it that way."

I was less enamored with Lacy's counseling skills because she brought them into our relationship. She would say during some of our talks, "If I put my counseling hat on..." I didn't want to talk to a counselor. I wanted to talk to Lacy. One time, she told Dave that "he lacked self-esteem," and I thought that was nonsense. I know that she helped several people through some very tough situations.

Junie did research on brain trauma and found the following, published by the Moody Neurorehabilitation Institute:

"Confabulation is a neuropsychiatric disorder wherein a patient generates a false memory without the intention of deceit. The patient believes the statement to be truthful, hence the descriptive term 'honest lying.' The hypothesis is that the patient generates information as a compensatory mechanism to fill holes in one's memories. It functions for self-coherence, integration of memories, and self-relevance. Confabulations can include small details such as birthdays, or they may be fantastical and more broadly based. They can be believable or bizarre. Presenting patients with contradictory information may further perpetuate confabulation in an attempt to explain their account."

Junie eloquently articulated what my instincts had been telling me: "Lacy had no more control over her lies (confabulations) as she did over her inability to create new memories or make sense of directions. This was a physiological condition rather than a moral lapse or, worse, an intentional betrayal. What was real and good and true in her remains." (Junie should write.)

Looking back, I wonder what stories Lacy told me were true and what were "confabulations." You know what? It doesn't matter.

What was real and good and true in Lacy remains.

Almost a year after her death, I started the painful process of going through all of Lacy's stuff and unearthed entries from a diary, all dated 1997. She would have been 12 years old... before her brain surgeries. All of the entries started out "Dear Diary..." Most of them were just a couple of sentences about her day, nothing revelatory...sometimes she apologized to her diary for not writing

297

more often. As I started paging through, I got tickled because the last sentence and sign-off were the same 100 times over. I had attributed her penchant for repetition, her comfort with stock phrases to be a product of her brain trauma, but I learned that her idiosyncrasy was built-in.

I'll let 12-year-old Lacy finish.

"Well, I guess I'd better go.

Love,

Lacy Van Zandt"

Mrs. Barnett and Faye

David Daniel wasn't from around here. He wore a suit and tie to school every day. His ensembles were frayed, bedraggled...I want to say one of them was corduroy...but suits he wore. I bet he was ridiculed, sophomorically, for his peculiar attire, and I bet he didn't care. David had an absent-minded Einsteinian air. A couple of years later, his 20-year-old Cadillac caught fire as he drove into the high school parking lot. He abandoned the burning vehicle and shambled onto class.

David sat next to me in Mrs. Barnett's 9th-grade English class at West Junior High School in Richardson, Texas. One day, he said "Pssst" and showed me a stick-figure, sparrow-like bird he'd drawn in pencil on lined notebook paper. Musical notes were playfully arrayed around the bird. Below the drawing, a caption read, "The bird sings with its fingers."

Something interesting was going on in that class...ideas sprouted and bloomed... and it all started with Mrs. Barnett.

One day a girl named Gretchen raised a ruckus. She was mad at Michael, one of the class stoners, about something. Mrs. Barnett stopped her lesson and said, "All right, Gretchen, what is the problem?" Gretchen said, "Michael thinks he's so much higher than everybody else." Mrs. Barnett said, "Well, he probably is...now, back to Shakespeare."

I remember several teachers who tried to scare the shit out of us kids on the first day of class, to cow us for the year, I suppose. Mrs. Barnett didn't do that, but we knew who was in charge. I have two distinct memories of her: One, she clearly enunciated every syllable she spoke, ("probably," not "probly"); her care with words jived with some instinct I had, as yet unidentified. Her bearing and speech were regal, queenly somehow. My second impression was there was mischief afoot in that mind of hers, between a certain twinkle in her eye, and the dimples that framed her smile. If she smiled at you it was like you two shared an inside joke nobody else knew.

Mrs. Barnett assigned us to read a poem in front of the class. I told Daddy about it, and he recited, off the top of his head, "Fog," by Carl Sandburg, "Richard Cory," by Edward Arlington Robinson, and "The Tyger" by William Blake. I chose "Fog" because it had only six lines. Unbeknownst to Daddy, I was desperately afraid of speaking in front of the class; the fewer lines the better. I took "Richard Cory" along as backup.

On the day of the poetry reading my friend Victor elbowed me and said, "Jones, Jones, you got something?" I tried to give him "Richard Cory," but he said, "No, no, gimme the short one."

I had a history with Victor Martinez. On our very first night in Richardson, after moving from Lubbock when I was nine years old, Junie, Carey and I walked from our apartment, the Shenandoah, across Spring Valley Road, to eat at Burger Chef. Junie had curlers in her hair in preparation for her first day at her new school the next day (Junie said later that she never, ever curled her hair...it was a once in a lifetime event). Three boys about my age in another booth started singing "Curlers in your hair, shame on you..." from a popular commercial of the time. Tense, unmoored from anything familiar, I defended my sister and told them to stop. They laughed and doubled down on their harassment. I told Junie and Carey to run home, and ended up skirmishing, in full retreat, with the boys in the parking lot. Victor was the ringleader.

The next day, my first at Dover Elementary, who showed up in class but the bully from the night before. Victor followed me to the pencil sharpener, "accidentally" bumped into me and managed to poke me just under the eye with a sharpened pencil, leaving the tip of the lead lodged in the soft tissue under my eye.

Victor and I became friends over the next few years, I don't know how. Maybe I'd earned his respect with our first encounters. Victor wasn't a big kid, but he was tough, wiry and strong. He would fight anybody, anytime. Later in high school, in the 7-Eleven parking lot, I watched him viciously, repeatedly, bash the head of a jock from our rival high school, Pearce, against a concrete light pole stanchion. His advice to me on fighting was, "You gotta throw the first punch." I spent the night with him one time so his father wouldn't beat him up.

Victor read "Fog," head held high, with dignity and respect. I mumbled through "Richard Cory" in a quivery monotone.

Mrs. Barnett taught "Romeo and Juliet". One day in class she summarized the plot: "So, on the first day, Romeo and Juliet met and fell in love, the next day they got married...", then I did something completely out of character for me, I smarted off in class. I said, "And the next day they had a kid." My flash of impertinence was Mrs. Barnett's fault; she fostered freedom of thought and expression.

I get to call Mrs. Barnett "Faye" now, because we've become friends, and because that's her name...her middle name. Norena is her first name. Her family, close friends and Jesse call her "Dear." Faye has multiple aliases.

Junie was in Faye's class the year after me and some of Junie's friends stayed in touch with Faye after their school days. At Junie's 50th birthday party somebody suggested they get together with her. I remember Junie asking me if I'd like to meet up with Mrs. Barnett again...it had been almost 40 years since I was in her class, and the question of meeting her was a no-brainer. "You name it, I'll be there."

Lacy and Jesse and I hit it off with Faye, who was just as I remembered...thoughtful, well-spoken, still with that subversive smile. The impression of being in the presence or royalty returned. I was reminded that you have to be on your toes with Faye. She has my favorite sense of humor...dry, understated...one of those people who says funny or insightful things in passing. You just have to listen.

One day, Faye treated us to lunch at Don Pedro's in Richardson, a perfect place for Jesse because it has a giant outdoor play scape just outside the door. Jesse managed to catapult a full bowl of salsa onto the window, the table and all over himself. Faye, a mother, grandmother and great-grandmother, took it with good humor; she'd been through that. She asked me how much we should tip, and I said, "$100, based on Jesse's behavior. Restaurants are going to start requiring a deposit to seat the little man."

Dear surprises Jesse with a toy every time we meet. Dinosaurs, a Spiderman watch...

Faye has hosted us for dinner several times at her house in Richardson. We'd end up on her back porch, talking, playing with Jesse and Faye's labradoodle, Coco. I am particular about dogs, but I would take Coco home with me in a New York minute.

I asked Faye about students she remembered. She didn't have Carey, whom she wouldn't have forgotten, but she did teach Carey's best friend of 50+ years, Glen Bakken. I remember a family trip we took to Grandmommie's house outside of Gilmer; Glen came along. Carey and Glen must have been 10 or so. For several days, every time you'd walk in a room, you'd stumble on to a no-holds-barred, knock-down-drag-out wrestling match between the two. Red-faced and sweating, they never got mad at each other, or if they did, it didn't last a minute. Glen and Carey have been through it all together; each as good a friend to the other as you could possibly have. Glen has been there for me too. Glen and his wife Laura made the 6-hour drive from Dallas to Levelland for Lacy's funeral. When I saw them sitting in a pew I couldn't believe it. I clumsily, abruptly ended a conversation I was having so I could go hug them.

Faye and Glen lived close to each other. Faye said that one time, she mentioned to Glen that she was building an addition to her patio, and soon after, Glen would arrive periodically with lumber he'd appropriated from construction sites.

One of Junie's friends who stayed in touch with Faye through the years was a girl named Gina, on whom I had a devastating crush in high school. Gina lived across the street from Victor, and I'm sure she knew him and his family much better than I did. I never did get to know her well enough to find out what she knew about Victor.

Lacy loved Faye, and Faye loved Lacy. Lacy said Faye was precious. Faye was as devastated as all of us by Lacy's death and made the 200-mile trip to Buchanan Dam for her memorial.

Over the years, I sent Faye some of the stuff I wrote, and she said she liked it, told me to keep writing. When you fear that most of what you write is crap, having someone like Faye encourage you is a kick in the pants. It was Faye who suggested I put together a memoir, so, dear reader, if you've suffered the material this far, blame it on Faye.

When life feels especially cruel and bewildering, I have to remind myself who's on my side. I am blessed that Faye loves us "boys," Jesse and me, that Faye is my friend.

Trial

The trial of Alejandro Molina began on November 4, 2024, a little over 15 months after the crash that killed Lacy Van Zandt. Folks in the DA's office said this was a relatively quick turnaround for an intoxication manslaughter case. During those 15 months, Molina still possessed a valid Texas license. He had spent a total of three days in jail for two DWIs, two felony possession arrests and intox manslaughter in the previous 25 months and never had his license revoked.

One summer day, I took Jesse to the park in Burnet, and who strolled up but Molina with a mother and child (his sister and nephew, I learned later). In court the previous week he had approached the judge limping badly, on crutches, still purportedly recovering from injuries suffered in the crash. He strode crutchless this day, miraculously recovered, like Kevin's Spacey's character at the climax of "The Usual Suspects".

I thought about introducing myself and Jesse, telling him that this was the boy whose mother he killed, but afraid I might do something to harm our case, I buckled Jesse into his car seat and left.

This event was just one of a score of cruelties visited upon us in the aftermath of Lacy's death:

--As I've said, Lacy's lifelong wish that her body be donated to science after she died went unfulfilled. We buried her in Sundown, Texas, near her Nanny and father.

--I wanted Lacy to be laid to rest with her engagement ring on her finger; I did not want to view her body, just her left hand. I knew it was an odd request, and I felt queasy asking the funeral director at the service in Levelland before the transport to the burial site. He said he would check and let me know. A few minutes later he called me in to his office and introduced me to the embalmer, who was visibly upset, from having viewed the body again, I assumed. She said that she was sorry but that Lacy's body was in very bad shape. She hadn't been able to do much with it; her left hand was so mangled that I wouldn't be able to place a ring on it.

--One of the most torturous ongoing ordeals has been dealing with Texas Crime Victim Compensation (CVC), run by the Attorney General's office. The charter of the CVC is to reimburse victims for crime-related costs financed by fines and penalties paid by those convicted. According to our Victim Assistance Coordinator, who deals with them every day, the CVC "is in shambles," and I've witnessed it up close and personal. I have filled out reams of paperwork, some documents completed six separate times; I have spent untold hours holding on the phone. 13 months after having completed all the documentation, I received nothing from the CVC.

Finally, enraged after having been on hold for 45 minutes and then hung up on by the same agent for the third time, I wrote letters to newspapers, TV stations and my state representative, who did indeed call the CVC on my behalf. Out of the blue, I got a call from my case worker, who had not returned one phone

306

call in the year I'd had him; I'd never spoken to the man. The paperwork had been sitting on his desk for months. I did finally receive compensation, about $1500 for funeral-related expenses.

The CVC in Texas is a bureaucratic torture chamber, heaping its exquisite agony upon victims who are already suffering beyond all measure. I have been told that the CVC will be reviewed by the Texas Legislature in the spring of 2025 and I would be eager to testify.

--Texas enacted a law requiring drunk drivers who killed a parent to pay child support to the family. The law went into effect one month after the crash.

--We never got a satisfactory answer to the most important question of all: Why was Molina still out on the streets after two DWIs and two felony possession charges one month apart, eight months later? It came out during the trial that in one of the arrests, Molina was passed out in his car at a stoplight in Burnet and had to be vigorously shaken by the police officer to wake him up. Lacy's family and I met multiple times with the county attorneys in charge of prosecuting the DWI and possession charges, trying to understand. They couldn't confirm it then, but it was finally revealed that the DWI involved cocaine and Fentanyl, not alcohol, so he was administered a drug patch. It seems that Burnet County attorneys felt their job was done with the patch, and they pursued the cases with no urgency thereafter.

At one point, Zana *alerted them* that Molina's bond could be revoked, and he could be taken off the streets, at least temporarily. The county followed Zana's advice and revoked his bond. He was arrested and immediately made bail.

After Molina killed Lacy, the felony took precedence, and the county washed their bloody hands of it. He would never receive any punishment for the DWIs and possession charges and would have no prior convictions on his record when we went to trial.

The trial was scheduled for August, 2024, almost exactly a year after the crash. Gil Stout, the Assistant District Attorney (ADA) who would be prosecuting the case (after the two other ADAs assigned had moved on to other jobs), said we should be prepared for a delay, and delayed it was because the defense attorney had pending murder cases that took precedence. The trial date was moved to October and we were assured there was a good chance it would go then.

Lacy's family and I met with Gil and agreed that Zana and I would testify. I would probably go toward the end. What I should have known but didn't was that you cannot be in the courtroom, nor even talk to those who sat in the trial before you testify. What a weird feeling to have agonized over a year about the event and then not be able to witness most of it.

In the meantime, at Molina's plea hearing, his defense attorney came to us with a plea deal of 15 years (the maximum sentence for intoxication manslaughter is 20). I was surprised that they came in so high and said we should at least consider it; Lacy's family was opposed. We did not accept the deal.

The week before the October trial date, we were informed that it would delayed again. There were three potential cases for two openings...ours, the sexual assault of a child case, and the verbal abuse of a policeman. I could understand the sexual assault case, but the other, no way. Our case came in third of three. As angry as I had been during the whole ordeal, I fired off a letter to the judge, asking for a reason for the prioritization and was told that, by law, if one defendant is in jail and the other is not currently incarcerated, the former takes precedence.

My letter to the judge was considered "ex parte" communication and had to be shared with the defense. Gil said the defense attorney might ask the judge to recuse himself, but it was never mentioned again.

I vented again in another letter to Gil and my family, saying that, according to logic of the law, if two jaywalkers were in custody at the time of the next trial, they'd go before ours, and that, if Burnet County jails remained full the case might literally never go to trial.

Then Gil passed along more bad news...there was a slight chance our case would go to trial in November, but the sexual assault case was up again, a continuance, and there was only one opening. If the trial didn't go then, the next possible date would be February 2025 because the defense attorney was going to be out of the country in December. We learned that a trial can be delayed six times each by the defense and prosecution. Six times each? Isn't that a bit excessive? I think that would have to be one of the root causes for the wheels of justice to grind so slowly.

Because there were no guarantees that the trial would go in February, I thought that the plea deal was the best way out, if it didn't happen in November. Helpless for 15 months, we could at least do something that the court couldn't seem to accomplish: Put the killer in jail once and for all. Lacy's family was still opposed. I understood.

Nothing made sense in the 500 days after Lacy was killed, and we got another surprise in late October: Our case was chosen for the November trial date.

Gil said Molina would plead guilty (which he did) because the evidence against him was indisputable and overwhelming. The trial would be punishment only.

Zana would testify first, and I would testify last. Maybe it was Lawyering 101 to choose this order, but regardless, I thought it was a shrewd decision on Gil's part. I had worried that if we testified back-to-back we might repeat the same stories, and the effect of our testimony would be muted. This way, Zana would introduce Lacy to the jury, the nitty-gritty details of the case would be presented, then I would bring Lacy back full circle.

I was supposed to meet face-to-face will Gil to prepare my testimony, but I caught a nasty stomach virus (Jesse named it the Naughty Bug) the week before the trial, and we had to do it over the phone. Lacy's family and I had written Victim Impact Statements that could be read, minus the jury, at the end of the trial and would be included in the documentation presented to the parole board when Molina went up for parole. Gil used the statement I had written as the template for my testimony.

In the week leading up to the trial I felt, at turns, extremely nervous, then confident, about my testimony. Public speaking is not my forte. I had feared it since junior high when I would be overcome with black-cloud dread when given the assignment to speak in front of a class. In college, I would scout syllabi for any mention of class presentations and cross them off my list.

On the positive side, I would be prepared. I had thought and written so much about Lacy that I knew what stories I wanted to tell and how to tell them. I had asked Gil what makes a good witness and he said, "Someone who tells the truth."

The one irrational fear I had was that I would slip up and say the word "Fuck" at some point in my testimony, appalling the judge, jury, and every soul in the courtroom, single-handedly blowing our case to smithereens, derailing justice for Lacy with one imbecilic blunder. I even knew the context of my catastrophic slip: One of the stories I wanted to tell was how Lacy was a person you just fell into a hug with. "Hug" and "fuck" sound alike. If I substituted the F word for "hug." Oh god...

It became an obsession almost…"Whatever you do, don't say "Fuck," don't say "Fuck," don't say 'Fuck.'" You know what happens when you tell yourself repeatedly not to say something…

Gil said that I would probably testify on Tuesday afternoon, late on the second day of the trial. Leaving nothing to chance, I drove to court with Junie first thing Tuesday morning, dressed in my best suit, and ended up walking, walking, walking the court parking lot all morning.

Finally, they broke for lunch, and I drove my aunt Sandy to lunch at Bill's Burgers, a local joint in Burnet. Sandy said, "I know I'm not supposed to tell you about what went on in the trial, but I think this is OK. They showed the trooper's body cam footage at the scene when he told you that Lacy had been killed. It was a very emotional moment." I was floored. In the 15 months I had to think of the events of that tragic night, I had never considered that I would have been filmed.

I didn't have time to think it through. Family and friends were there. We visited. I didn't want to get full and sleepy before testifying, so I ate little, drank a latte' instead.

How would you feel if you were filmed, without your knowledge, during the most vulnerable moment of your life…the saddest, most shocking, most bewildering moment of your life? How would you feel if the film was shown to family, friends and complete strangers? You haven't seen it yourself, but 50 people have. Would you want to see it? How would you feel?

I don't know that I'll ever wrap my head around it, but I do know that I do not like it. That was a private moment, not for public consumption. I understand why Gil showed it, and from what people say, it made an impact on the courtroom. As you will see, I gained the utmost respect for Gil, but he should have at least let me know in advance that it would be shown. I suppose I would have approved it, given the choice, for the sake of our case, but it would have been an agonizing decision.

I testified after lunch. I shouldn't have drunk the latte; it made me feel jicky and even more nervous than I had been. I took deep breaths.

I did not say "Fuck" on the witness stand.

Three jurors cried during my testimony, I was told. I didn't see them because another juror caught my attention: A stoic middle-aged man with a straight-backed posture and blonde, crew-cut hair. I thought "military." What struck me was he never once looked in my direction, as if ignoring me completely, as if I wasn't there, as if his mind was already made up. I felt like I was speaking to a cipher, a rock.

I think I did all right. I think I told Lacy's and Jesse's and my story with animation and emotion, not in the monotone drone I feared. As Gil questioned me, I felt free to venture off into stories we hadn't even discussed, then he would prompt me gently for another one. The courtroom audience laughed one time, which made me feel good, but I can't remember the context of the humor.

The one regret I have about my testimony feels incongruous...I'm telling a desperately tragic story of the loss of my love, Jesse's mommy, yet what I wish I'd said was an attempt at humor. I think it speaks to my instinct as a writer; I want to make people laugh.

Gil was questioning me about the 25-year age difference between Lacy and I and how we came to fall in love. I said, "Love is blind." What I wish I'd said was, "Either love is blind, or Lacy was."

The first witness Wednesday morning, the third day of the trial and my first to observe, was a forensics expert who would testify about the autopsy. I left the courtroom. Lacy's niece, Shelbie, followed. About five minutes later, Terri came out, ashen, and headed straight to the bathroom. Shelbie went to the Ladies' Room to care for her stricken grandmother.

We re-entered after the forensic testimony and heard several character witnesses for Molina. One was a lady friend from church who had known Molina for years; she said she prayed with him often and that he was a changed man after the "accident." After the defense finished questioning her, Gil, still seated at his table, asked two questions:

"Do you know the victim's name?" "No."

"Did you and Molina ever pray for the victim?" "No."

I thought that it was brilliant of Gil to repudiate her entire testimony with two succinct questions.

Another telling witness was Molina's probation officer, called by the defense. She was the most competent of all the witnesses I saw; no-nonsense, straight to the point. She had been his probation officer for over two years since his first offenses. After the defense questioned her and earned no real points that I could see, Gil asked about a positive test that had occurred when Molina was on the drug patch. The probation officer explained that the patch tests at much lower levels than the state drug test, which proved negative. I don't know the exact nomenclature, but the patch test showed a level of over .1xx in his system; the state verification test starts at levels of .5xx. It's just a glitch in the system, she said.

If the state had a better drug testing mechanism, Molina might have been arrested, and Lacy might still be alive. This was just one of a half-a-dozen "what ifs," had they occurred, Lacy would be here today.

Next, Gil asked her if Molina had reported to her after the crash. She said he had reported to her on August 7, 11 days after. Gil asked what Molina said. The probation officer said that Molina reported that he had been in a car wreck and had a steel rod in his leg from the injuries. He did not mention that he was drunk and had killed someone.

I thought that said everything you needed to know about his character: "Changed man," my ass.

As Gil began his closing statement, I had to do a double-take...I realized he was crying. I'm certain it was not an act. Over the months of meetings we'd had with him and all the Lacy stories we'd told, he had come to know and love her too. I gather that he is a man of faith, and I believe he admires Lacy's example. Gil settled into his cross-examination. The defense attorney had suggested that five to 12 years might be a reasonable punishment and that Molina deserved mercy. Gil argued that the state had shown mercy by limiting the maximum sentence to 20 years and that he deserved that and more.

The jury ended up deliberating for six hours. We waited around, killing time, inside the courthouse and out in the parking lot. I didn't see it, but Zana said Molina's family and friends laughed at her and made fun of her as she walked through their crowd. She reported it to the bailiffs.

During the wait, I called Junie at home with Jesse and Zana's boys (yet another selfless act of Junie's, volunteering to watch the kids on the last crucial day of the trial), and we agreed that she should bring Jesse to the courthouse. I'd asked Gil if that was OK and if he wanted to meet Jesse. He said "Yes," and they met. Jesse was preoccupied with the toys in the waiting room, so Gil didn't get to meet the charming, engaging Jesse I'd hoped he'd encounter.

Junie had attended the first two days of the trial and told me later how heartened she had been by the compassion of the two Bertram police officers who were first on the scene and of the witnesses of the crash. She said that one of the officers was so devastated by what he saw that he had begun counseling. The message she got was, "We are not alone in this." She suggested that I reach out to the officers and witnesses and thank them, which I have done.

Gil said that he had never seen a punishment deliberation take so long. The fickleness of the human element of a jury hit home. There might be eleven people who agreed on a decision, but one outlier could queer the whole shooting match. Was the outlier the man I couldn't reach in my testimony?

Finally, about 9:00 that Wednesday night, we were summoned back to the courtroom: The jury had reached a verdict. Molina laughed and joked with friends in the audience before taking his seat beside his attorney. Dumbfounded by his behavior, I wondered, "Does this guy understand that he will be going to prison in 10 minutes?"

Molina received a sentence of 18 years (eligible for parole in nine) in the state penitentiary. He wasn't laughing when the verdict was announced.

The jury was dismissed, and Terri, Christi, and Zana read their passionate, painful Victim Impact Statements to Molina and the courtroom. Zana spoke directly to him, and she said he never met her eye. I told Gil I'd said my piece already and did not read mine.

A few days after the trial, our MADD representative, who had attended, called me with some information she wanted to pass along... Molina was still in the county jail because Texas prisons had no room for another inmate. A space was expected to open in three to six months. Meanwhile he'll remain in the county jail, just a couple of miles from his home.

I am asked if I feel a sense of closure, and I suppose I do. I finally got to tell Lacy's story in front of friends, family, strangers, a judge and a jury. That's what closure means to me: Telling Lacy's story.

Jesse, Junie and Me

I could rewrite this piece every single day and never say enough. There is a new story, twist or dumbfounding moment every day in the development of a four-year-old child, as every parent on the planet would attest. I try to draw a line in the sand, saying, "OK, I'll stop here." Then, the next day, Jesse gives me a new story to write.

During one of our front-porch conversations, Junie said, "Jesse wants to please you." I was momentarily gratified…Junie got the inside information from Jesse that he wanted to please me.

But wait.

I said, "OK, then explain this: Whenever we play pretend ice cream shop or pizza delivery, he is always, always, always out of what I order. In an entirely pretend world, he cannot pretend to have what I want."

Junie laughed and said, "That's hysterical."

I think it's pretty damned funny too.

Based on the trajectory of Jesse's development and my inevitable decline, Jesse will be able to beat me up by the time he's eight. I will be 68.

How to dissuade him from geezer daddy abuse besides being a loving father? I think about the "on to it" lady from my childhood, who tagged "on to it" at the end of most of her sentences. Perhaps I could co-opt the usage with my own particular spin to implant a concept in Jesse's mind. "Time for a bath, buddy, kids don't beat up their daddies"... "Eat your corn dog, kids don't beat up their daddies".... "Let's go to the park, kids don't beat up their daddies"....

How did it feel to be a first-time father at age 60? I felt energized to paint rooms, rearrange furniture, install shelves, take Lacy to doctor appointments, sell sports cars and buy baby cars.

I felt inspired to write a 40-page letter to my unborn son, telling him about his father, his mother, the fabulous Joneses from whence he came, what I've learned in life...in case I won't be there to tell him in person.

I felt scared for Lacy's health during her pregnancy and Jesse's health thereafter, but it was going to work out. Human beings adapt; I would adapt. Lacy and I loved each other and would love Jesse as deeply as a child can be loved. Lacy, the born mother, would be the backbone. I would lean on her to educate me on how to raise a child. She knew, from having helped raise half a dozen nieces and nephews, I had instincts but no practical experience. I would have my own opinions and methods. Lacy and I would argue and compromise. We were a good team despite our differences and conflicts. We'd raise a great kid. It was going to work out.

Long since reconciled that I would never have kids, and knowing that Junie and Carey wouldn't, I think I carried a subconscious sadness that the Jones line would end with us; that our unique strain of human being, our character and intelligence and hilarity and life would no longer animate the world at large.

Jesse's birth meant, "Hooray, Joneses will grace the world a little bit longer."

The only way Jesse will know his Jones ancestors is through Junie and me, and our extended family to a lesser extent. Junie says confidently, "I carry them with me," but I worry that I can't live up to their example, can't represent them in all their glory. All I can do is tell him stories and try to be the father they would want me to be.

How does it feel to be a lone parent at age 64? I know "single parent" is the term used to define my status, but "single" connotes some kind of freedom or availability that I don't feel. "First-time parent" and "lone parent" are different universes. Being a lone parent is exponentially more terrifying and difficult. "First-time parent" resounded of inspiration and hope, like the line from the Lou Reed song, "the beginning of a great adventure;" "lone parent" feels deadly serious, forever eliminating "carefree" from my lexicon of self-description.

I have felt like I was free-falling and had no idea when, where, if...I would land on stable ground. I have felt lost as if once I knew how to live life, but now I don't. I use the perfect tense because feelings evolve. Lacy has been gone 15 months now, and while my grief remains, the unreality of her sudden death has faded, and I am accepting reality. It feels like a step toward figuring out how to live again.

I feel like my "lightness of being," my exuberance, has been gouged out of my heart. I feel like I need to rekindle that, for Jesse, for me. I think of how, on my Saturday drives to Fredericksburg for the races, I would crank the music as loud as it would go and sing my guts out; I haven't felt like singing my guts out since Lacy died.

My answer to every question now is, "I don't know."

Where will we live? I don't know.

Our house used to be out in the country, but growth from Austin is stampeding toward us, and I don't like it. I don't like the traffic, the construction, the feeling of everything closing in. I need space.

The political and weather climates of my home state have worn me out, too. I won't go into a political rant, but I've had enough of the mean-spiritedness, gun worship, prizing of ignorance over education, haves over have-nots...

I think we're feeling the effects of global warming in Texas with one brutally hot and dry summer after another.

I've looked around, and New Mexico and Colorado seem the most likely alternatives, but I don't have a feel for where the "sweet spot" to live happily and raise Jesse would be. I did propose to friends and family that we all pitch in and buy a castle in Ireland.

If I get some kind of outrageous offer for my house, I may say "Adios"... where to, I don't know.

One thing I do know: Junie, Jesse and I will make the decision together.

What is the trajectory of the life of a child? What skills do they develop when? I have no frame of reference. I don't know.

I do have one vivid memory of a stage in a child's development from when I was 20 or so. I say the memory is vivid, yet I don't remember who the kid was. He was a boy about five, a little older than Jesse is now. I spent a few hours with him and he was delightful, unintentionally hilarious. We all laughed at him and with him. I saw the boy six months later and found that a tragedy had occurred…he had become self-conscious. He *tried* to be funny and it fell flat; his innocent charm was gone.

I'm afraid I'm seeing the same development of self-consciousness, the effort to be funny, in Jesse and it makes me a little sad. I know it's a positive development in the long run, but I mourn the loss of innocence.

How will the loss of his mother at age three affect Jesse? I don't know.

These are his words:

"I love my mommy."

"I miss my mommy too much."

"I was in the hospital, and I needed my mommy."

"My dad and I are hurting because we don't have mommy anymore."

"My mommy's in heaven, but I want her here with me."

"Make my mommy come home."

"I try to draw her picture, and I get so mad, I hold my crayon tight, and I make big mad marks. I don't want a picture; I just want mommy."

"I'm going to invent a rocket ship that takes me up to heaven so I can see Mommy again."

He seems to be thriving, somehow. He's a happy, creative, loving boy, and I'm trying not to screw him up too much.

How is the death of Lacy affecting me and my relationship with Jesse? Am I dealing with it properly? I don't know.

I'm sure writing has been therapeutic for me. Neither Jesse nor I have talked to a counselor, and I'm not inclined to go in that direction...yet. I've always lived by my own counsel, and that instinct remains.

Lacy had evolved into the bad cop, and I was the good cop, the fun one. I had the freedom, spatially and emotionally, to recharge and to bring the little kid in me to the relationship. Now, there's just one cop...I originally wrote "and he's a bad cop" because it was easy and concise, but it's not true. The one cop is impatient, ill-tempered, and moody...but he's a pushover; Jesse gets almost everything he wants in the end.

The little kid in me doesn't show his face as much as he used to.

I have a better understanding of Lacy's depression now because, for the first time in my life, I get depressed. Of course I've had down times and lows in my life, but this is different...Out of the blue, some thought or event will strike me down, and hopelessness I've never felt sinks in for a couple of days.

Let me tell you about a day I had: It started off with Jesse wetting the bed, so I spent the next several hours washing bed linens and going to the laundromat to wash the comforter that won't fit in the washer. For months, we'd planned for a relative to take Jesse for a few days, and I would get some glorious free time to write, to think, to rejuvenate. I'd done Jesse's packing, and he was ready to go. One hour before the longed-for moment, I got a call saying there'd been an illness in the family. We had to cancel. Despondent, lost without a plan again, I headed to the park with Jesse for something to do. I stopped for a latte, and the lid popped off, drenching my lap in scalding coffee. Sitting on a bench in the park, my thighs pink from the coffee burn, I draped my arm over the backrest and was swarmed by wasps, stung six or eight times on the arm...a wasp's nest was hidden underneath the backrest.

I don't know how to be chipper on a day like that. I don't know how to present a happy face to my son. All he sees is a morose, angry daddy, and that can't be good for him.

I believe that energy is the way out if I can generate it. Throwing myself into a project helps. Right now, Jesse and I are working on a yard beautification enterprise that keeps us sweaty and occupied. I've thought about putting an ad in the paper to drum up more activity: "Old fart/toddler comedy handyman team available for house and yard projects...."

How will we make it financially? I don't know.

A very scary unknown...Lacy and I were both working part-time when she died. We've lost both of those incomes and now live entirely on Social Security and taxable IRA withdrawals, which have landed me in debt to the IRS. I routinely commit financial management atrocities. I can't afford daycare, so we're in survival mode until Jesse goes to kindergarten, when I can start working again. I'll be 65 then; 65-year-olds are a hot commodity in the labor market, right?

I make a conscious effort not to think too far into the future. If I do, I think things like...Jesse will live most of his life without his parents, and it makes me desperately sad for him. How do you possibly prepare him for that? Extended family and friends will be even more important to him than most people. How do I inculcate in him the ability to be a good judge of character and find the right friends and mentors?

If I think about the future, I think about the deaths of his very closest loved ones that Jesse will have to endure in the next couple of decades.

Jesse will have to grow up quicker than most kids, won't he? Another development that I don't like to consider is the eventual decline of my health and how it will impact Jesse. He'll have to take a hand in the care of his father at a relatively early age. How is that going to work? Will he be resentful? If he's like Lacy, he'll step right up and lend a hand.

Obviously, it behooves me to stay in good physical shape and live as long as I can, and I am failing. I've become a tub-a-lard. My self-discipline has evaporated. I am a creature of habit, I suppose, and my habits used to include walking three miles or doing some kind of strenuous yard work every day. Developing a daily routine with a toddler has been very difficult for me. Surprises, delays, and unplanned diversions rule the day.

Junie spends more than half of her time here with us in Bertram, uprooted from retired life and friends in Plano. Her presence makes all the difference. I can't picture Jesse's and my lives without her taking a major part of the load, giving me breaks as I need them. The dynamic between Jesse and I improves when Junie is here; it's not just me scolding Jesse when he does something wrong.

Our names have become interchangeable with Jesse. He often calls me "Junie" and Junie "Daddy" by accident.

Junie makes no pretenses about being Jesse's "mother." She honors Lacy at every turn. She misses being the "fun aunt" whose primary role was entertaining her nephew. She does the dirty work now, too, gets frustrated with him like I do and disciplines him when necessary. I trust Junie 100%.

Having her as a sounding board is invaluable, too. She knows his foibles, his delights, his antics, and if we see something amiss, we talk about it. We talk about everything when it comes to raising Jesse.

At a t-ball practice, Jesse hit another boy, Kaden, in the face with the bill of his helmet. I didn't see it, so I didn't know if it was accidental or intentional. The boy had a bump on the bridge of his nose and cried; his parents, one of whom was an assistant coach, consoled him. At the next practice, Jesse was playing tag with Kaden and pushed him too hard, shoving him to the ground. Junie was in the stands and told me later that the boy's mother was angry at Jesse.

What a weird, uncomfortable feeling to have another adult angry at your child.

Were disturbing tendencies emerging, Junie and I wondered. Could we be seeing a latent reaction in Jesse to losing his mother? We were worried. We both talked to Jesse about it, and he told Junie, "I just want Kaden to be my friend." Junie told him that next time at practice, he should first ask Kaden if he wanted to play tag and to tag him lightly. Jesse did exactly what Junie suggested….asked Kaden to play tag and touched him gently. Junie and I were gratified that Jesse listened and responded appropriately.

Jesse and Kaden played tag before games the rest of the season, uneventfully.

After we learned Lacy was having a boy, I developed a picture in my mind of what he would be like...dark-haired, quiet, studious, shy, short of stature...Jesse is almost exactly the opposite...blond-haired, garrulous, tall for his age, a ham...once he gets over his "pretend" shyness with a stranger hiding behind my back, he'll bust out his "awesome cool moves" and dance all over a convenience store, a courthouse.... He put on a rock'n'roll concert "for all his fans" at his 4th birthday party.

This is my kid? How did that happen?

Because of his premature birth, his speech was a little slow to develop, and we enlisted speech and vocational therapists who worked with him. I don't know that their efforts made much difference (no offense to the therapists)...it seemed it was just a matter of natural development, and the speech came...boy did it come. He talks up a storm now, reminiscent of Lacy. Now, I wonder if there are speech therapists who specialize in inhibiting a child's speech.

I joke, but the constant distraction is a problem for me. I am a thinker and enjoy endeavors requiring concentration...reading, writing, crossword puzzles, doping out the racing form.... Being unable to pursue any train of thought for more than three seconds frustrates me, and I get testy. That's not fair to him. Jesse will reliably go to sleep for an hour or two if I put him in his car seat and drive late in the afternoon, so we go driving most afternoons.

I am an insomniac, so I do get thinking time from about 4:00 am to 8:00 am, but being awake most of the night means geezer daddy might need a nap in the afternoon. What has evolved is this: I will lie on the couch and doze off while he watches TV. He will lie next to me for 10 seconds, get up, lie down again, get up...then wake me up at every commercial. It probably sounds irresponsible to sleep with a temporarily unsupervised four-year-old in the room, but he has earned my trust. Junie agrees; Jesse is responsible.

Lacy would tell you that Jesse has Nanny's ear lobes, her father's teeth, Junie's nose, Carey's cheeks, her uncle's belly button, her great-grandfather's toenails, her niece's knees...Lacy saw resemblances everywhere, and I don't. Jesse has just one dimple on his left cheek, a replica of Lacy's. She said Jesse looks most like Junie, and I've seen that in flashes. The only time I've thought he looked even remotely like me was one time when he was concentrating on catching a baseball...the expression on his face startled me. I saw myself.

A barber who cut Jesse's hair told me, "Without his glasses on, he looks like you." I was surprised how good it made me feel. I want him to look like me, I just don't see it.

Lacy took me to task for talking to Jesse like he was an adult, again, the "too many big words" complaint. I plead guilty but don't think I will change much. I make a point of repeating things he says back to him to make sure that I understand the words he just said and to speak his language in some sense. Junie speaks "four-year old" much better than me.

I think he does show signs of an advanced vocabulary. Junie and I praised a drawing he did, and he said, "This is one of my masterpieces." He uses "hypothesis" in context. One day we were strolling through IKEA and overheard the word "bamboozle," which we taught Jesse. He later proclaimed, "Bamboozle is my name and bamboozle is my game."

Jesse is my son, and for better or worse, he will be shaped by me. I'm going to be me.

Jesse's "I love you" started in the Intensive Care Unit of the Dell's Children's Hospital in Austin. On our second day there, out of the blue, Jesse said, "Daddy," I said, "Yeah, buddy." "I love you," I said, "I love you too, more than you can imagine." It broke my heart...my sick, scared little boy telling me he loved me. I didn't remember him ever saying "I love you" before, but he said it 50 times that day and continues to favor Junie and me with his vow every day.

Jesse had been staying with his aunt Zana and family in Giddings, and Zana called saying Jesse wasn't feeling well...she was on her way. I met them at his pediatrician's office in Marble Falls, and the minute I saw him, I knew he was seriously ill...labored breathing, fever.... His pediatrician immediately called an ambulance, and I rode with him to the Emergency Room at Baylor Scott and White. We spent a couple of harrowing hours there, where Jesse had his blood drawn, an oxygen cannula inserted in his nose, an epi-pen injection and suffered other innumerable pokes and prods, still struggling to breathe. I cried for his pain.

Jesse wasn't responding, and the ER doctor said they weren't equipped to treat a two-year-old properly and said we needed to go to Dell Children's Hospital. Jesse and I took our second ambulance ride of the day.

Jesse was diagnosed with viral pneumonia at Dell, gradually recovered and was finally released three days later. I had stayed up with him for 30 hours straight at one point. Jesse charmed every nurse and doctor who treated him and was cared for assiduously.

A few months later Jesse sneezed all day, then started coughing, his breathing becoming labored. We headed to the Dell ER at about 1:00 am. Jesse threw up on the front desk and was admitted immediately.

This time, Jesse was diagnosed with virally-induced asthma and released on the second day with an Asthma Action Plan. He takes a preventative inhaler treatment twice a day, with an Albuterol backup, in case he shows signs of difficulty breathing, which he has not. We see a pulmonologist every three months. He runs and plays like any other four-year-old. When I hug him, I'm amazed at his musculature, how strong and fit he is.

Alarm bells still go off in my head if he sneezes or coughs.

Jesse has been diagnosed with a peanut allergy, another scary development. He is also allergic to walnuts, and perhaps shrimp and salmon, to a lesser extent. I read the ingredient summary on every piece of candy he is given; he is aware of it, too, thankfully, and is on guard. Our allergy doctor says he has a 10% of outgrowing it in his lifetime. We keep an epi pen that I pray we never have to use in his backpack.

One of my favorite TV shows was "Inside the Actor's Studio," hosted by James Lipton. He would conduct an hour-long interview with famous actors and actresses and end with the same ten questions, one of which was "What sound or noise do you love?" If the interviewee had children, the answer was almost always, "I love the sound of my child's laughter."

I love the sound of Jesse's laugh, but what tickles me most is the sound of his "gulp" when he drinks lustily. He tilts his head way back and audibly inhales the drink, his Adam's apple thrumming like a piston.

I think, "Drink in life like that, buddy, and you can't go wrong."

"A long time ago, when I was your age..." is Jesse's introduction to the stories he tells. Junie and I don't know where he came up with that; it's not a phrase we use. I considered that he might be living life in reverse chronology, like the doctor in Martin Amis's *Time's Arrow*, but no, I've seen him grow up. After his intro, he launches into a 10-minute fantasy made up on the fly. One of the stories was about his friend, a cat named "Oatmeal," that sits in the bathroom and talks with him while he's pooping if I'm not there. Oatmeal is not here right now, he said; his driver, Vinny C, took him a long way away to Mexico, but he'll be back soon.

Jesse tells stories about his grandsons, about how he built our house...

Jesse has umpteen imaginary friends besides Oatmeal. One night, he had us pull out our toolkits to fix Robodog. Jesse summoned an invisible dog to hand him his wrench. I asked him about it, and he said, "Oh, I have dogs who give me tools. They are service dogs."

Jesse prefers me to stay in the bathroom with him when he poops; he often stays with me. I'd never been hugged by anyone while sitting on the toilet until Jesse came along. One of our poop conversations went like this:

Jesse said, "Daddy, did you ever dream about having a little boy or little girl?"

I said, "Yeah, buddy, I always thought, when I was young, that I would have kids."

With a mischievous gleam in his eye and a tone of voice that had the ring of a challenge, Jesse said, "Well, you got a little boy."

T-ball was Jesse's first organized activity of any sort with other kids. I was an assistant coach. It was a valuable learning experience, not necessarily for him, but for me.

We'd practiced beforehand, and Jesse could smash a ball off a tee in our backyard both right-handed and left-handed. I thought he'd be one the best players because of the practice and the sports gene he must have inherited from me. For me to have had expectations of competence was ludicrous, I learned. There were too many distractions. Dirt, for example... My god, I had no idea how interesting dirt was until every kid on the team showed me...and the whole damned infield was made of dirt. Jesse would be running from third base to home plate in the middle of a game and stop to make a dirt pile.

Jesse was one of two three-year-olds on the team; most of the others were four, and one girl had just turned five. The developmental differences of just one year or so were remarkable. The five-year-old girl and one of the older boys were the best throwers, catchers, and batters.

Sometimes I found myself getting angry at Jesse because, in the field, he paid no attention to the batter, ever. I told him at least 100 times, "Watch the batter, pay attention," but it didn't matter; he would not, could not. I learned that the longevity of a three-year-old's attention span is equal to one flit of a hummingbird's wings.

One game, when Jesse found out that his team wouldn't be batting first, he lay face down on the dugout bench and refused to come out. When we finally got him out on the field, he walked way out in the outfield, far removed from the game, and sat down. I let the other coaches talk to him.

We would try soccer next. Soccer is played on grass.

One day before t-ball practice, I watched an older boy on the field next to us hitting ball after ball to the outfield. His lazy-ass dad sat on a bucket, pitching to him while his mom gamely chased baseballs from one foul line to the other, flagging from the effort.

The mother reminded me of Lacy...she would have chased balls down for Jesse till the cows came home.

Junie, my aunt Sandy and I took Jesse to a local pizza joint after one of our games. Sandy gave Jesse all of the coins she had, a dollar's worth or so. He played with them on the table. A player on the opposing team came in with his family, and Jesse struck up a conversation with him. As we were leaving, Jesse tried to give the boy all of his change. Oh lord, shades of his mama.

Jesse was following me through my master bedroom one day and said, "Daddy, who is that?" pointing to a picture on the dresser. I said, "Oh, that was my dog, Mordecai," and told Jesse what a great dog Mordecai was, how he'd go on "joy runs," just so happy to be alive...that one time Mordecai was on a joy run and ran head-on into a parked car, knocking himself out...that I was worried, but Mordecai woke right up, saw me laughing at him and joyfully attacked me.

I told Jesse how Mordecai listened more intently than any creature I've ever known. Earnest brown eyes locked on mine, ears perked, head cocked if I said something he didn't understand or was really interested in...that Mordecai had taught me something about being a father...that the reason I talk so much shit to Jesse was that I did with Mordecai and he loved it, loved being engaged, hearing his own name, no matter the nonsense I spouted.

I thought the conversation was over and began to walk away, when I heard a sob. I looked back, and Jesse was crying real tears.

What happened? I knelt down beside him, hugged him, and said, "What's wrong, buddy?" Jesse said, "I miss Moh-de-ky."

I've enrolled Jesse in golf, tennis and baseball academies in preparation for a professional career in one of those sports. If, by age 10 or so, he doesn't show signs of major-league talent...well, there's always child slavery.

It seems gratuitous to say that I will support Jesse wherever his heart and head lead him. Isn't that what any sensible parent does? I will expose him to as many things as I possibly can and see what sticks, see where his talents and passions lie. If he becomes enthralled with knitting, I will encourage and support him to be the best knitter that he can possibly be.

The one thing he must do that will break my heart if he doesn't do...is read, read, read. Reading has meant everything to me in my life: educated me, given me different perspectives, made me laugh and cry, made me fall in love, enriched every facet of my life, made me who I am.

The first book that shaped me was *Babbitt*, a Sinclair Lewis book that Daddy gave me when I was about 10 years old. What I got out of it was that you don't have to live your life like everybody else, to reject conformity. *Babbitt* is the most important book I ever read because I read it so young and it informed the rest of my life.

I will teach him something about reading that wasn't as important in my childhood: To consider the source. Is the source trustworthy? There is so much utter bullshit out there now on the internet, social media, national news networks... and now the bald-faced lying by our politicians that has become standard operating procedure... Consider the source.

One time Lacy asked me if I would attend Jesse's kindergarten graduation, and I said the first thing that entered my mind: "Kindergarten graduation? Hell no." I'd never even heard the term before. I launched into a good-natured rant about it being one of those helicopter parent inventions where every child must always win, and just getting up in the morning merits a standing ovation. Doing something that everyone in the world does is not an achievement. I said that I would praise Jesse to the heavens for anything real that he accomplishes at any age, but graduating from kindergarten ain't it.

Lacy was upset at first but lightened up after talking with friends...other fathers scoffed at the idea, too, but they ended up going.

I envision Jesse's kindergarten graduation like this: Junie, Murphy, and I are standing at the back, sincerely applauding the teachers and kids, blameless in the whole charade; Murphy and I nudging each other with sarcastic commentary on the rest of the spectacle, as the tiny scholars proceed down the tiny aisle in their tiny caps and tiny gowns that cost $200 for the one-time gig.

Then we'll chaperone the graduates to a party at their hangout by the lake, where they chug beer from Paw Patrol cups, knock back tequila shots from thimbles...

They'll reminisce about the old days...their favorite superheroes...the milk they drank...the naps they took...the dirt piles they built...the butterflies they chased...

Then they'll wax philosophical, pondering the future...life in the real world...they'll ask themselves the momentous questions that every five-year-old must ask...

-- "What do I want to do with my life...policeman or doctor, ballerina or nurse?"

-- "Should I go on to first grade or find a job and start making a living?"

-- "Am I built for first grade?"

-- "Can we afford first grade?"

-- "Where will I matriculate?"

--"Can I place out of any classes?"

--"Is Humdinger Elementary a party school?"

--"Can I afford an apartment, or will I have to sleep with my brother in the bunk bed?"

Kindergarten graduation...I can't wait.

Finish

Thank you for reading, and good on you. Finishing a book, any book, is an accomplishment, an education completed. Your takeaway may be, "I'll never read this kook again," but you learned something, and you finished. Jesse and I took on a 220-page, painful slog of a book, but we will persevere, we will finish, we will learn something, and we will choose better next time. Daddy said, "If you start a book, finish it." I think he meant it as a life lesson as much as a lesson about reading. Finish, and move on.

To those who worry about Jesse, my audience of one, reading this book and being negatively influenced by the foul language and questionable choices his Daddy sometimes made: Well, he shouldn't read it when he's 9…or 12…or 15…or 18 (lord no, not 18)…or 21…or 24. 27? He can read it when he's 27. He'll have my 40-page letter to keep him company in the meantime.

Junie asked me if I was sure I wanted Jesse to read everything I'd written about his Mommy. I agonized over one Lacy story since the day I wrote it and ended up removing it, but the answer is certainly "Yes." I believe Jesse should know everything he can possibly know about his mother; he didn't get to know her in real life, but she lives on in him and in all of us, and I want him to know *how* she lives on.

I think about the stories I didn't tell. I think about the formative people, the beautiful, loony characters in my life I didn't mention or didn't paint as complete a picture of as I would have liked. In some cases I tried and failed, but my dereliction stems mostly from what I noted in the Preface…my ambivalence about a memoir. Do you really want another 100 pages of ME? Mercifully, I finish here, but you formative ones, you beautiful loons, you know who you are, be warned: I will write on; you're not out of the woods just yet.

Acknowledgment

I thank Jesse for being Jesse. You bamboozler you, you surprise, delight and inspire me every day…and, yes, we can go to the park today.

I thank Junie for…where do I begin? For being my oasis of sanity, my partner in raising Jesse, my editor, my best friend. In darkest times, a light.

I thank all the fabulous Joneses who came before me. Nanny, Daddy Sam, Grandmommie, Dave, Carolyn, Daddy, Mother…your character, your class, your life…I couldn't be prouder to be a Jones.

I thank Carey and Paula for being the benevolent forces of nature that they are. Jesse will be sleeping against Carey's shoulder again in no time.

I thank Sharon and Murphy for being the best friends a person could ask for. Sharon, your timing was impeccable, and your feedback invaluable. Murphy, who do you like in the 8th at Kentucky Downs?

I thank Faye Barnett for her love and the spark. Faye, you might be more careful of what you wish for.

I thank Terri, Zana, Christi and the entire Van Zandt family for making me their own, for their love and support of Jesse, and for the gift of Lacy. We went through hell together, and still we thrive. I am honored to be a member of the Van Zandt family.

I thank my aunt Sandy for embodying Mother, for her enthusiasm, her toughness, and her unconditional love of Jesse and me. Sandy, you amaze me.

I think of Mickey Rourke's rousing toast in the movie "Barfly"... "To all my friends." How I didn't write about some of you beautiful loons, I don't know, but I want to thank Jeffrey, Nicole, and Audrey Jones, Richard and Sandra Key, Steffen and Paul Saustrup, Kevin and Anna Warren, Billy and Liz Crow, Glen and Laura Bakken, Melinda and Lou Hervey, Nora Henson, Faye Sansom, Jay Williams, Richard Scott, Kelly Sommer, Trampus Isom, Shelli and Jeff Dill, William and Maria Haskell, Tom Allen, Johnny Lucas, Mondo Max, Susan Hatfield, Joe Ozello, Trey Stiles, Robert Vaade, Truman Crane, Kamyr Fernandez-Diaz, Cynthia, Carole, Joelle, and Erika Cruz, Jeff Fincher, Sharon Scott, and "Bean Bag" Sarah Watkins...for your friendship. To all my friends!

About the Author

Jay Jones is the bestselling author of...nothing, yet. His instinct is to write humor, but sometimes life gets in the way. A 65-year-old single, befuddled father of a 5-year-old boy, Jesse, he knows the names of all the Paw Patrol characters, against his will. In past lives he was a Project Manager and greens keeper. He enjoys horse racing and golf. He and Jesse live in Bertram, Texas.